LEARNING STRATEGIES IN UNIVERSITY SCIENCE

Learning Strategies in University Science

International Council of Scientific Unions Committee
on the Teaching of Science (ICSU—CTS)

Edited by Derek McNally

 University College Cardiff Press

First published 1979 in Great Britain by
University College Cardiff Press,
P.O. Box 78, Cardiff, CF1 1XL, in association
with Christopher Davies (Publishers) Ltd.,
52 Mansel Street, Swansea, Wales

ISBN 901426 90 3

Printed in Wales by Salesbury Press, Llandybïe, Dyfed.

List of Contributors

Professor Paul Bamberg (Director of Science Instruction Development) — Harvard Science Center, Harvard University, Cambridge, Mass 02138, U.S.A.

Professor A. Becher — Education Area, Education Development Building, University of Sussex, Falmer, Brighton, BN1 9RG.

Professor T.J. Black (Director) and Dr. J. Ogborn — Centre for Science Education, Chelsea College, University of London, Bridges Place, London SW6 4HR.

Professor W.H. Dowdeswell — School of Education, University of Bath.
Dr. N.D.C. Harris (Director) — Educational Services Unit, University of Bath, Claverton Down, Bath BA2 7AY.

Professor Dr. Brigitte Eckstein — Institut fur Mineralogie und Lagerstättenlehre, Rheinish-Westfälischen Technischen Hochschule Aachen, Wüllnerstrasse 2, 51, Aachen, West Germany.

Professor M.J. Frazer (Professor of Chemical Education) and Dr. R. Maskill — School of Chemical Sciences, University of East Anglia, Norwich NR4 7TJ.

Dr. A.T. Rogerson (Director) — Schools Mathematical Project, Westfield College, Kiddipore Avenue, Hampstead, London NW3 7ST.

Dr. A.R. Stokes — Department of Physics, King's College, London, The Strand, London WC2R 2LS.

Professor V.M. Showalter (Director) — The Center for Unified Science Education, Ohio State University, Box 3138, University Station, Columbus, Ohio 43210, U.S.A.

Dr. W.F. Williams (Director) and Mrs. J. Lipscombe — Combined Studies, Faculty of Science, The University of Leeds, Leeds, LS2 9JT.

Dr. D. McNally (Assistant Director) — The University of London Observatory, Mill Hill Park, London NW7 2QS.

Contents

Foreword

This series of articles had its origins in discussions of the Committee on the Teaching of Science of the International Council of Scientific Unions, which is concerned with science teaching at all levels and in all sciences. The committee was aware of many innovative schemes and ideas at University level but felt that, on the whole, University Teachers in the various sciences were less aware of new learning strategies than their colleagues in other levels of education. It is hoped that this series will stimulate thought and discussion which will in turn lead to greater effectiveness in our extremely responsible tasks both of developing our disciplines and of preparing future generations of scientists.

The committee is grateful to all the authors for the work done in preparing the articles. Thanks go especially to Professor Becher who wrote the introduction from the professional educationist's viewpoint after reading the nine core articles, and to Dr. Derek McNally who performed the difficult task of persuading authors to write, of editing the resulting texts and of reacting, as a teacher of a specific discipline in the U.K., to the series, in the final article. Thanks also go to Unesco for the financial support that made the publication possible.

C.A. Taylor
Chairman, I.C.S.U. C.T.S.

9

Preface

Concern was expressed at a meeting of the ICSU Committee for the Teaching of Science (CTS) in 1975 that the teaching of science at University level was carried out in a wholly traditional way and that the results of research into teaching practices had made little impact. It was recognised that much research on teaching methods was expressed in a terminology alien to most science teachers who had a dual role to fulfil — namely keeping abreast with current research in their speciality and maintaining adequate courses in their subject. Since greater emphasis was placed on achievement in research, it was impractical to suppose that many University teachers would keep up with the literature explosion in two such disparate areas.

The CTS decided that the most efficient way of proceeding was to produce a set of articles, aimed at the hard pressed working teacher, giving a digest of the current state of art in some particular method of encouraging learning in students. Some of these methods are not new; some are still controversial. However old, however controversial, the treatment would be in everyday terms free of educationalist's jargon and endeavouring to weight the advantages and disadvantages (while not disguising completely the enthusiasm and bias of the authors!). A short (or long) list of appropriate references would be included to direct further research if a particular teaching method was found to be suitable for a particular situation.

11

It would be wrong to suppose that the CTS wishes to incite wholesale revolution in teaching methods in University science. However, it is undoubtedly true that scientists are conservative in their approach to teaching. Opportunities are being missed in traditional approaches to presenting material to students. New approaches for their own sake are not necessarily a good thing — a dull teacher is dull whether of the traditional or *avant garde* type. The CTS would like all teachers to rethink their teaching methods, to decide afresh what is the best method of presenting their current course. Whether it is traditional talk-and-chalk or small group tutorials, or merely a supervised reading programme, at least the course will have benefited from a rational rethink. The number of teachers encouraged by this series to rethink their teaching methods, irrespective of what changes are actually made, will be a measure of our success.

The fundamental problems of teaching are international and we are deeply indebted to UNESCO for the enthusiastic grant support for this project. We are also deeply grateful to our authors who have responded so well to our brief.

A superb teacher may only be the result of a genetic accident; competent teachers can result from taking thought, applying the same scientific spirit of enquiry to teaching as research and, above all, having sympathy for the enthusiasm, aspirations and needs of their students.

The Context of Change in University Science Teaching

A. Becher

Any piece of a jigsaw puzzle can be examined in terms of its own properties. It can also be looked at within the setting of the other pieces into which it fits — and this gives it a different significance. What before was seen as a particular conjunction of colours and shapes becomes part of a wider design, usually one which is capable of a coherent general interpretation.

The central aim of this introductory survey is to suggest how the piece — or perhaps better, the set of interlocking pieces — delineating contemporary science teaching in higher education fits into the rest of the jigsaw of degree-level education as a whole. Or, for those who prefer blunt statements to fancy metaphors, it tries to relate the nine following contributions in the series to developments in curriculum and teaching approach in the broad range of other academic subjects.

In order to do so, it will be necessary to survey contemporary trends in academic courses and methods, and to explore the rationales behind them. But the paper also has two subsidiary themes, each related to its main purpose. First, there is a need to sketch in a framework of theoretical ideas against which the developments under consideration can appropriately be viewed. The opening section accordingly offers a brief resumé of the present state of research into the process of innovation itself, with particular reference to higher education. Second, there is a case for giving some attention to an important but neglected aspect of change, namely the difficulties associated with implementing novel and promising ideas. Those who read, in the following articles, about innovations which they would themselves like to try out may also find it useful to anticipate the practical problems of putting them into effect. With this in view, the concluding section is devoted to a consideration of the main barriers to change, in relation both to academic structures and to prevailing attitudes and beliefs.

1. What is Academic Innovation?

The concept of innovation in higher education

The majority of those interested in research into higher education as a topic in its own right have tended to concentrate on its macrostructure. In particular, there have been numerous studies of forward planning at the level of the system as a whole, or of the individual institution. There have been economic analyses of differential costs, investigations into access and transfer policies, follow-up enquiries into graduate employment, and case-studies of the role of the university in the community. But even the vast programme of research sponsored in the late 1960's and early 1970's by the Carnegie Commission on Higher Education in the USA barely glanced at what one might have thought to be two central functions of universities and colleges: namely the design of courses and the teaching of students.

This tendency to focus on the high oratory of policy-making and planning rather than to get down to the everyday world of the transactions between teachers and taught is understandable enough. Looking at the specific detail of curricula and methods is a troublesome business, because the necessary information is not easily available: in fact it is often not accessible at all except on the basis of direct personal contact with large numbers of individuals. In contrast, the pronouncements of government bodies responsible for higher education, the public statements of university presidents and vice-chancellors, the statistics of student numbers and academic budgets, are readily to hand. Even if the exegesis and the critical discussion of such material makes virtually no contribution to the betterment, or even to the better understanding, of higher education, it sounds impressive and is not too difficult to do.

Nevertheless, there have been some researchers — and not least the various contributors to this series — who have turned their attention constructively to one aspect or another of curriculum development in universities. While their activities can be grouped, for descriptive purposes, into a number of distinct categories, what they all have in common is a readiness to question established assumptions and explore untried possibilities.

Most studies of the academic curriculum take a predominantly practical approach, concentrating on the critical evaluation of a particular teaching method or course pattern, or on the planning, testing-out and revision of a substantially new set of curricular ideas. We shall however start by considering the more theoretical efforts to pin down the elusive nature of innovation (with special reference to academic innovation) before going on to look at more empirically-based attempts to document the variety and apparent direction of curricular changes.

Studies of the innovation process

The past two decades have seen a steadily-accumulating literature on how innovation should best be defined, what its essential characteristics are, and what conditions have to be fulfilled for it to take place. The earlier writings adopted what might be called a philosophers' stone approach to the subject. They sought to track down the elusive component which, once found, would guarantee successful change. It was assumed that what was true of agricultural reform would apply to business management; that what was learned from innovation in medical practice would be transferable to education. Case studies were diligently assembled of all manner of changes, and anxiously scanned so that their common features could be discerned. Some useful ideas emerged, though they were predictably at a very general level of abtraction. One of the best-known accounts in this genre is Donald Schon's *Beyond the Stable State.* [1]

When hopes began to be disappointed that the hidden essence of change could be revealed by such procedures, a more modest and pedestrian style of enquiry developed. The emphasis now fell on compiling taxonomies and cook-books. Distinct types of change and diverse strategies for reform were differentiated one from another, and various recipes were offered for the relationships between "change-agents" "gate-keepers" and other cut-out characters in the game of innovation. But, as all too often in attempts to develop recipes which might replicate complex human interactions, the explanatory models and the operating processes failed to fit any real-life contexts: and so the fashion changed again.

Much of the current research on the innovation process is limited and tentative in comparison with the ambitious confidence of earlier work. It tends to concentrate on identifiable and bounded domains — such as a given sector of medicine; a specific group of business firms; or a large public enterprise — and to explore the possibilities and constraints of change within that particular setting. It assumes innovation to be dependent on the possibility of modifying in particular ways the existing pattern of values within the domain under review.

One interesting exemplar of this approach is a recent Swedish study of change in higher education. [2] It may be worth giving some space to a resumé of its main arguments.

On the basis of seven detailed and closely-documented case studies of a variety of recent curriculum innovations in Swedish universities, the authors of the report put forward suggestions which they quite explicitly do not consider as valid for any context other than higher education itself. Their claims are further limited, since they are to be taken as applying only to changes which depart significantly from established norms (i.e. are not merely technical or organisational readjustments) and which affect "contents and methods of education". Within these limitations, their preconditions for significant change are, first, that there should be some lack of conformity among the individuals or interest groups within a given situation; second, that some of the individuals or groups concerned should have contacts with the environment outside their own particular domain.

The authors then introduce what might be seen as a geological-cum-fluid-mechanical analogy. The first precondition (lack of conformity) gives rise to " 'cracks' or conflicts in the system"; the second (external contacts) allows "impulses from the environment [to] flow into the 'cracks' in the system and 'break' the system by creating a potential for movement". This potential for movement is also identified as "unfreezing". If some innovative idea takes hold — and this depends on a complex of factors which the study enumerates — there is then "a continuous disequilibrium, caused by the dominance of the driving forces over the restraining forces". This stage is followed by "re-freezing", in which "balance is created round a new equilibrium".

Much of the analysis of the case studies themselves depends on the discussion of expected losses and gains to the individuals involved, the extent to which they come to feel ownership of, or identification with, the change proposed, the pattern of leadership which develops round a new cause, and the extent to which political power can be invoked in support of such a cause.

Discussions of this kind, focusing on the common constraints which militate against change in institutions of higher education, and of the ways in which these constraints might be modified, are useful among other things in promoting a better understanding of how universities actually function as communities. There have in recent years been some curiously naive attempts — we shall return to a discussion of them later — to impose change on universities from above. It is possible, but alas unlikely, that the improved understanding resulting from work such as the Swedish study quoted above will communicate itself to academic administrators and decision-makers, and so prevent comparable errors of judgement in times to come. Even if not, those directly involved in teaching may benefit in terms of a clearer recognition of which new ideas are likely to be viable in a given context and which must be expected to have very limited life chances.

The natural history of curriculum change

It is easy, by concentrating on the complexities of bringing about any kind of change in higher education, to fall into a state of despair in which almost nothing seems possible. A necessary antidote is provided by those inquiries which, rather than looking directly at the process of change, concentrate mainly on its consequences. Any investigation which sets out to document some of the innovations which have already established themselves in the overall pattern of university teaching and learning is liable to create a notably more optimistic frame of reference. The fact is that, for all the legendary conservatism of the academic profession, a remarkable number of new developments has taken place in recent years; the countenance of the curriculum has changed, if not out of recognition, then at least in many clearly discernible ways.

A fairly substantial recent attempt to map the pattern of innovative changes in course structures, curriculum content and teaching approach in one particular higher education system — that of Great Britain and Northern Ireland — was underwritten by the Nuffield Foundation. It involved one-week visits, by individual members of a team varying in size between four and six researchers, to every university institution and to twenty of the thirty British polytechnics, over the four-year period 1972-1976. The baseline of the team's work was to document any departures from the traditional pattern of lectures, laboratories and tutorials which might have relevance outside their department of origin. Over the period of the study, on the basis of detailed discussions with well over 1,000 individual academics, approximately 400 such changes were documented. After each documentary account had been revised by the original informant (the person primarily concerned with putting the idea into practice) it was published in one of a series of seven newsletters. These were distributed by the Nuffield Group to a mailing list of approximately 2,000 which was built up on the basis, very largely, of word of mouth between actively interested teachers.

This steadily-growing dossier of new developments fairly soon enabled the Group to identify major areas of common interest and to follow them up in various ways. During the latter part of its existence, it published a variety of short reports, collections of working papers and analytic studies of particular types of course organisation. It also attempted, in its interim report, [3] to identify the salient trends in academic innovation.

It should perhaps be emphasised that the Nuffield Group's attention was focused, as are the studies in the present series, on the day-to-day processes of teaching and learning. Its categories did not therefore include any reference to changes in the management of the higher education system as a whole (such as reforms in patterns of governance and control) or to innovations at the level of the institution (such as changes in planning processes or in committee structures). The Group distinguished between three main contexts in which significant changes could be discerned: that of the organisational framework within which particular courses might be developed; that which was related to methods of teaching, learning and assessment; and that which was concerned with various forms of background support for staff and students. This threefold classification is straightforward enough to form a useful basis for the discussion which follows in Section II, on the main directions of change.

2. What are the Main Directions of Change?

Common changes in curriculum patterns

The majority of innovations documented by the Nuffield Group fell into a number of fairly obvious clusters. The first of their categories — changes in curricular framework — reflected departures from the single-subject honours degree which has traditionally characterised British higher education. Three major, and distinct, curriculum patterns could be identified.

The first was interdisciplinarity. A remarkable number of new degree programmes had recently been, or were currently being, developed in both arts and science in which a broad theme or area was taken as the subject of study from a variety of intellectual perspectives. Thus a European Studies degree might embody an understanding of the politics and economics of a particular group of European countries, alongside a study of their language and their culture. Urban Studies could involve looking at the conditions of city life from the standpoints of geography, sociology, social administration and planning. Comparable degree patterns were also to be found in growing frequency within science and technology. Such examples as Environmental Chemical Engineering, Industrial Science, and Energy Studies come readily to mind. The phenomenon of interdisciplinarity in science at the tertiary level is very fully discussed in V.M. Showalter's contribution to this series. [4] The only point which needs to be underlined here is that it is part of a wider movement involving arts and social science subjects as well. Many of the advantages and difficulties experienced in designing and implementing an interdisciplinary degree in science are reflected in a surprisingly direct way on the other side of the arts/science divide — and especially perhaps the problem of trying to introduce a degree structure which challenges disciplinary boundaries within an institution which is strongly departmentalised. [5]

The second innovative curriculum pattern noted by the Nuffield Group was related to the development of modular or unit course structures for degrees. Modularity is quite distinct from inter-disciplinarity. In the latter, a deliberate attempt is made to achieve intellectual cohesion, and to use different approaches in the service of a unifying idea. The curriculum in consequence tends to be tightly structured, with relatively few student options. It is a strictly *table d'hôte* offering. In contrast, unit or modular degrees, while they may in practice impose some timetabling restraints and demand prerequisites for certain advanced courses, set out first and foremost to offer the student freedom of choice. He is meant to put together his own degree, out of a range of standard-size components. Normally, no attempt is made to link the components with one another. It is very much an *à la carte* menu. Although, in a somewhat different form, the unit course has been a familiar and long-established basis for degree programmes in the USA, its first introduction to British higher education occurred only just over a decade ago. Its origins, and its subsequent development within the sciences, are documented in the contribution to this series by A.R. Stokes. [6] Again, however, it should be emphasised that unit or modular courses also exist in some arts-based degrees, and that one of the most ambitious and far-reaching modular programmes in Britain (that at the City Polytechnic in London) allows students to take almost any mix of courses, including ones which span arts and science. (A similar, but more limited facility is offered by the Open University).

The last of the three curriculum patterns — breadth — is less neatly definable than the first two: indeed, it might be said to be a general goal or ideology more than a particular type of course structure. The quest for breadth can in practice take a variety of forms. In the arts and social sciences, the most common strategy for putting a specialised single-subject degree in perspective, and enlarging its frame of reference, is to begin the degree programme with a broadly-based "foundation course". Thus, for example, arts students might spend their first year following parallel intro-ductory courses in any three disciplines of their choice (as in

University College, Cardiff); social science students might be exposed in their initial term to a series of intensive two-week introductions to each of six disciplines before deciding on their subsequent choice of specialisms (as at the Polytechnic of Central London); or new entrants might follow a carefully-designed one-year interdisciplinary unit within their broad subject field (as at the Open University).

In professional subjects such as medicine, engineering and law, however, broadening more often takes the form of introducing ancillary courses which look at the role of the professional in its broader social setting. As with their counterparts in the humanities and social sciences, such broader-based degrees seem to be on the increase. Thus one finds courses within a number of Law Schools on socio-legal problems; many Medical Schools now provide some discussion of community medicine, doctor-patient relationships and the social determinants of ill health; and engineering courses increasingly offer students the chance to develop additional skills in management and cost-benefit techniques. The most far-reaching of such developments have stemmed from the "social studies of science" movement. W.F. Williams and J. Lipscombe have undertaken a comprehensive review of the issues in their contribution to this series. [7] It may incidentally be noted that among the examples they quote there are instances of all three curricular patterns discussed above. There are interdisciplinary programmes (as at Manchester University and Griffith University), modular schemes (as at North East London Polytechnic), and broadening elements involving social studies in science (as at Leeds University, and a number of other institutions involved in the SISCON programme).

Innovations in teaching and learning methods and assessment techniques.

In looking at significant variations on the familiar pattern of lectures, set experiments, tutorials and three-hour unseen examinations, the Nuffield Group was again able to document a wealth of new ideas and promising experiments. The range of variation was predictably greater at this level (where individual teachers are often able to set up their own innovative schemes) than at the level of degree course patterns (where new departures have to be collectively approved by the appropriate Faculty or Faculties and usually argued through Senate as well). But despite this wide canvas, a number of common areas of interest could be clearly discerned.

In relation to teaching methods as such, two very pronounced trends were identifiable. The first was a remarkable growth in the amount of project work undertaken in laboratory-based and field-based subjects, and a comparable increase in the significance of dissertations and long essays in library-based disciplines. This had the effect, for example, of focusing a degree programme around a series of mini-dissertations by each student, often revised and extended on the basis of tutorial and seminar discussion (as in History at Reading University and German at the University of Warwick). A number of courses in science and technology adopted a sequential growth from open-ended experiments and small-scale projects in the first and second years to major pieces of individual or group work in the third. The account by W.H. Dowdeswell and N.D.C. Harris in the present series [8] analyses this development, explores its rationale, reviews the problems to which it can give rise, and looks closely into the important issue of assessment.

The second major trend was towards new and more open styles of small group teaching. These might involve co-operative "workshops", running over a term, in which a team of students explored a topic of their own choice (as in the Department of Sociology at Keele University); or experimentation with a variety of group learning techniques (simulation, learning games, role play, analysis of case studies, syndicate work); or student-initiated discussion of a problem posed by the tutor (as in Chemistry at the University of East Anglia). Many of the approaches discussed by B. Eckstein in her knowledgeable survey of seminar methods [9] are peculiar to science subjects, but her general comments on methodology and on the case for small group work are relevant to undergraduate teaching as a whole.

The Nuffield Group, in their various reports and newsletters, also drew attention to some less pronounced, but nevertheless significant innovations in traditional teaching methods. One related to the aims and techniques of laboratory work, which appeared at the time of the study (the early to mid 1970's) to be undergoing major changes — even leaving aside the development in project work to which reference has already been made. The nature and significance of these changes is admirably brought out in the contribution to the present series by P. Black and J. Ogborn. [10] Another development — which is perhaps as much a matter of curricular organisation as of teaching method — concerned the exploitation, in a number of departments quite independently of one another (e.g. English at Exeter University and Biology at Imperial College, London), of the benefits of concentrated study. This calls for the students' intensive and undistracted attention over two or three weeks to a single theme — a kind of academic total immersion, usually involving a variety of different teaching approaches and study techniques.

We turn next from changes in teaching approach to innovations in methods of learning — that is, situations in which the teacher is not directly in contact with the student. Here the development of audio-visual facilities, together with the advent of programmed instruction and computer-assisted learning, have made a noticeable impact (though one considerably less far-reaching than the change attributable to the introduction of projects and dissertations). In most cases science-based departments have opted for closely-structured types of independent learning material — whether of the Audio-Tutorial variety or based on the Keller Plan pattern, or in some other combination (P. Bamberg's [11] paper notes a range of possibilities). In contrast, some examples of resource-based learning are more open-ended, being patterned predominantly on the library mode of study. In a few instances (as in the Chemistry Learning Resource Centres in Aston University, Queen Elizabeth College, London and South Bank Polytechnic), students have access to a diversity of independent learning materials, from model kits and tape-slide sequences to interactive computer terminals.

It is still relatively rare, in British universities, to find complete courses structured round an integrated set of learning materials. The time and effort called for in designing such materials is substantial, and the teamwork required is beyond achievement without a sizeable group of likeminded and highly motivated colleagues. However, the possibilities and advantages of this kind of study programme have been convincingly demonstrated by a number of institutions (notably the Open University, all of whose degree offerings have of necessity to take this form, but also for example by the departments of Zoology at University College Cardiff, Engineering at Exeter University and Biochemistry at the University of Dundee).

Finally, in this review of methods (as opposed to curricular patterns or the mechanisms of background support), we come to changes in assessment procedure. Although degree-level examinations might be expected to remain the most jealously-guarded bastions of academic conservatism, the evidence clearly shows that a major shift took place in the five-year period spanning the late sixties and the early seventies. In part this was a direct consequence of the growth of project work, which introduced a novel basis for accreditation. In part it derived from new curricular models — and especially from unit course patterns, which had an intrinsic requirement for intermittent assessment, rather than for a global examination in the final year. But as in other countries, student militancy, in 1968 and beyond, also played a direct and important role in examination reform.

As a consequence of these factors, the present structure of degree assessment in the UK departs in a variety of ways from the earlier stereotype of a series of three-hour unseen examinations, calling for essay answers, with accompanying all-day practical exercises, concentrated in the final term of the student's final year.

Firstly, the nature of the examinations themselves has changed (though not necessarily always for the better). They may allow the students full access to reference material, pocket calculators and the like (to reduce memorising by rote and low-level routine operations). They may be set as "take-away papers", which allow students two or three days to answer questions, with full access to library resources. Or else their format may be that of a series of several multiple-choice questions, and/or of questions demanding short one-or-two sentence answers (which present the student with a quite different task from that of writing three major essays in as many hours).

The second and more radical change has been a general downgrading in importance of the final examinations themselves. While in the majority of departments they still account for the largest proportion of marks for final assessment, there is a strong tendency towards reducing their numerical significance to fifty percent of the total or below. The remaining marks now go to course-work submitted for assessment during the student's second and third years (and, exceptionally, the first year also). In a few cases so-called "continuous assessment" really *is* continuous, and virtually the whole of the work assigned to a student is taken into account. But for the most part this is found to exert undue pressure on both teachers and taught, and the practice is for work to be assessed and marked intermittently rather than continuously.

The types of coursework required vary a great deal from institution to institution and subject to subject. Projects and major dissertations naturally tend to earn a sizeable proportion of the total credit — usually being equivalent in weight to at least one finals paper — though specially-commissioned end-of-term essays or labwork reports will often carry some share of degree marks. In the case of modular patterns, of course, the assessment is spread over the whole degree programme, most units being accredited (by examinations or other means) at the end of the term or semester in which they are taken. The weighting between units will often vary with their level in the system, with final-year components almost invariably carrying more marks than those taken in earlier years.

A third innovation in assessment procedures is to be found in only a relatively small minority of departments, but is nonetheless significant in its implications. It comprises various types of involvement by students in their own assessment. In its more restrained form, student participation is limited to an individual choice of assessment methods. Especially where a large year-group is involved, a department may allow individual undergraduates to decide the manner in which they are to be assessed. Thus some may elect to submit papers written during the term; others to work on a short project; and others again may prefer a conventional end-of-course test. Even though obvious problems of comparability arise, it is claimed that the procedure is fairer in allowing students to show their abilities in the mode in which they feel personally most at home.

Other forms of student participation are more far-reaching. "Peer group assessment" — which calls upon students to mark each others' work — is practiced in some departments' group projects (usually by giving a total of, say, 100 marks to a group of five students who have worked together, and requiring them to distribute these as equitably as possible amongst themselves).

"Self-assessment" or "negotiated assessment" requires the undergraduate and his or her member of staff to make independent evaluations, and then to achieve an agreed mark (as two independent examiners normally have to do). Although a few instances of this practice are to be found in British higher education, it seems surprisingly rare, when one considers the emphasis in many degree prospectuses on preparing graduates to evaluate their own performance in their subsequent careers.

Support for staff and students.

The third category of changes identified by the Nuffield Group was a somewhat miscellaneous one. It comprised those innovations which were designed to have a bearing on the improvement of undergraduate education, but which consisted neither of new curricular patterns nor of departures from the established procedures of teaching, learning and assessment. They might perhaps best be described as contextual changes — that is, attempts to modify the institutional framework within which staff-student interaction takes place.

A number of such developments were centred upon helping students better to cope with the demands of higher education. In particular there appeared to be a steady growth in the support provided for newly-arrived undergraduates in adjusting to an unfamiliar (and, for some, totally alien) environment. Even where this provision took a form which clearly failed to meet the needs of new arrivals,[12] a good deal of time and effort was devoted to it. In some universities, second- and third-year undergraduates volunteered to act as "sponsors" for individual students in their first term. When the arrangement worked well, it helped to create a positive attitude to academic life, and by the same token to improve motivation and performance.

A somewhat similar development, catering for students later in their university careers as well as in their difficult first year, is the substantial growth in counselling provision. This may have a variety of emphases. In some cases personal counselling, with a largely psychiatric basis, is offered as part of the student health services. In others, the counselling is predominantly academic (there is a particular need for such help where the course pattern is complex, calling for a considerable amount of student choice, as in modular degree schemes). Or else both forms of provision may be linked, and combined also with careers counselling in a comprehensive service (such as that available at Keele University).

Academic counselling has its unofficial counterpart in the growing number of "consumers' guides" to courses, usually prepared by the Students' Union on the basis of reports from satisfied or dissatisfied learners. Predictably, such "underground" publications were at first strongly condemned by the academic establishment. However, on more mature judgement they have been generally agreed to be sensible, responsible and useful additions to the range of existing evidence on which students can base a choice of courses.

Another notable growth area in the provision of help for learners is the availability of "study skills" courses. These are usually optional: they aim to give direct guidance — and a limited amount of supervised practice — in such activities as rapid reading, essay writing, note taking, and participation in seminars. The rationale is that since many of these activities are peculiar to higher education, undergraduates are unlikely to have had previous experience of them, and can therefore benefit from exercises designed to make themselves more familiar with the necessary techniques.

A similar argument has been directed, in most universities, to the needs of new recruits to the academic teaching profession. It is certainly true that postgraduate research — the usual channel into a university lectureship — gives no systematic practice in how to lecture, run a seminar, or give a tutorial (though in some science departments graduates have a rudimentary introduction to laboratory teaching as demonstrators). Accordingly, as a counterpart to the provision of "study skills" training for students, many UK universities have in the past few years offered some course of initial training in teaching techniques for staff. The level and quality of such courses varies considerably from one institution to another. Few of them involve more than about a dozen sessions, and virtually no established academics (despite their own lack of training) opt to participate in them. The retrenchment of the mid 1970's has now caused the rate of recruitment of new staff to fall to an almost insignificant level, with the result that even the modest existing provision for training university teachers has ceased to be economic.

Less direct forms of support for teaching have, however, proved generally acceptable to academics. In some universities (Sussex is one example) facilities are available, on request by any teacher or group of teachers, for the independent and confidential evaluation of their courses or their assessment procedures. Such facilities are normally called upon when a course seems to be working unsatisfactorily, or when the mechanisms for assessing students appear unreliable or ineffective. An informative diagnosis of the problem can often lead on to a request for help in the techniques of curriculum development (an activity which, though basically straightforward, seems to be handled in an extraordinarily amateur and naive way by most academics). Central support facilities of this kind — which usually involve the active part-time help of interested faculty members — serve to encourage staff to recognise that the improvement of the quality of courses and of teaching is well within their reach. It can be shown to depend on taking an intelligent and inquiring interest in what happens in the lecture hall, seminar room and laboratory, and on trying to picture the situation from the learner's point of view,[13] rather than on acquiring any special set of "tricks of the trade".

3. What are the Potentialities and Limitations of Change?

"Top down" and "Bottom up" Innovations

The preceding section has aimed to give a fairly full resumé of the trends in British higher education during the first half of the 1970's. One of its most remarkable features has been the way in which innovative ideas have transcended disciplinary as well as institutional boundaries. The ideas of resource-based learning, for example, might first take root in a department of engineering and then infiltrate into a course in English literature. A successful experiment with an interdisciplinary programme in European Studies might create a helpful precedent for one in Environmental Sciences; and so on.

It was one of the main conclusions of the Nuffield Group [14] that although the scope and pace of innovation during the period of their research had proved to be greater than they initially expected, the flow of worthwhile and generally-applicable ideas was disappointingly haphazard, and the means of communicating them primitive in the extreme. Series of publications such as the present one clearly offer a useful approach towards tackling the problem. They may however need to be supplemented over time with more permanent means of disseminating curricular innovations and of allowing for their more cumulative and systematic development.

For our current purposes, it may be useful to round off this exploration of the concept of change in higher education with a survey of some of the potentialities, as well as some of the practical limitations, of testing out apparently promising innovations in a university setting. We will begin by looking at attempts to impose innovations from a higher authority, go on to review the effects of structural constraints, and end with a discussion of prevailing academic values and their relationship to new developments.

"Top down", as opposed to "bottom up", innovations have a generally poor record of success in higher education. The primary reason is perhaps because the basic academic units — departments, course teams and the like — are in most institutions professionally autonomous. Given that they are resilient both to external coercion and to exhortations from higher authority, it is not in practice possible to impose any curricular changes on them, however desirable such changes may be thought to be. Two illustrative examples, very different in nature and scale, can be given from recent UK experience.

In the mid-1960's, a number of sustained attempts were made, on the basis of an officially-sponsored enquiry into audio-visual aids in higher education, to encourage academics to make more extensive use of new media, and especially educational television. The support of a number of politically powerful vice-chancellors (many of whom were instrumental in establishing closed-circuit links and sizeable central studios in their own universities) suggested that this change was likely to take firm root. But as yet, television has provided only a marginal embellishment to undergraduate teaching. Few staff think of it as a resource, on a par with textbooks and journal articles, to be closely woven into the fabric of the curriculum. More than a decade after its installation, it would be difficult to claim that the investment has anywhere near paid off.

A "top down" innovation on a more massive scale was consciously and deliberately injected into British higher education by the establishment of the polytechnic sector between 1969 and 1972. The new polytechnics were required, by the terms under which they were designated as degree-level institutions, to carry out a distinct set of functions. Their courses were meant to be more industrially-oriented, more responsive to local and regional need, and more socially relevant than those of universities. But over the years, universities have become more competitive in their links with industry; polytechnics have recruited nationally rather than locally, and their curricula have reflected this; a continuing concern with academic respectability has muted the original quest for social relevance. The professional values of polytechnic teachers are little different from those of other academic groups, and they look outside their own institutional structure for their identity as specialists. So, as the result of a steady process of "academic drift", the actual differences between the polytechnics' curriculum programmes and those of the universities have now become blurred and difficult to discern.

If changes introduced from outside, or from above, run into trouble because of the strength and persistence of the academics' sense of professional identity, those introduced from within, or from below, have a different set of challenges to overcome. Some promising ideas may founder because they go too far in questioning established assumptions; but many fail because they are unable to accommodate to existing structural constraints.

Academic structures and regulations for the most part evolve to protect the legitimate interests of researchers and teachers. They help to define, and also to defend, the main areas of professional concern within an institution. But once established, they can prove surprisingly rigid and difficult to change. Even when an innovative idea is generally accepted on intellectual grounds, it may face severe difficulty if it appears to conflict with conventional practice, or to challenge some existing organisational constraints. Thus, both W.H. Dowdeswell and N.D.C. Harris [15] and W.F. Williams and J. Lipscombe [16] independently remark on the difficulties experienced by some teachers in introducing project work because of the problems of assessment. (The Nuffield team, for its part, came across a number of departments which had decided against group project work, while extolling its educational merits, because it could not meaningfully be assessed in accordance with conventional practice). Again, B. Eckstein [17] refers in her discussion of the seminar method to the tension which can be set up between the co-operative ethos of group teaching and the institutional demand for competitive grades.

A similar conflict, on a more extensive scale, can arise in the course of attempts to introduce new curricular patterns. In some institutions, the introduction of a unit-based degree pattern can be interpreted as a threat to the autonomy of existing departments: indeed, some institutions introducing modular courses on an extensive scale have found it necessary to change over to a matrix structure in which teaching resources go to course teams and research resources to discipline-based groups. Interdisciplinary courses present even greater problems, since they challenge the whole set of organisational assumptions on which traditional discipline-based universities have evolved. Workable compromises have been reached in a number of cases. However, the ideal solution of establishing broadly-based schools of study, adopted in some newly-created universities in the 1960's, appears to be out of reach of most institutions with an entrenched departmental framework.

Changes in attitude and belief

It is one thing for those promoting an innovative idea to compromise with the regulations and the structures of particular academic institutions, but quite another to negotiate significant changes in the prevailing values of university life. In most cases of change, this is the first, and most important task: very often, it is also the most difficult. But unless those individual academics who are being urged to adopt a new practice, or to teach a novel type of course, can accept its rationale — unless they can "internalise" the change so that it becomes part of their professional identity — the experiment will almost inevitably be short-lived. So it is important, in understanding the nature of academic innovation, to be aware of the different elements which go to shape the climate of attitudes and beliefs among those engaged in higher education.

We will concentrate here on three different but related clusters of values — which might for convenience be labelled disciplinary, professional and personal — before embarking on a fuller discussion of a fourth category, namely educational values.

Disciplinary values constitute the unseen, taken-for-granted inner life of academia. They are portrayed in operation in A.T. Rogerson's interesting review [18] of the relationships between mathematics and statistics on the one hand and individual science subjects on the other. It emerges clearly, from his account, that this is the really innovative facet of higher education. Change in the nature and content of disciplines is not only expected but positively sought after and valued. Except in the rare cases where a whole frame of reference is being called into question (as with Darwin, Einstein or Heisenberg), new ideas are assimilated relatively painlessly. Thus, as Rogerson shows, the nature of mathematics is constantly evolving; the intellectual territory occupied by geography and biology has expanded and changed almost out of recognition. Of course, the growth of some disciplines is affected by internal dissent, while others may at a particular point in time become static, or reach a dead end. But overall, the picture is of constant shifts in value and of a steady incidence of new ideas which — once they have met the criteria of validity — are positively welcomed.

The openness by its practitioners to new ideas within an individual discipline is in marked contrast with the attitudes of those same practitioners towards change in their professional domain. Thus, if it seems that the integrity of a particular field of interest is being undermined, or that its status is being questioned, or even that its power is being curbed, the ranks close and the marauder is beaten off. The existing "pecking order" of academic prestige, which is more a product of historical accident than of anything else, is as jealously preserved as if it embodied the eternal necessities of logic.

This professional defensiveness is understandable in terms of academic politics; and it might be harmless enough, were it not that it very ofen conflicts with curricular requirements or with the demands of good teaching. For example, "service" courses in mathematics of the type discussed in the papers by A.R. Stokes [19] and by A.T. Rogerson [20] may well be essential from the students' point of view: but they are notorious for three common failings. First, they are usually taught within an inappropriate conceptual framework by professional mathematicians. Second, because they are seen as second-rate courses by the mathematics department, the teaching is apt to be assigned to the most inexperienced, or the most incompetent member of staff available. Third, because the staff of the students' parent department also tend to see such courses as a tiresome necessity, taking up time which could be more profitably spent in pursuit of the prime discipline, they too downgrade them. It is not difficult for the student to "get the message" and so to fail to take such courses seriously.[21] As W.F. Williams and J. Lipscombe [22] show in their perceptive analysis of the problem of introducing broad courses, a somewhat comparable mechanism operates in the case of many combined honours degrees.

Academic departments — and professional associations with a wider national role — can be a potent means of obstructing ideas which challenge professional, rather than disciplinary, norms. Their main influence is at the level of the curriculum, especially in relation to reforms which appear to call into question existing patterns or to modify established boundaries.

Innovations which relate to teaching method are less likely to be affected by such professional constraints. On the whole, departments (and the professional bodies which operate as watchdogs for their corporate interests) allow the individual academic a good deal of freedom to decide how he will present the required curriculum content within a predetermined structure. So changes concerned with the day-to-day strategies of teaching and learning are in some respects easier to establish than changes in curricular organisation. In other respects, they may be harder. They depend on winning the consensus of a large number of individual teachers, as opposed to negotiating a collective agreement at the level of the institution. It is in changes along these lines that the personal values of academics tend to be a key factor.

Personal attitudes, wants and beliefs are sometimes hard to separate out from disciplinary ideologies and professional loyalties; they may be even more difficult to distinguish from the educational views and standpoints which we shall go on to discuss in the following section. However, each academic — in his capacity as a human being — has certain individual notions of right or wrong, good or bad. He also has personal preferences as between one kind of activity and another, and his own particular idea of what it means to be doing a worthwhile and rewarding job. All these factors can condition his judgement of any new and unfamiliar proposal. Thus, for example, an academic strongly committed to research and relatively uninterested in teaching may show little enthusiasm for developing a programme of "skill sessions" which are time-consuming to work out. Similarly, a teacher who believes strongly in preserving the authority of staff members will be reluctant to embark on the democratic procedures inherent in some forms of seminar group.

Luckily, even the most strong-minded and apparently entrenched individuals have been known to change their minds: as have the most apparently dyed-in-the-wool departments. Were this not so, the prospects for developing and trying out promising ideas would be bleak indeed. In practice, the optimal strategy for the innovator — whether he is setting out to initiate a change in the existing routine of undergraduate teaching or attempting to establish and win creditibility for a complete new institution — seems to consist in maintaining a strong continuity of values along one dimension while promoting a discontinuity along another.

Thus, the undeniable success of the Open University — which must on any count be rated as a highly innovative institution — can be attributed at least in part to its firm insistence on matching the standards of academic excellence in more conventional UK universities. Because it could not be faulted on the stringency of its assessment criteria, academic opinion allowed it to get away with the flouting of several other established conventions. At the other end of the scale, the rapid rate at which undergraduate project work was accepted — despite its radical departure from the previous conventions of undergraduate teaching — depended in large measure on its consistency with another well-established and respectable procedure, namely the graduate thesis. As P. Black and J. Ogborn [23] put it, "Projects seem immediately valid to teachers: they can easily be assimilated to activities which are highly valued, namely research and research training. . . project work has succeeded by challenging just enough, but no more, accepted ideas of undergraduate teaching''.

Views about knowledge and the nature of teaching

Having looked briefly in turn at disciplinary, professional and personal values in relation to academic innovation, it seems appropriate to conclude by considering in more detail the beliefs and attitudes which have a direct bearing on educational issues. Educational values might be said to fall into two broad categories: those which concern the structure of knowledge and the nature of teaching; and those which relate to the characteristics of the learning process. The contribution to this series by M.J. Frazer and R. Maskill [24] takes both categories fully into account.

It is scarcely possible to be a university teacher without having some view (implicit and subconscious, if not explicit and conscious) about such questions as whether knowledge is relative or absolute, and whether teaching is a matter of transmitting facts efficiently or stimulating a desire to learn. What academics actually do in the process of presenting lectures, planning and supervising laboratory work, and conducting seminars and tutorials is a general indicator of their educational values. Surprisingly often, such values are not the result of careful debate, or of philosophical reflection — they seem to have been acquired uncritically, mainly from personal experience of the educational process and through the example of influential colleagues.

Two long-standing academic traditions, which reflect contrasting views of what undergraduate education is about, can be characterised in a number of different ways. We shall take the notions of validity and relevance as the main determinants of the two curriculum approaches in question (it may be noted that Frazer and Maskill mark the same distinction in terms of didactic and heuristic teaching strategies).

The tradition which emphasises validity as a prime value tends, appropriately, to pay a high regard to original research and to the generation of new knowledge within the discipline. Teaching is evaluated primarily in terms of the efficient transmission of established knowledge to a largely passive, receptive audience. The curriculum is defined in terms of content and coverage rather than of methodology, or of matching the learners' needs.

In contrast, the tradition which emphasises relevance as a general goal — which sees the academic enterprise as being in some measure socially-determined, rather than defined by purely disciplinary considerations — has a different set of priorities. It is as much concerned with the critical analysis and appraisal of existing ideas within a given field as it is with "pushing back the frontiers". That is, it values scholarship and knowledge regeneration at the expense of research and knowledge generation. Teaching is seen as a transaction between students and staff, in which new ideas and interpretations have to be developed in the context of a growing understanding by the students of what the subject is about. The curriculum is shaped by a concern with exemplifying processes of inquiry — by enabling students to appreciate the characteristic methodology of the field in question, rather than requiring them to master its contents.

The two traditions can of course coexist within the same institution (and sometimes even within the same department), though this can give rise to problems. Within the tradition of validity, specialisms tend to be narrowly defined and to generate a hierarchy in which the more expert hold dominion over the less expert. Professors know better than lecturers; both are authorities over their students. The tradition of relevance leads to more collegial structures, in which the professor is only first among equals. Anyone (including students) can have a good idea or make a worthwhile academic contribution. Not only are professional values different as between allegiances to the different traditions; what count as legitimate personal wants and expectations will differ as well.

Although these rival traditions may be thought to have played some part in defining what C.P. Snow called "The Two Cultures", they can certainly not be equated with science and technology on the one hand and arts and social science on the other. They cut across the boundaries, not only of subject-matter and type of institution, but also of different phases in the history of higher education. Indeed, one might say that every period embodies some compromise between the two. At some stages, as in the medieval universities, the tradition of relevance might be strongly dominant. At others, as in the reforms first inspired in Germany under Humboldt, the idea of validity may gain ascendancy. But for the most part, there is an uneasy balance struck between them, with the actual point of equilibrium moving in one direction or another over time.

Views about learning

The discussion by M.J. Frazer and R. Maskill [25] of psychological learning theories brings out the wide range of values implicit in different views of how students learn. At one extreme lies the highly mechanistic conception of human understanding developed in behavioural psychology and exemplified by the work of B.F. Skinner.[26] It is implied that the complexities of undergraduate and graduate level work are ultimately reducible to the stimulus-response mechanisms by which pigeons and rats can be trained to perform routine sequences of tasks. At the other extreme of the spectrum is the humanistic approach developed by Carl Rogers,[27] working within the psychoanalytic tradition. On this view, the emotions and attitudes of the learner are paramount in creating the conditions for learning.

These "hard-line" and "soft-line" positions about the learning process are related, ideologically, to differing views on human intelligence. One long-established school of thought, basing itself on the technology of mental testing, argues that most intellectual abilities are innate and immutable — though admittedly, the degree to which their potentialities are realised may depend on circumstance. Suitable tests can be devised to assess in precise, numerical terms, the mental properties of any individual; and these properties are held to be invariable and genetically-determined. In recent years, however, the intellectual fashion has shifted away from psychometry in the direction of sociological techniques of investigation: and this has given rise to a vigorous questioning of earlier findings (as witness the recent controversies, centred round A.R. Jensen, on intelligence and race).

The claim that contextual factors play an important part, both in creating intellectual confidence and in promoting effective learning, is explicitly put forward in the papers by B. Eckstein [28] and P. Black and J. Ogborn.[29] It is reinforced by the — as yet — relatively few studies of student learning which have taken interviews with undergraduates as their starting-point, rather than opinion surveys of university teachers or observations of how laboratory animals behave. The findings of the study conducted within the Higher Education Learning Project (Physics) on "Students' reactions to undergraduate science" are discussed briefly in Black and Ogborn's review article. They bear a marked similarity to the conclusions in the independent study by the Nuffield Group, "Learning from Learners".[30]

Students — perhaps not altogether surprisingly — turned out to be highly perceptive and articulate commentators on the courses in which they had taken part. They were most at home, and considered that they worked effectively, in those contexts in which some direct personal contact existed between teachers and taught — and where they accordingly felt more easily able to ask about points which they did not fully understand. In those situations where the atmosphere was uncompromisingly formal, they tended to feel alienated and inhibited. Overall, the impression given by such studies is that a number of straightforward opportunities to improve university teaching are missed as a result of the teacher's paying inadequate attention to the student's perspective.

4. Conclusion

This introductory contribution to the series has given roughly equal emphasis to three different aspects of change in higher education. It began by tracing the development of recent research on academic innovation as a phenomenon in its own right. It went on to summarise the main trends of innovative developments within one particular system (that of the UK), as identified in a recent Nuffield-sponsored study. Here, the main categories chosen for the analysis were: changes in curriculum pattern (such as inter-disciplinarity, modular courses and breadth); developments in teaching and learning methods and assessment techniques; and new forms of support for staff and students (counselling, study skills courses, course evaluation facilities and the like). Finally, an attempt was made to review some of the practical limitations and possibilities of putting new ideas into effect. This involved looking at structural constraints and also at four clusters of academic attitudes and beliefs — disciplinary, professional, personal and educational.

The papers which follow provide between them instances of nearly all the main trends which can be identified in higher education as a whole. They also, understandably enough, represent a diversity of educational stances. It may be helpful to round off this introduction by offering an account of two basic philosophical positions against which the characteristics of most such developments can be charted. The dichotomy which these rival world-views represent is at a more fundamental level than any of the values considered earlier, but can nevertheless be seen as related to them.

Among those with a professional concern in higher education, one group tends to see the issues in terms of developing an appropriate technology — of finding predictable generalisations about the nature of learning, and clear-cut causal connections in the process of initiating change. The quest is for discrete entities and absolute values. The other group, contrarily, is prone to emphasise the organic nature of changes in teaching, and the complex, contextually sensitive and essentially unquantifiable character of the learning process. In this view, the environment is maintained to be extremely important. Phenomena which are abstracted from it are claimed to lose many of their essential characteristics. The emphasis is on relativity, interconnectedness and the wholeness of things.

To take some specific examples within this series, broad courses along the lines described by W.F. Williams and J. Lipscombe [31] allow for a considerably higher level of uncertainty and relativism of content than traditional degree programmes. Programmed learning and audio-tutorial techniques of the type discussed in P. Bamberg's paper [32] are ideologically at an opposite pole to the seminar approaches described by B. Eckstein.[33] Again, Black and Ogborn [34] draw a clear distinction between objectives-based and open-ended approaches to laboratory teaching. The ideological stance of an individual teacher, or of a department as a whole, will powerfully condition which innovations will be found acceptable and which not.

The conflict is in some ways reminiscent of the methodological contrasts between classical physics and ecology. There can be no expectation that one view or the other will eventually emerge triumphant, though they are unlikely to enjoy a comfortable coexistence. Of course, fundamental value positions, like political allegiances, can be changed in individual cases, and even their general characteristics can become modified over time. But such basic divergences as those between right and left, non-compromiser and negotiator, quantifier and qualifier, will always re-emerge in some guise. All that the present series can reasonably expect to do is review the existing disposition of forces and nudge it in the direction which seems most conducive to the betterment of university science education to-day.

REFERENCES

[1] D.A. Schon, *Beyond the Stable State,* Penguin, 1971.

[2] B. Berg and B. Östergren, *Innovations and Innovation Processes in Higher Education,* Swedish National Board of Universities and Colleges, 1977.

[3] T. Becher *et al, The Drift of Change,* Nuffield Group for Research and Innovation in Higher Education, The Nuffield Foundation, 1975.

[4] V.M. Showalter, *A Challenge for Interdisciplinary Science*, p. 241.

[5] G. Squires *et al, Interdisciplinarity,* Nuffield Group for Research and Innovation in Higher Education, The Nuffield Foundation, 1975.

[6] A.R. Stokes, *Integration and Separation as a result of Unit Courses*, p. 321.

[7] W.F. Williams and J. Lipscombe, *Broadening Courses*, p. 279.

[8] W.H. Dowdeswell and N.D.C. Harris, *Project Work in University Science*, p. 203.

[9] B. Eckstein, *Group Methods in University Science Teaching*, p. 117.

[10] P.J. Black and J. Ogborn, *Laboratory Work in Undergraduate Teaching*, p. 161.

[11] Paul G. Bamberg, *Adapting Instructional Method to Class Size*, p. 97.

[12] Some instances of this are documented in M. Parlett *et al., Learning from Learners,* Nuffield Group for Research and Innovation in Higher Education, The Nuffield Foundation, 1976.

[13] M. Parlett *et al., op.cit.*

[14] T. Becher *et al, Making the Best of It,* Nuffield Group for Research and Innovation in Higher Education, The Nuffield Foundation, 1976.

[15] W.H. Dowdeswell and N.D.C. Harris, *op.cit.*

[16] W.F. Williams and J. Lipscombe, *op.cit.*

[17] B. Eckstein, *op.cit.*

[18] A.T. Rogerson, *Mathematics and Statistics in Relation to Science*, p. 65.

[19] A.R. Stokes, *op.cit.*

[20] A.T. Rogerson, *op.cit.*

[21] W.F. Williams, *op.cit.*

[22] P. Black and J. Ogborn, *op.cit.*

[23] M.J. Frazer and R. Maskill, *Learning Theory and Practice*, p. 43.

[24] M. Frazer and R. Maskill, *op.cit.*

[25] B. Eckstein, *op.cit.*

[26] P. Black and J. Ogborn, *op.cit.*

[27] M. Parlett *et al, op.cit.*

Learning Theory and Practice

M.J. Frazer and R. Maskill

1. Introduction

This review has two purposes. The first is to provide brief reviews with key references of: (i) current methods of teaching and learning science at university level *(practice)* and (ii) the present state of the psychology of how people learn *(theory)*. The second purpose is to show the extent of the gap between *theory* and *practice* and to indicate where the gap is being, or might be, bridged.

There is now a vast literature on the psychology of learning and yet for the many reasons listed below, it is either unknown to, or is ignored by, university science teachers.

(i)   Many studies are made on learning in early childhood and there is a justifiable doubt whether there can be application at university level.

(ii) University science teachers are so busy researching and teaching their own subject that they do not have time to master the language and literature of another subject.

(iii) There are various theories of learning which superficially seem to contradict one another. It is naive to suppose that there will ever be *one* theory of learning but possibly some university teachers are waiting until someone will come to them and say: "... this is how students learn"*.

* Scientists tend to assume that a "theory" will be prescriptive, whereas social scientists usually claim no more for a theory than that it should be descriptive.

(iv) Some of the published work is so theoretical that there seems to be no way in which the ideas can be applied in the classroom or laboratory. Furthermore the validity of some of the research is doubtful and it is not always easy to distinguish between deductions from experimental results and the opinions of the writer.

It is hoped that this review will act as a guide for the busy university science teacher so that he can obtain an overall view of the diverse theories of how students learn in order to see where there may be links with his teaching methods, which he has usually adopted either intuitively or by imitation.

The review is in three parts: practice (section 2), theory (section 3) and bridging the gap (section 4). There are a number of books and papers [1-5] which give an overview of the connections between teaching practice and learning theory.

2. Teaching methods in university science

Twenty five years ago a first degree student of science would have been taught mainly by formal lectures using nothing more than blackboard and chalk and by working through a standard set of laboratory experiments. Although lecture plus laboratory still forms the basic diet for most science students, they will now certainly experience some other teaching methods. Several factors have led to these innovations:

(i)   expansion of universities, particularly in the number of science students during the 1950's and 1960's, leading to larger classes and to a wider spectrum of student ability and motivation;

(ii)   the decline in popularity of science in many developed countries in the 1970's causing university teachers to seek ways of making their courses more attractive;

(iii) pressure from employers of science graduates who required students to be able to think and apply knowledge not simply to recall knowledge (i.e. a slow recognition on the part of university science teachers of the importance of considering the aims of their courses and of matching these aims to teaching/learning strategies):

(iv)   the constant expansion of scientific knowledge and

increasing complexity of modern research techniques and instrumentation causing university staff to seek ways to "teach" more in the same unit of time:

(v) increasing financial pressures on university science departments so that ways of becoming more cost effective were sought;

(vi) the availability of a great variety of audio-visual techniques.

Hardly any of the innovations have come about as a result of applying knowledge of the theories of learning. Innovations have been centred on teaching and not on learning. It is to be hoped that the next twenty five years will see a change in emphasis so that educational development is based on an increasing understanding of how people learn. This is fundamental, but as this review will reveal we are only at the beginning and there must be a change of direction in educational research. At present, much research is directed not at problems of learning but at the efficacy of particular techniques of teaching.

It seems generally recognized that there are two broad strategies for teaching although it is also accepted that there is a spectrum of approaches between extremes. The ends of the spectrum are labelled with words such as:

didactic	heuristic
formal	informal
passive	active
knowledge based	research based (i.e. guided discovery approach, problem solving)
teacher centred	student centred

It is not suggested that these labels are equivalent. They mean different things to different people and so in this review we shall use an alternative classification of strategies based on three categories:[6]

classroom (i.e. group) methods,

laboratory methods,

individual methods.

Within each category the didactic — heuristic dimension applies, and within each category there are a number of sub-divisions as shown in Table 1.

In addition to the key references listed in Table 1, a general view of current teaching and learning methods in university science teaching can be obtained from other references [17-20] and from specific examples.[21-25] References [7-25] have been selected more to give coverage, and it is therefore striking that none of these references refer in any depth to theories of learning. In the next section we review what is currently known about these theories.

Table 1. Strategies of teaching and learning

Strategy	Characteristics	Key References
1. *Classroom (i.e. Group) methods*		
1.1 Lectures	A formal situation in which students listen, watch, take notes, but are otherwise passive. Visual aids and written "hand-outs" are often used. Useful for conveying knowledge to large numbers of students.	Bligh [7] gives a comprehensive account of the variations, limitations and advantages of this method and shows how lectures can be made active.
1.2 Seminars	A small group discussion centred on a prepared theme. It may be tightly controlled and structured by the teacher, or be very informal, and at the extreme leaderless (i.e. peer teaching). Useful for learning "to present an argument" and to develop critical thinking.	
1.3 Problem classes ("workshops", example sessions)	Small group sessions in which students attempt problems and receive solutions.	Critical accounts of these methods are given. [7-10]
1.4 Syndicate methods	Students are divided into groups of about six members who then work on problems and produce a report or answer, to present to the assembled students. Useful for developing communication and problem solving skills.	

| 1.5 Simulations, games, case studies, role playing, etc. | There are many variations. Useful for motivation, teaching applications of knowledge and decision making, and may help in changing attitudes. | Critical accounts of these methods are given.[7-10] |
| 1.6 Tutorials | Very small groups (usually less than four) of students meeting with a teacher to discuss difficulties, present essays etc. | |

2. *Laboratory methods*

2.1 Individual set experiments	The essential feature is that students follow instructions. Various audio-visual aids and computer assisted learning (3.4) are sometimes combined with this approach. Used for teaching manipulative skills and general under-standing.	[11, 12]
2.2 Open-ended practical work	Intermediate between 2.1 and 2.3	
2.3 Individual projects	An open ended investigation. Useful for teaching decision making and for changing attitudes (self-awareness etc.).	
2.4 Group projects	As for 2.3 but students work in groups. Also useful for teaching team work.	

3. *Individual methods*

| 3.1 Reading and essay writing | Useful for acquiring knowledge, ability to seek, select and present knowledge. | |
| 3.2 Programmed instruction | Usually a structured, written text requiring active student responses, but may also involve audio-visual tech-niques. Useful for teaching knowledge and simple applications. Helpful for remedial work. | [13] |

| 3.3 Keller plan (Personalised system of instruction) | Students work at their own pace through a highly structured course and proceed from unit to unit only on passing a criterion referenced test at a suitably high level. | 14, 15 |
| 3.4 Computer assisted learning | Similar to 3.2 but students have a two way communication with the computer. Often used for simulating data. Useful for teaching decision making and problem solving. | 16 |

3. *Theories of Learning*

3.1 Overview

The major theories of learning and their principal proponents are shown in Table 2.

Table 2. Major theories of learning

Section	Proponent	Description	Key reference
3.2	Skinner	Behavioural psychology	26
3.3	Gagné	Hierarchical task analysis	27
3.4	Lewin	Gestalt (Field) psychology	28
3.5		Cognitive psychology	
	Ausubel, Bruner	General	29, 30
	Piaget	Developmental	31
	Lindsay and Norman	Information processing	32
3.6	Rogers	Humanist psychology	33

3.2 Behavioural Psychology

The basis of the behavioural approach to the psychology of learning is found in the work of E.L. Thorndike.[34] Learning was considered to be the association, by some neurological process, of a *response* to a *stimulus*. The research which lead to this view was done mostly on animals and it was implied that the research results so obtained could equally well be used to rationalise human learning activity. This was, and still is, debatable.

Many of the early statements and laws of the behaviourists have since been shown to be either wrong or over simplistic, but the movement has been carried up to the present by the work and ideas of B.F. Skinner.[26] He is generally accorded the title of neo-behaviourist since his ideas, though based in a behaviourist philosophy, have developed considerably and have many new facets. In common with Thorndike, Skinner has no place for theories of the mind or of thinking. He does not deny their existence but chooses not to study them. For Skinner psychology is the science of overt behaviour. Psychological issues must rest in, and be settled by, the study of observable behaviour and the situational variables to which they are linked. The two major terms used in this type of study are *operant* and *reinforcer*. An operant is simply a behaviour, a performance or an act which a human is capable of. A reinforcer is anything which will increase the likelihood of a particular operant occuring in a given situation. One of the essential differences between Skinner's views and those of the early behaviourists is that he concentrates on what follows the desired operant, i.e. the reinforcer, whereas Thorndike concentrated on the stimulus which preceded the response. For Skinner, it is the consequences of an act in the past which governs the likelihood of it taking place in the future. If an operant has been reinforced in the past then it is more probable to happen in the future. A reinforcer is therefore *anything* which will increase the likelihood of an operant recurring. Reinforcers are discovered empirically and cannot always be predicted to be useful in the future. Skinner believes that all human learning can be studied in the framework of operants and reinforcers and that a technology of teaching should be developed on this basis.

When applied to teaching, the message of behaviourism is simple — reinforce what you want; ignore what you don't. In order to achieve this effectively, complex learning is usually broken down into a sequence of small steps. At the end of each step the learner is asked to make some response which requires the content of that step to have been mastered. Correct responses are rewarded and therefore reinforced by a sense of achievement and by the learner being allowed to continue. Incorrect responses give no such feeling and also stop progress. In this way the learner is receiving constant reinforcement of correct operants and hopefully will effectively learn the sequence to achieve the overall learning task. This approach has become known as "programmed instruction" and has been usefully applied in many situations.

That simple programming is not the whole answer has however been apparent for some time. It is likely that in very many learning situations the context of learning, (i.e. the learner's attitude to, and perception of, the learning task) is far too complex. Programming methods actually presume that the learner is a constant factor. It seems, however, that people have unpredictable purposes and that this can make simple behaviouristic principles inappropriate.

3.3 Hierarchical task analysis and the conditions of learning

The psychological theories of R.M. Gagné [27] have their roots in the behavioural tradition and in the methods of task analysis. His ideas are not however strictly behavioural in outlook and he does have quite a lot to say about thinking as well as about learning.

Gagné classifies learning into categories, namely information learning, intellectual skills, cognitive strategies, attitudes and motor skills. In the type of learning designated as intellectual skills there is a further sub-classification. It is this final scheme for which Gagné has become best known and which holds out promise for the organisation of teaching at university level. The suggestion he makes is that intellectual skills are subdivided into a hierarchical sequence and that teaching should follow this sequence in order to be effective. The higher sub-classes of intellectual skills are (i) discriminations (of concrete properties), (ii) concepts (which are real and concrete), (iii) rules (which are concepts by definition) and (iv) problem solving. [35] The implication is that to teach problem solving requires the previous teaching of the prerequisite rules, which in turn require the prerequisite concepts and so on.

Skills are defined in terms of performances and the key question to be asked is always:

> "What must the learner be able to *do* in order to achieve what is required, given only simple instructions?"

If this question is asked for any learning task, a prerequisite set of tasks is produced. The same question can then be asked of each of these prerequisites and so on, until eventually a level of tasks is arrived at which can be taken as already in the repertoire of the learner. The structures of capabilities produced in this way for the various levels of intellectual skill are described as learning hierarchies. The implication of Gagné's work is that hierarchies are in some way psychologically valid as descriptions of the best way of approaching the teaching and learning of the capabilities in question, but so far the evidence for their validity is not very strong.[36] There is reason to suppose that learning hierarchies have their best application in the very rule oriented disciplines of the pure sciences.

3.4 Gestalt Psychology

The essence of Gestalt psychology[28] as outlined by K. Koffka, W. Köhler and more recently extended into Field Psychology by K. Lewin is the study of human perception. A perception is what an individual makes of a happening. It is what his past experience causes him to interpret, or to pay attention to, or to ignore in any situation. Thus, seeing is not perceiving (as everybody knows well enough) and Gestalt psychologists are concerned with unravelling the factors in human experience which govern changing perception.

The need to come to an acceptable understanding of a previously ambiguous situation is seen by the Gestalt psychologists as fundamental, biological and universal. The resolution of ambiguity is the driving force of learning and no other reinforcement should be necessary. Here immediately is a sharp contrast to behaviourism, which insists on a reinforcer which is external to the learning event and which itself may have no relationship to the learning event (except that it acts as a reinforcer). Gestalt psychologists say that the reduction of ambiguity inherent in any learning task will itself provide all the motivation required. In other words, learning is its own reinforcer.

The word Gestalt has no literal translation in English. It means a combination of perceptual impression and insight. A learning act is seen as the formation of a good "feel for" a problem, or the gaining of an insight into the true nature of a problem. This insight includes everything, both in memory from past experience and in the surroundings as accepted by the senses and interpreted by the brain, which is taken into account when a particular problem is encountered. This perceptual totality has come to be called the psychological field which should be taken into account when studying any learning problem.

The atomistic, step by step approach of programmed learning is rejected. In its place is put a stress on whole situations and a guided discovery methodology which emphasises meaningfulness. Meaningfulness is necessary if learning is to be other than trial and error — it is essential for learners to be able to think about the learning problem, otherwise the highly developed human capability of forming insights can never function.

Insight, it is suggested, cannot be learned except from personal experience. It cannot be learned from a presentation of other's insights — information can be learned but insights must develop themselves. This clearly points to an activity based approach to teaching with large scale, meaningful problems as the main tool. Learning will then take place by learners surveying the total field and grasping via insight the implied and the necessary relationships. This is different from the style of teaching which comes out of the behaviourist tradition. Gestalt psychology has not however been applied to teaching very extensively, having been pre-empted by the force of the behaviourist movement and it is only possible to speculate on the pros and the cons of likely applications.

One question which has to be asked is why learning as described by the Gestalt psychologists should be self-motivating, (i.e. why is this reduction of ambiguity a universal reinforcer?) Piaget, who may have been influenced by the early work of Gestalt psychology, takes this question and puts it into a biological context to give the necessary justification. This is discussed in the next section.

3.5 Cognitive Psychology

3.5.1 Cognitive Structure

Cognitive psychology is a term used to describe the branches of psychology which try to investigate and describe *thought processes*, to distinguish them from the behavioural studies which do not. It is something of an umbrella term, and possibly the theories of Gagné and the Gestalt psychologists could be included. Cognitive psychology is concerned with developing theoretical models of thought processes.

The work of D.P. Ausubel[29] clearly places him as a cognitive theorist. His concern has been mostly with what he calls meaningful verbal learning. Information coming into the mind fits into an existing structure (cognitive structure) and so Ausubel has stressed the importance in teaching of relating new information to this existing structure. J.S. Bruner[30] also emphasises the importance of relating incoming information to a previously required frame of reference. He stresses the importance of the learner being active — selecting and transforming incoming information, constructing or rejecting hypotheses relating this information to the existing structure in the mind.

The views of Ausubel and Bruner about the way people learn are not dissimilar to those of Piaget which is now described in more detail.

3.5.2 Piaget

The part of Piaget's work[31] which is most commonly quoted is the theory of human cognitive development. In this theory individuals pass through two stages during childhood, the sensory motor stage and the concrete operations stage, on the way to adult functioning which is characterised as the formal operations stage.

However, Piaget also has a lot to say about the ways "thinking" takes place. Indeed it is out of this more basic work that the stage theory itself emerges.

Piaget believes that human cognition develops via a process which is closely similar to the Darwinian notion of adaptation in the development of species. Piaget insists that the principles which apply to cognitive development must be those which apply to biological development. Essentially, Piaget suggests that animals develop their capabilities by retaining those abilities and ways of operating which "pay off" and work. Those ways of operating which do not are lost, or not developed. As an individual matures he is required to do many things in order to come to terms with his existence. Experience selects in a natural way, those modes of thinking, of manipulating information and of representing them, which are of optimum efficiency.

Mental adaptation is seen by Piaget to take place via two complementary processes, assimilation and accommodation. In any intellectual happening certain things will be experienced, either from outside via the senses, or internally via thought. Whenever this happens Piaget, like the Gestalt psychologists, suggests that the new happenings are taken in in some interpreted form which depends upon the past experience of the individual. The experience is said to be "assimilated"; it is accepted by the individual in some interpreted form. Inevitably, after experiencing some new happening or event, the individual now knows more than he did before; his mind has a greater store of experience to call upon; he may even have completely reorganised a previously held view or opinion or have rejected some previously accepted fact or data. He is said to have "accommodated" to the new experience. These complementary processes, assimilation (of the event) and accommodation (by the individual) are how Piaget sees cognitive progress being made.

For teaching, this model of cognition suggests a graded problem solving approach. Problems in a particular area ought to be graded so that introductory ones, approachable from general experience by novices should lead by stages to the kind of mental operation required to solve the most involved and difficult problems. This is very similar to the guided discovery approach advocated by the Gestalt psychologists.

Another aspect of Piaget's more general view of cognition is his view of the structure of the mind. Schemes of operation which come into effect in particular circumstances and which have been built up out of experience by the adaptive process, are the building blocks of the mind. Thus in any situation a given scheme will govern reaction. Feedback may change the scheme, or it may not, depending upon the consequences. These schemes make up the totality of a mind and it is this which Piaget terms "structure". It is his study of the properties of "structure", characteristic of individuals of different ages, which has lead to the famous stage theory.

3.5.3 Cognitive Style

The study of what has come to be called cognitive or learning style has produced a number of interesting descriptions of how human beings tend to go about solving problems of various kinds. Usually a dimension of difference is described along which learners can be placed according to how they think. For example the oft quoted work by Bruner, Goodnow and Austin [37] which categorised learners according to how they set about a concept formation task; the work of Hudson [38] which looked at certain problem tasks, and that by Pask [39] which investigated how people set about learning a complex set of relationships and definitions, all produced dimensions which seem to have much in common. The focussing/scanning dimension of Bruner, the convergent/divergent dimension of Hudson and the serialist/holist dimension of Pask all seem to be distinguishing between people who prefer to think about one thing at once and others who appear happier considering a broader spread of possibilities. If this kind of categorising is valid then it would seem only sensible for teaching styles to reflect learning styles and hence for teachers to take note of the results. Pask has experimentally demonstrated the relation between learning style and teaching style. Evidence of other learning styles has also been published by Witkin [40] on field dependent/field independent learners and by Kagan [41] on impulsive/reflective learning styles.

3.5.4 Information Processing

There is currently a very clear trend in psychology towards the so called information processing approach. The emphasis on the behaviourist preoccupation with performance/environment measurables has given way over the last twenty years to a strong interest in "how the mind works". The cognitive view has now developed to the point where computer simulations of cognitive functioning are being produced which try to model, with some precision, the way in which human beings solve some problems. [42] The point of this work is that if the computer programme is able to solve problems in a human-like way then it will offer a model for human cognitive functioning. The models so far produced, though sophisticated, are a very long way from offering any generality and the implications for teaching are not yet very extensive.[43] There is no doubt however that this is the way in which psychology is progressing and that implications for teaching and learning will be forthcoming.

3.6 Humanist psychology

The humanistic approach to learning is described most fully in the book *Freedom to Learn*[33] by the psychotherapist Carl Rogers. The essential idea is that learning is personal and emotional. If the right emotional conditions can be found for each individual, then meaningful learning will take place. A simple slogan to sum up humanist psychology is *a person will learn what he wants to learn*. In other words, crucial to learning is the desire to learn. This desire can be generated in a number of ways.

(i)   Individuals are naturally curious and want to discover or experience something new. Rogers believes that many traditional educational processes inhibit curiosity and so make learning more difficult. Learning will be at a maximum when each individual's curiosity is liberated.

(ii) The subject matter should relate in some way to the individual. If a student can see that the knowledge or skills he could acquire by learning will help to solve a problem which has been troubling him, then he is more likely to learn than if there is no such personal link. Thus motivation to learn can be developed by presenting appropriate problems.

(iii) An individual will want to learn if learning does not constitute a threat or danger. For example a person who practises (makes mistakes) alone, or in a sympathetic group, will be more willing to attempt learning than when under threat of exposure, ridicule, etc. Thus encouraging self-criticism as opposed to assessment by others is essential to effective learning.

(iv) Individuals are more willing to learn if they can be involved in selecting the methods and processes of learning. Encouraging students to think about how they, as individuals, learn will in turn improve their ability to learn.

Humanist psychology condensed into these four ways of generating a desire to learn is less a theory but more a series of hypotheses based on experience. In summary, learning is at a maximum when the individual is involved emotionally and actively in the learning process. A condition for becoming so involved is freedom — freedom to choose how to learn, freedom from fear of failing to learn and, to some extent, freedom to choose what to learn.

4. Bridging the gap between learning theory and teaching practice

4.1 Overview

University science teachers use, and expect to use, several teaching strategies depending on the situation. Furthermore for each strategy, listed in section 2, there is a range of styles available so that quite different situations for learning can be presented to students. (For example; (i) lectures can have wide variations in the amounts of structure and student activity and (ii) computer assisted learning can be used simply to present programmed instruction, to place a student in a novel problem solving situation or to simulate complex data.)

What factors influence the choice of strategy and style? For most university science teachers the answers would be mainly (i) tradition, (ii) intuition and experience, and (iii) non-educational factors (such as costs, convenience, availability of equipment etc). Much less emphasis would be given to (iv) the purpose (aims), (v) consideration of the abilities, personalities and aspirations of the students, (vi) knowledge of theories of learning and (vii) the results of research into the efficacy of a particular strategy. However factors (iv), (v) and (vi) are the most important. They are interconnected. Indeed the newcomer trying to apply the disparate theories of learning outlined in section 3 to the task of selecting a teaching method would inevitably have to consider also the aims and the interests of students. This is shown diagrammatically in Figure 1.

The non-educational factors to be considered in selecting a teaching strategy have been outlined in an earlier paper[6] and are outside the scope of this review. Also excluded is any discussion of research into teaching methods.

Fig. 1. Factors affecting the selection of teaching strategy.

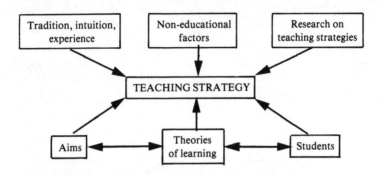

In Table 3 are presented some examples of current teaching methods for university science teaching related to learning theories. This Table is neither intended to be comprehensive, nor to imply that teaching methods have been adopted as a result of theories of learning. It simply reveals where there is a consistency between psychological theories of learning and how science is taught in universities. That is, it reveals where the gap between theory and practise is being bridged, whether by tradition, intuition or experience of the teacher on the one hand; or by a considered application of theories of learning to a situation involving particular aims and students on the other. A particular strategy may appear under the heading of more than one theory usually because it is being used in a different style.

4.2 Application of learning theories

In this section we attempt to show how the theory-practice gap might be bridged.

What essential advice can be distilled from learning theories? The teacher should consider three factors.

(i) *The aims should be known.* Having a clear aim to work on is an essential requirement for the application of any learning theory to teaching practice. For example, if the aims relate mainly to recalling and understanding knowledge then the behavioural and task analysis theories are likely to be helpful, but if the aims are more socially oriented, such as developing

Table 3. Examples of consistency between theory and practice

Theory	Practice	Comment
1. Behavioural psychology.	Use of behavioural objectives.	There are a number of examples of university science courses which make use of objectives. Examples, and a summary of advantages and disadvantes, have been given.[44]
	Programmed instruction.	This might be in the form of Keller plan, programmed texts or computer assisted learning.
2. Hierarchical task analysis.	Highly structured courses.	Where teachers plan their courses with explicit attention to prerequisite knowledge and abilities they are consistent with Gagné.
3. Field psychology.	"Guided discovery" courses.	In many laboratory situations, but also sometimes in a group or individually, the teacher arranges for the student to gain insight (discover for himself).
4. Cognitive psychology.	Situations where students work actively on meaningful problems (e.g. projects, problem solving classes).	The essence here is that the students learn by being active and working in situations where what is to be learnt relates to what they already know or can do.
5. Human psychology.	Informal leaderless small groups. Continuous assessment instead of final examinations.	These remove the threat from the student and so encourage learning.

the ability to work in a team, then advice from humanistic psychology could be useful.

(ii) *The presentation should be structured.* Most learning theories suggest that capabilities are built up in some kind of sequential, hierarchical fashion. Gagné's theories (section 3.3) contain this idea most explicitly stated, but it is also apparent in most other models. Past experience is the *sine-qua-non* of learning. In order to achieve the optimum sequencing of study it is necessary to ask at each stage such questions as:

What do the learners need to be able to do to learn this?
Does this relate to their past experience?
Will they perceive and understand what is to be learned?
Will the relevance of this learning be clear?

Included in this kind of analysis must be questions not only about knowledge and abilities but also about attitudes and personality. Clearly students must be disposed to learn (section 3.6), and how ideas are presented can often have a large influence on this.

After considering factors (i) and (ii) the teacher should have a clear idea of where he is aiming and the sequence of steps on the way. Now comes the all important question — what teaching method is appropriate? This is factor (iii).

(iii) *For any teaching method the learner should be active.* The clearest message from all the theories is that students learn by being actively involved. In the behaviourist view (section 3.2) it is active responding, in cognitive psychology (section 3.5) it is processing into the memory, and in Piaget's scheme (section 3.5) it is mental adaption. These very similar ideas hold a major key to the relationship between teaching and learning. This is that the teaching method selected should make the students do something as close as possible to what it is they have to learn. For example if the expectation is that students should be able to design experiments, it is no good simply showing them how others have designed experiments. They must experience designing experiments for themselves.

5. Summary

There may be little relation between theories of learning and teaching practice at the present time. During the last 25 years development of teaching strategies in university science education has been largely empirical. This may change because the next 25 years is likely to see some advances in fundamental knowledge of how students learn.

Because of the diverse aims and subject matter of university science education and because students differ in personality and cognitive style, we can expect that science teaching will continue to use a wide range of teaching methods. As theories of learning develop we should be able to make more rational decisions about how to teach — that is how to help students learn.

REFERENCES

[1] Entwistle, N. and Hounsell, D., *How Students Learn,* University of Lancaster (1977).

[2] Proceedings of a conference, Newcastle, U.K., June 1977, *Cognitive Psychology: Its Impact on Learning and Teaching in Higher Education.* (Available from Dr T. Benjamin Massey, University of Maryland U.S.A.) (1977).

[3] Beard, R., *Teaching and Learning in Higher Education*, Third Edition, Harmondsworth, Penguin (1976).

[4] Perry, W.G. Jr., *Forms of Intellectual and Ethical Development in the College Years*, New York (1968), Holt, Rinehart and Winston.

[5] Belanger, M., Learning Studies in Science Education, *Review of Educational Research*, 39, 377-395 (1969).

[6] Frazer, M.J., Educational and other factors affecting the selection of techniques for effective teaching in *Educational Technology in the Teaching of Chemistry*, (Editor: C.N.R. Rao), Oxford, International Union of Pure and Applied Chemistry, (1975).

[7] Bligh, D., *What's the use of lectures?* Harmondsworth, Penguin (1972).

[8] Simons, H., (Editor) *Small Group Teaching*, a publication of the Group for Research and Innovation in Higher Education, The Nuffield Foundation (1975).

[9] Ogborn, J., (Editor) *Small Group Teaching in Undergraduate Science,* (Nuffield Foundation, Higher Education Learning Project — Physics), London, Heinemann Education Books (1977).

[10] Abercrombie, M.L.J., *The Anatomy of Judgement*, London, Hutchinson (1969). Abercrombie, M.L.J., *Aims and Techniques of Group Teaching*, Third Edition, London, Society for Research into Higher Education (1974).

[11] Anon., *Studies in Laboratory Innovation*, a publication of the Group for Research and Innovation in Higher Education, The Nuffield Foundation (1974).

[12] Ogborn, J., (Editor), *Practical work in Undergraduate Science*, (Nuffield Foundation, Higher Education Learning Project — Physics) London, Heinemann Educational Books (1977).

[13] Elton, L.R.B., An analysis of aims of self-instructional methods in undergraduate science courses, *Aspects of Educational Technology, VIII*, 105-110, London, Pitman, (1975).

[14] Bridge, W., Self-study courses in undergraduate science teaching: the report of a survey, *Higher Education, 5*, (2) 211-224 (1976). Hills, P.J., *The Self-Teaching Process in Higher Education*, London, Croom Helm, (1976).

[15] Bridge, W. and Elton, L.R.B., (Editors), *Individual Study in Undergraduate Science*, (Nuffield Foundation, Higher Education Learning Project — Physics), London, Heinemann Educational Books (1977).

[16] Tawney, D.A., New Light in Old Corners — reflections prompted by observing some computer assisted learning developments, *Studies in Higher Education, 2*(1), 69-77 (1977). (References to other papers on computer assisted learning are given.)

[17] Lockard, D., McNally, D., and Taylor, C., *New Approaches to Teaching/Learning Strategies in University Science*. Booklets published by UNESCO, (1977).

[18] Becher, R.A., *et al., Making the Best of it,* Final Report of the Group for Research and Innovation in Higher Education, London, The Nuffield Foundation, (1977).

[19] Anon., *Improving Teaching in Higher Education, London,* University of London Teaching Methods Unit, (1976).

[20] Mackenzie, N., Eraut, M., and Johns, H.C., *Teaching and Learning: an Introduction to new Methods and Resources in Higher Education*, Paris, UNESCO (1971).

[21] Postlethwait, S.M., and Murray, H.J., *The Audio-Tutorial Approach to Learning*, Minneapolis, Burgess (1971).

[22] Fisher, K.M., and MacWhinney, B., AV Autotutorial Instruction: a review of evaluative research, *AV Communication Review*, 24, (2), 229-261 (1976).

[23] Brewer, I.M., SIMIG: A case study of an innovative method of teaching and learning, *Studies in Higher Education*, 2, (1), 53-54, (1977).

[24] Haynes, L.J., Hills, P.J., Palmer, C.R., Trickey, D.S., (Editors), *Alternatives to the Lecture in Chemistry*, London Chemical Society, (1976).

[25] Roach, K., and Hammon, R., Zoology by Self-Instruction: *Studies in Higher Education*, 1 (2), 179-196, (1976).

[26] Skinner, B.F., *About Behaviourism*, London, Johnathan Cape, (1974).

[27] Gagné, R.M., *The Essentials of Learning for Instruction*, Dryden Press, Hillsdale, Illionois, (1974).

[28] Bigge, M.L., *Learning Theories for Teachers*, New York, Harper Row, (1964).

[29] Ausubel, D.P., *Educational Psychology: A Cognitive View*, New York, Holt Rinehart and Winston, (1968).

[30] Bruner, J.S., *Toward a Theory of Instruction*, Cambridge, Massachusetts, Harvard U.P. (1967).

[31] Flavell, J.H., *The Developmental Psychology of Jean Piaget*, Princeton, New Jersey, Van Nostrand, (1967).

[32] Lindsay, P.H., and Norman, D.A., *Human Information Processing*, New York, Academic Press, (1972).

[33] Rogers, C., *Freedom to learn*, Columbus, Ohio, Merrill (1969).

[34] Thorndike, E.L., *Human Learning*, Cambridge, Massachusetts, MIT Press, (1931).

[35] Gagné, R.M., *The Conditions of Learning*, London, Holt Rinehart and Winston, (1970).

[36] Gagné, R.M. and White, R.T., Past and Future Research on Learning Hierarchies, *Educational Psychologist, 2,* 19-28, (1974).

[37] Bruner, J.S., Goodnow, J.J., and Austin, G.A., *A Study of Thinking*, New York, Wiley, (1967).

[38] Hudson, L., *Contrary Imaginations; a psychological study of the English schoolboy*, London, Metheuen, (1966).

[39] Pask, G., Conversational techniques in the study and practice of education, *British Journal of Educational Psychology*, 46, 12-25, (1976).

[40] Witkin, H.A., Moore, C.A., Goodenough, D.R., and Cox, P.W., *Field-Dependent and Field-Independent Cognitive Styles and their Educational Implications*, Princeton, New Jersey, ETS, (1975).

[41] Kagan, J., *Development Studies in Reflection and Analysis*, in *Perceptual Development of Children*, Kidd, A.H., and Ricoire, J.L. (Editors), University London Press, (1965).

[42] Newell, A., and Simon, H.A., *Human Problem Solving*, Englewood Cliffs, New Jersey, Prentice Hall, (1972).

[43] Broadbent, D.E., Cognitive Psychology and Education: *British Journal of Educational Psychology*, 45, 162-176, (1975).

[44] Frazer, M.J., *Up to date and precise learning objectives in chemistry*, New trends in chemistry teaching Volume IV, Paris, UNESCO Press (1975).

Mathematics and Statistics in Relation to Science

A.T. Rogerson

1. Introduction

The purpose of this article is twofold: to provide information for scientists and mathematicians, and to encourage personal communication between them. Much can be gained by both sides in realising the large area of overlap between mathematics and science, and the specific areas of mathematics which can be useful to a particular science. This article is no substitute for personal contact between mathematicians and scientists with common interests, however, and ideally such contact can take place locally, within individual universities or industries. As a prelude specially organised meetings, seminars or conferences can be organised, [1, 2] such as the Oxford Study Groups with Industry.[3] At an international level, working groups have been set up at the ICME conferences at Exeter, 1972, and Karlsruhe, 1976, to discuss and encourage communication and cooperation between mathematicians and scientists. Similar working groups have met at international science conferences (for example the ICPE meeting at Edinburgh, 1975).

This article will relate mathematics to the Physical Sciences (Physics, Chemistry and Engineering), the Biological Sciences and the Earth Sciences (mainly Geography), although mention will also be made of the Social Sciences, Economics, and Architecture.

While it is hoped that what is said about the relationship between mathematics and the sciences will be relevant in an international context, it is clearly impossible to do justice to such a vast area within the scope of a few pages. This article will inevitably be a highly selective summary, but the temptation to escape into generality has been resisted, and wherever possible specific references are given for fuller documentation.

Mathematics *and* Statistics is nowadays a helpful bifurcation since statistics (which should be linked with probability) has its own philosophy, techniques and areas of application and has recently grown into a separate and independent subject from mathematics. Both mathematics and statistics are now increasingly being integrated with particular sciences at an interdisciplinary level (e.g. the department of biomathematics at Oxford University). While such integration is warmly welcomed, this article is directed more at the *relation* between contemporary mathematics/statistics and the sciences as separate disciplines. We will first look at mathematics/statistics as a whole and then the separate sciences and their inter-relationship with mathematics.

During this century, and in the last twenty years especially, *mathematics* has grown and changed in many ways both at university and school levels. This change has not always communicated itself clearly or quickly to scientists (or even mathematicians!) and present day mathematics (as practised at university and taught in schools) differs considerably from the subject that scientists themselves may have studied. The consequent information gap has tended to affect the physical or pure sciences most — since their use of (and interrelation with) mathematics is well established. It is instructive that the newer areas of application of mathematics — the biological and social sciences (including economics and geography) have assimilated more rapidly and effectively the concepts and models offered by "modern" or contemporary mathematics (especially statistics).

2. Contemporary University Mathematics

It is difficult to generalise about university mathematics internationally.[4] It is often claimed that mathematics itself is an "international language" and so bridges national and cultural barriers. This is only partly true. In as much as mathematics is a symbolic language or activity (akin to chess) it is more easily *communicated*. Nevertheless it is striking how different the content, emphases and learning methods for mathematics are in countries such as the U.K., U.S.A., France, India and Scandinavia. In as much as mathematics is one of many academic subjects it must fit the different national and cultural attitudes to education within any separate country. In India, for example, mathematics seems to have a lower status relative to technology or the social sciences (economics in particular), it is learnt much more formally by committing theories and proofs to memory, and the subject content is an unusual mixture of very modern topics such as topology and linear algebra, with more traditional work. In fact the mathematics in any two countries may differ not only in content and emphasis, but may be learnt and taught in differing ways and the place of mathematics in education and society as a whole may differ radically. Despite these national and cultural differences, there is growing international agreement on what constitutes contemporary mathematics — largely determined by the quantity and quality of mathematicians studying any particular area.

2.1 Pure Mathematics

To some extent the more traditional pure mathematics categories of arithmetic (number), algebra and geometry still exist. Nothing has been more striking in the twentieth century, however, than the expansion of the mathematics associated with computing. This growth has been so enormous that whole new disciplines have arisen in numerical methods, computing, computer science and data processing. Apart from the commercial and social revolutions effected by the computer, it now plays a major role in contemporary mathematics and has a growing influence on other disciplines. Many would claim that the separate departments of Numerical Analysis and Computing Science [5] are no longer part of mathematics itself; but even within mathematics departments the influence of the computer has been seminal.[6] The recent computer "proof" of the "four colour theorem" (a classical problem if ever there was one) is a striking example of the growing awareness within mathematics of the opportunities and uses of a powerful modern computer. A computer is no longer simply a fast arithmetical calculator, or a convenient data storage and processor. It can be programmed to carry out virtually any mathematical process, formulae or algorithm, it is ideal for iterative processes in algebra or calculus that require repeated numerical work, and it can engage in creative searches by extensive numerical trial and error. Computer simulation of situations that are at present impossible to model precisely or analytically is a growing and vital use of the computer. Indeed, the ability of the computer to "solve" by successive trial and error has caused a revaluation of what mathematics itself is. There is now less concern for exact methods of solution involving complicated manipulation if a numerical method can be devised for which the computer can be programmed. This idea is of great generality and power and can (in principle) be applied to almost any brand of mathematics.

In this sense arithmetic/number is assuming a growing importance in mathematics research and teaching:

> Today, however, we are concerned with the other half of the computer revolution: the use of computers to perform tasks that, before, had never even been attempted.
>
> Among these tasks, the most usual (and most useful) has been the reliable, quantitative analysis of a big, complex system, taking into account the mutual interactions between hundreds of different elements of that system. The ability to make such a reliable quantitative analysis of a large complex system is equally important in all the different branches of engineering; as well as in the economics and management sciences and in all of the natural sciences.[7, 8, 9]

2.2 Algebra

Algebra began as generalised arithmetic but has now become a subject whose symbols can stand for any appropriate objects: numbers, sets, vectors, matrices, forces or geometric transformations. Modern algebra is the general study of *structure*, in principle it need not identify what its objects are, but in practice of course it very often provides a model for specific situations. Modern algebra is no longer merely the manipulation of equations and formulae, but the study of pattern of an abstract kind (hence modern algebra is often called "abstract algebra"). It is not always true that algebra deals with the discrete, and *calculus* (or analysis) with the continuous, but this is generally a helpful dividing line. Within modern algebra there are many separate specialisms: the study of sets, groups, rings, fields, vector spaces, algebraic number theory, and so on.[10] By far the most important topic as far as its interrelationship with science is concerned, however, is *linear algebra*.

Linear algebra is a major mathematical method for Physics, Biology, Economics, Geography and Engineering.[11] In many problems if a variable t depends on a known number of other variables (x, y, z --) say, the simplest model we can make is a *linear* one. We assume the variable t is related to ($x, y, z,$ --) *linearly*:

$$t = ax + by + cz + \cdots$$

where $a, b, c,$ etc. are fixed numbers or coefficients. Linear algebra is concerned with the implications and ramifications of such a general model and it includes work on vectors, matrices, vector spaces, and linear transformations. The power of linear algebra is the way in which the same well known and simple mathematical techniques can be used for an enormous variety of problems in science. This includes electrical networks, vibrations, pendula, oscillating systems and stochastic systems. As Trevor Fletcher points out in his excellent introductory text "Linear Algebra Through Its Applications": "Over and over again we will see that the use of matrices enables methods of calculation in one variable to be extended to many variables". Here are three of many examples he provides and solves in the book.[12]

(1)   Three particles, each of unit mass, are equally spaced at distances l on a light horizontal string fastened rigidly at the ends, resting on a smooth horizontal table (Fig. 1.). How do the particles behave if
(i) they are displaced by constant horizontal forces, perpendicular to the string, of magnitudes f_1, f_2, f_3 ;
(ii) they are perturbed by periodic horizontal forces, perpendicular to the string, of magnitudes p_1 sinkt, p_2 sinkt, $p_3$sinkt,
(iii) they oscillate freely, moving perpendicular to the line of the string, in the horizontal plane?

(2)   Three particles, each of mass m, are spaced at distances l on a light vertical string which hangs freely from a point of support (Fig. 2.). All subsequent displacements are in a fixed vertical plane. How do the particles behave if
(i) they are displaced by constant horizontal forces of magnitudes f_1, f_2, f_3 ;
(ii) they are perturbed by periodic horizontal forces of magnitudes p_1 sinkt, p_2 sinkt, p_3 sinkt
(iii) they oscillate freely?

The same mathematical ideas occur, but on a very different physical scale, in the analysis of the vibrations of suspension bridges and of the network of cables which are the main load-carrying elements in certain designs of large-span roofs.

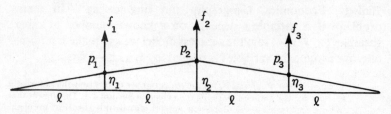

Fig. 1.

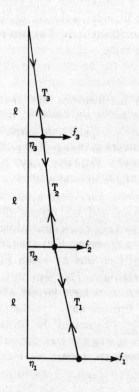

Fig. 2.

(3)   Consider the electrical filter shown in Fig. 4.5. This consists of inductances in series with capacitors in parallel. If there are N stages of the kind shown, and all the inductances have value L, and all the capacitors value C, then, denoting the voltage across the r_{TH} capacitor by V_r, the current into it by i_r and the current in the r_{TH} inductance by j_r, electrical theory shows that the circuit equations are:

$$CV_r = i_r$$

$$j_r = j_{r-1} - i_{r-1}$$

$$Lj_r = V_{r-1} - V_r$$

The main point of interest is that the equations are of precisely the same form as those for the particles vibrating on a chain in Section 4.3. This means that the previous mechanical discussion applies also to this electrical problem. Furthermore, just as the continuous vibrating string may be regarded as the limiting case of a light string loaded with particles, so a transmission line is the continuous analogue of a filter made up of lumped components. The differential equations of the transmission lines and vibrating strings are of the same mathematical form, although one system is electrical and the other is mechanical.[13]

2.3 Geometry

No topic within mathematics has changed as radically as geometry during the twentieth century. It may seem that since geometry is the study of space and shape (which is empirically determined) it is less likely to change, but geometry is itself a model of the external world and the very fundamentals of our mathematical model have now altered. For something like 2000 years "geometry" meant Euclidean geometry; based on Euclid's axioms and definitions and his formal didactic and deductive methods of proof in two and three dimensions. Euclid's system was philosophically (not mathematically) shaken by the invention of non-Euclidean geometries, one of which Einstein found a more suitable basis for relativity. This was not, however, the major reason why mathematicians have largely abandoned and ignored Euclid's geometry. Present day "geometry" is transformation geometry which offers (instead of the formal deductive proof) a dynamic geometry involving the transformations we can make on geometric figures: rotation, reflection, translation, enlargement, shearing and glide-reflection. Transformation geometry has become popular as an object of study because of its close affinity with modern algebra, its deeper structural basis and its capability for much easier and wider generalisation. [14, 15, 16] In particular transformation geometry links easily with matrix and vector algebra. Modern geometry encompasses the study of topology, affine geometry, projective geometry, euclidean geometry and transformation geometry as structures which can be algebraically expressed. Topology is the most generalised form of geometry, sometimes pictured as the study of networks or "rubber-sheet geometry". It links in turn with *analysis* which is the generalised study of calculus.

2.4 Calculus

One of the key changes from traditional to modern algebra has been the displacement of the "equation" by the new concept of "function". A function is a simple way of expressing a rule on variables, thus $f(x, y, z)$ denotes a function of x, y, z which is defined by some rule, formula or expression (e.g. $x^2 + y^2 + z^2$). The major advantage of this notation is its generality and its ease of use. Function ideas and notation now underlie the whole study of calculus or, as it is now called, *analysis*.[17] Analysis is not merely the study of rates of change and motion of *points*. Modern analysis is the study of rates of change of general objects, which, like modern algebra, may be points, vectors, functions and so on.[18] Thus many of the most useful models for use in science involve differential equations, partial differentiation, multiple integrals and other major areas of calculus. Alongside linear algebra, analysis is the most widely used part of mathematics in science and within analysis differential equations is one of the most widely used topics.

2.5 Set Theory and the Foundations of Mathematics

The early work of Frege and Russell has led to a growth of interest in the connections between logic and mathematics and considerable contemporary research within mathematics, "meta-mathematics" and philosophy. For a full exposition of Russell's ideas see Russell [19] but an enlightened and more profound critique is found in Wittgenstein.[20] At present there seems to be little direct link between these fields and science except for the connections of logic and Boolean algebra with computer circuitry.

2.6 Applied Mathematics

Traditionally mathematics in Britain has been "pure" or "applied", and most university departments are split into separate departments of those names. The effects of this have been difficult to determine, although polarisation has sometimes taken place, into the pure (beauty for its own sake) and applied (usefulness is vital) schools of thought. In some countries mathematics means "pure mathematics" while applied mathematics is done by the scientists. Other countries have a genuinely integrated pure *and* applied mathematics. Whatever institutional divisions occur there is often a distinction of *content* that can be drawn between pure mathematics: algebra, geometry, analysis etc. and applied mathematics: mathematical methods, mechanics, electricity etc. Some mathematicians would include probability and statistics under applied mathematics, on the grounds that they *apply* mathematics to the external world in the form of statistical data.

The most obvious and traditionally strongest branch of applied mathematics is *mechanics*, which is still central to contemporary work although it is now expressed using function, vector and matrix notation.[21] Alongside mechanics, a number of subsidiary models are used in hydrostatics, hydrodynamics, electricity, electro-hydrodynamics, aerodynamics etc. Indeed any physical phenomena (water, gases, heat, charge, etc.) amenable to mathematical analysis has a place in applied mathematics, and the borderline with physics and chemistry becomes increasingly harder to discern. In theoretical physics and nuclear physics, cosmology and astronomy there is a particularly strong interrelationship between mathematics and science.

Since the *content* delineations of applied mathematics have become more and more blurred, it has recently become more popular to concentrate on the process of applying mathematics (or mathematical models) to the world. This process is sometimes called "applicable mathematics" or simply "modelling".

> I want to suggest that educators may have most benefited their pupils when they have succeeded in giving a feel for what is involved in the process of applying mathematics. This is the process of building a bridge between the abstract ideas and inferences of mathematics and the concrete problems arising in some field of application. It seems to be increasingly recognised that there may be more skill, more art, in that bridge-building process than in the associated mathematical problem-solving. Computers may be of great

value in problem-solving, but apparently the human brain alone is able to tackle the subtler aspects of creating an effective correspondence between the mathematical world and the world of experiment and observation.[22, 23]

2.7 Probability and Statistics[24]

Probability concerns itself primarily with theoretical models and statistics with the analysis of numerical data, but these important areas of mathematics rightly belong together. Like computer science, probability/statistics has grown *out* of mathematics to be a major subject area in its own right,[25] and like computer science it has been developed by (and for) scientists outside of mathematics.[26] Much of the contemporary theory of statistics was developed by Fisher and Spearman to analyse data from agriculture, medicine and biology. In addition to widespread applications outside of mathematics, probability and statistics have had some effect inside, notably in number theory and mechanics.

In content terms, mathematics today can be broadly categorised as consisting of pure mathematics (number theory, algebra, geometry, analysis (topology) and probability theory) and applied mathematics (mechanics, electricity, thermodynamics etc., and statistics). There are of course numerous subdivisions and specialisms, some of which (such as catastrophe theory and graph theory) seem to be growing in popularity. The most fundamental and far reaching mathematical ideas conceptually are the ideas of function and algorithm, algebraic structure, the algebratisation of geometry, the arithmetisation of analysis and the art of mathematical modelling.[27] Institutionally, mathematicians are now found in departments variously labelled as Pure, Applied, Statistics, Operations Research, Acturial Sciences, Computing Science and Numerical Analysis.[28] Content aside, there is a growing disquiet amongst mathematicians about the style and type of education a mathematician receives. McLone reported in 1973 on the low level of communication of mathematicians in industry, their lack of ability in problem formation[29, 30] and a general dissatisfaction with their university courses.[31]

2.8 Modelling

The last section has attempted to survey contemporary mathematics as a prelude to discussing its relation with individual sciences. It may be helpful for scientists to be aware of the topics in mathematics that are widely used in their science and others, and also those areas of mathematics that seem at present to have only a limited application. There is so much happening in the development and use of new mathematical models, as well as the growth of interdisciplinary subjects, that a topic in mathematics today which is little used by the sciences may be widely adopted in a few years time. The growth of vector analysis as a universal technique stemmed from an engineer (Tait) adapting some pure mathematics of Hamilton and Grassmann. Similarly the growth in importance of linear algebra is a direct consequence of its adoption by physics, economics and related subjects. Undoubtedly other branches of mathematics are "available" as possible models or techniques for sciences to use and this potential can only be developed by a two way communication between practitioners in mathematics and science. The impression given by Biology and Geography in particular is that they are only just beginning to explore and exploit mathematics.

That this process may not work *one way only* is illustrated by "catastrophe theory" in which a relatively traditional and staid branch of mathematics (three dimensional analytical geometry) has been renamed and offered as a "model" for a wide variety of situations in subjects as diverse as medicine and history. Whether or not this "model" will find a suitable and mutually agreed application in the future, the process can be criticised as being too one sided — a model in search for an application as it were.[32] Appropriate models arise more naturally from specific problems in the sciences in the first instance, and by communication with mathematicians searching for and finding an appropriate model (or models) to apply to the initial problem.

3. The Sciences Considered Separately

3.1 Physics

Physics has already assimilated the new mathematics ideas of vector analysis, matrix algebra, functions etc., and these (with a substantial amount of calculus) constitute the major overlap between mathematics and physics. A university physics course normally presupposes an elementary mathematical background (functions, graphs, calculus, trigonometry, kinematics, mechanics etc.) roughly between the U.K. O and A level mathematics standard.[33] On this basis most physics undergraduates study a core of work consisting of vector methods, differential equations, mechanics, multiple integrals, partial differentiation, linear algebra, all applied to a variety of physical problems.[34, 35]

In addition many other mathematical ideas and techniques are developed within a normal physics degree course, and the conceptual interdependence is a profound one.

> This state of things, i.e. the relation of mathematics to physics — is excellently expressed by Reed and Simon in the preface to their beautiful book "Methods of Modern Mathematical Physics": "It is a common fallacy to suppose that mathematics is important for physics only because it is a useful tool for making computations. Actually, mathematics plays a more subtle role which in the long run is more important. When a successful mathematical model is created for a physical phenomenon, that is, a model which can be used for accurate computations and predictions, the mathematical structure of the model itself provides a new way of thinking about the phenomenon. Put slightly differently, when a model is successful it is natural to think of the physical quantities in terms of the mathematical objects which represent them and to interpret similar or secondary phenomena in terms of the same model. Because of this, an investigation of the internal mathematical structure of the model can alter and enlarge our understanding of the physical phenomenon. Of course, the outstanding example of this is Newtonian mechanics which provided such a clear and coherent picture of celestial motions that it was used to interpret practically all physical phenomena. The model itself became central to an understanding of the physical world and it was difficult to give it up in the late nineteenth century, even in the face of contradictory evidence. A more modern example of this influence of mathematics on physics is the use of group theory to classify elementary particles."[36]

In the same paper the author lists 100 mathematical topics which he feels makes up the "mathematical structure of physics". The danger here is to see *explicitly* in a physics course the mathematical ideas which may be there only *implicitly*. In other words there is often neither the time, relevance or motivation to uncover and discuss the underlying mathematics in a physics course. There is also no time or need for formal proofs and a rigour more characteristic of a mathematics degree course. This is in no way to decry the physics treatment which is valid in its own terms. Proof and rigour are *relative* to the context of the subject and it is both impracticable and unhelpful to attempt to "mathematise" physics in that way. The vital aspects are the central skills, techniques and concepts needed for solving *physics* problems and an explicit emphasis on the *process* of modelling and problem solving. In this way the true interaction of deductive and empirical disciplines takes place.

The relationship between mathematics and physics is of long standing; many of the techniques and much of the subject matter of physics is essentially mathematical and a great deal of applied mathematics is physics. Many first year undergraduate physics courses contain as much or more mathematics than physics. It is interesting that in a survey of "topics talked about" by physics undergraduates:

> "In the first year, mathematics easily led the field. It just retained its lead in the second year, but where there had been more than twice as many instances in 'bad' stories as in 'good' ones, the numbers were now more equal."[37, 38]

This interdependence of physics and mathematics is well established and well known, but it may now be undergoing a change. Mathematics itself has altered during the last two decades but physics is undergoing its own metamorphosis. In the developed countries (the U.K. and U.S.A. in particular) a growing emphasis on the environment, pollution and the social responsibility of science has challenged the power and status of the pure sciences and there is an increasing trend for students to study the professional subjects and the biological and social sciences rather than physics or chemistry. Even in a developing country such as India there is a strong emphasis on economics and the social sciences as well as basic technology. So either through an excess or deficiency of technology, physics is being threatened.

The responses to this problem vary. In the U.K. and U.S.A. a number of projects have been initiated to "humanise" physics, or to relate it more closely to human affairs, society and technology. The Nuffield Science projects in the U.K. were designed to revitalise physics teaching in schools but although the number of physicists at school level may be holding steady, there has been a continuing fall off in university entrance to read physics. Part of this global problem may be the rise in popularity of the biological sciences and their related disciplines (biochemistry, biophysics etc.) and a steady decline in financial commitment to the pure sciences. It is certainly difficult to see what physics can and should do at university level without in effect losing its present identity and being merged with or swallowed by other growing disciplines.[38] The traditional link between physics and mathematics may therefore be altered in future years, as physics itself alters and adapts to these pressures.

3.2 Engineering

The mathematical content of many engineering courses (particularly in the first year of an undergraduate degree) is similar to that of physics.[39, 40] The mathematical needs vary depending on the branch of engineering. Electrical engineers need considerably more work on differential equations and network analysis while mechanical engineers will take mechanics further. What is generally less evident in engineering courses is the *depth* of study of mathematical ideas, and there is less explicit modelling using mathematical ideas. Thus a physicist may well study some mathematics for its own sake (e.g. complex numbers, linearity or matrix algebra) and then relate this to the physics. The engineer is usually more interested in *techniques* for solving his own problems and sometimes may neglect or be unaware of the mathematical background, except as far as it is required for his own purposes. One example is the routinised ways (Cramers rule, relaxation methods) in which linear algebra may be used to solve linear equations. Another is the formula or technique orientated approach to solving electrical network problems found in many engineering texts. The underlying mathematical ideas, involving matrices, vectors and topology, are *in this case* illuminating in solving the problem, but are hardly ever mentioned, much less explained.[41, 42, 43]

These remarks apply mostly to the undergraduate study of engineering and are perhaps in any case inevitable in view of the pragmatic and professional aspects of the subject which physics lacks. It is precisely this professional factor which has enabled engineering to escape the unpopularity that has beset the pure sciences. Students in increasing numbers apply to study engineering which offers more secure (professional) employment after graduation. One of the recurrent problems affecting engineering and other sciences is who should teach undergraduates: mathematicians or scientists?

Teaching mathematics to first year engineers has become an increasingly difficult and unpopular task, both because of the large spread in the mathematical background and ability of engineering students and lack of desire to study mathematics at all. As A-level syllabuses become more divergent and as more people enter higher education through other routes, the problem of inhomogeneity is likely to intensify. It was our conviction that in this situation the conventional lecture framework was quite inadequate, making it extremely difficult to provide sufficient help for the weaker students without being repetitive for others.[44, 45]

3.3 Chemistry

The interaction of chemistry with mathematics at an undergraduate level is similar to that of physics and engineering. It uses the same mathematical topics but to a lesser degree. The applications of linear algebra, for example, are more limited but they do exist:

Hydrogen and oxygen react according to the formula

$$2H_2 + O_2 \rightarrow 2H_2O.$$

Chemists now believe that molecules H_2 and O_2 will not react this way on their own; the reaction is attributed to the presence of radicals H, O and OH, which participate in three simultaneous reactions

$$O + H_2 \longrightarrow OH + H,$$
$$OH + H_2 \longrightarrow H_2O + H,$$
$$H + O_2 \longrightarrow OH + O.$$

A single radical starts a chain reaction according to the pattern shown in Fig. 6.1. The uranium nuclear fission reaction is a somewhat similar branched chain reaction where the propagating particles are neutrons.

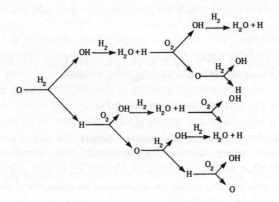

Fig. 6.1

For mathematical simplicity we will assume that all three reactions take place at the same speed, and that there is an unlimited supply of oxygen and hydrogen radicals. At time t_0 we will start a chain reaction with one oxygen radical, and calculate how many O, OH and H's there are at each successive stage.

Denote the number of O, OH and H radicals at stage n by o_n, $(oh)_n$ and h_n respectively.

Then

$$o_{n+1} = h_n,$$

$$(oh)_{n+1} = o_n h_n,$$

with $o_0 = 1, (oh)_0 = 0, h_0 = 0, (6.1)$

and

$$h_{n+1} = o_n + (oh)_n.$$

This is a set of simultaneous difference equations, which may be tackled with techniques of varying sophistication.

If

$$\mathbf{q}_n = (o_n, (oh)_n, h_n) \quad \text{and} \quad \mathbf{A} = \begin{bmatrix} 0 & 1 & 1 \\ 0 & 0 & 1 \\ 1 & 1 & 0 \end{bmatrix}$$

then

$$\mathbf{q}_{n+1} = \mathbf{q}_n \mathbf{A},$$

and in general

$$\mathbf{q}_n = \mathbf{q}_0 \mathbf{A}^n.$$

This provides a formula for the number of radicals present at successive stages of the chemical reaction. Conceptually the formula is very useful because it shows that we may think of the successive stages of the reaction as being described by a geometrical progression of vectors

$$\mathbf{q}_0, \quad \mathbf{q}_0 \mathbf{A}, \quad \mathbf{q}_0 \mathbf{A}^2, \quad \mathbf{q}_0 \mathbf{A}^3, \dots,$$

If we wish to have some easy way of calculating the general term of this sequence, without calculating all of the previous terms successively, further techniques are called for. These will be discussed later in this chapter in Section 6.6. For the moment we wish merely to investigate a number of situations, all of which lead to the same problem — the evaluation of powers of a matrix.

Show that the matrix

$$\mathbf{A} = \begin{bmatrix} 0 & 1 & 1 \\ 0 & 0 & 1 \\ 1 & 1 & 0 \end{bmatrix}$$

which describes the chemical reaction in Example 6.3, has eigenvalues y, -1, $1 - y$, where y denotes the golden ratio number $1 \cdot 618$ (approximately), which is the positive root of the equation $x^2 = x + 1$. Show that y is the dominant eigenvalue, and compute the related row and column eigenvectors. In what ratios are the O, OH and H radicals produced in the chemical reaction in the long run?[46]

In addition to mathematical methods, linear algebra and calculus are the major topics as well as some interesting *applications* of linear algebra and group theory in crystallography.[47] Like many other sciences today, chemistry is moving away from its descriptive nature towards a more interactive role involved with mathematics at a quantitative and modelling level. Whether this change has come too late to save the subject from neglect and unpopularity or whether it will be subsumed in interdisciplinary studies it is too early to say. Its existence at university level appears to be more threatened today than at any other time.

3.4 Biology

One of the most striking transformations during the past twenty years has been the rapid development of the relation between mathematics and biology. A sudden realisation has occurred that a vast field of previously unexploited data is available for mathematical modelling. In the past biology has been largely a descriptive science with a conspicuous lack of interaction with mathematics. There is now an extensive interaction of biology with various branches of mathematics: graphs, algebra, calculus, differential equations, vector analysis and statistics. The relationship falls into two distinct categories: *modelling*, data analysis and computer simulation using statistics/probability.[48, 49] The analysis of population processes in time, for example, requires the use of integration, 2nd order differential equations, flow diagrams, matrices, graphs, double summation and the exponential function. Population genetics, on the other hand, uses mainly statistics, probability, stochastic processes, and computer simulation.

The delicate problems inherent in this interaction were well summarised in Bartlett and Hiornes:[50]

> The mathematician and the biologist have an almost inevitable confrontation in the formulation of a model for any biological situation for, whereas the biologist will probably begin with the actual and complex set of facts that he has observed or otherwise become aware of, the mathematician is likely to be looking for an idealized model capable of theoretical investigation. This kind of dilemma has become more obvious as the use of mathematics has moved from the physical to the biological (and also to the social) sciences, and I do not believe that there is a facile answer . . . .
>
> It is absolutely essential that both the experimental biologist and the professional mathematician should establish a close relationship. For biological material does not exhibit the nice regular reproducible behaviour ideally anticipated by the simple-minded mathematician. Instead it is almost infinitely variable. I recall very vividly how this impressed itself on me more than 35 years ago, at a time when I had turned away from the physical sciences to become for a while an experimental bacteriologist. Bacteria of a given kind were clearly not all the same, in size, or activity. So the concepts to be used in studying them could not be the same sorts of concepts as would be appropriate in the physical sciences. We could summarize by saying that the mathematician needs the restraining hand of the experimental biologist, and the biologist needs the rigorous competence and analytic power of the mathematician. Without this mutual interaction we have all too often bastard mathematics or "sloppy" biology. Nowhere is this more clear than in the study of population dynamics: nowhere is it more necessary to establish an effective liaison.

The subject of biomathematics is a particular case of a rapid academic growth point creating a new discipline with its associated opportunities and growing pains. One report characterised this as "the biomathematics shock front" where

> pressure in a particular area from "employment" has led to changes in "education" at tertiary level in the biological sciences and these changes may well propagate into secondary level. "Employment" should be interpreted broadly to include work sponsored by the research councils as well as work within the manufacturing industries. References to biology or the biological sciences should be similarly interpreted to embrace medicine, agriculture, pharmacy and environmental studies as well as the more obvious disciplines of biology and biochemistry.[51]

Biologists are increasingly aware of the conceptually wider foundation of their models compared to the "traditional" users of mathematics: physics and chemistry.

> "Perhaps the richest fields for application of mathematical thought and techniques to biology, and conceptually perhaps the most important, lie outside the framework of physics".[52, 53, 54]

Two examples in particular are given in mathematical genetics (dynamics of populations in time) and the theory of neural nets. One consequence of the adoption of mathematics in biology has been a more positive and vocal support for "modern" mathematics — in particular the ideas of functions, vectors, matrices, statistics and probability.[55]

Here are some examples of the use of mathematics in biology:

Two Competing Species

Let $A(x, t)$ and $B(x, t)$ denote the population densities of two species with the same diffusivity and let $r_A(x, t)$ and $r_B(x, t)$ denote their compound interest growth rates locally at those densities. The total population

$$N = A + B, A = yN \text{ and } B = (1 - y)N. \text{ If}$$

and

$$\frac{\partial A}{\partial t} = \frac{\sigma^2}{2} \frac{\partial^2 A}{\partial x^2} + A r_A.$$

$$\frac{\partial B}{\partial t} = \frac{\sigma^2}{2} \frac{\partial^2 B}{\partial x^2} + B r_B,$$

then

$$\frac{\partial y}{\partial t} = \frac{\sigma^2}{2} \left\{ \frac{\partial^2 y}{\partial x^2} + 2\eta \frac{\partial y}{\partial x} \right\} + sy(1 - y),$$

where

$$\eta = \frac{\partial}{\partial x} \log N(x, t) \quad \text{and} \quad s = r_A - r_B.$$

Two Competing Autosomal Alleles

A, B, C stand respectively for the population densities of the genotypes $[a, a]$, $[a, a']$, $[a', a]$ in the breeding population, all classes having the same mobility and mortality when adult.

Selection takes place prior to recruitment into the breeding population, and Hardy-Weinberg proportions apply at fertilization.

$N = A + B + C$ and $y = (2A + B)/(2N)$. If

$$\frac{\partial A}{\partial t} = \frac{\sigma^2}{2} \frac{\partial^2 A}{\partial x^2} - \mu A + \gamma_A y^2 N,$$

$$\frac{\partial B}{\partial t} = \frac{\sigma^2}{2} \frac{\partial^2 B}{\partial x^2} - \mu B + \gamma_B 2y(1 - y)N,$$

$$\frac{\partial C}{\partial t} = \frac{\sigma^2}{2} \frac{\partial^2 C}{\partial x^2} - \mu C + \gamma_C (1 - y)^2 N,$$

then

$$\frac{\partial y}{\partial t} = \frac{\sigma^2}{2} \left\{ \frac{\partial^2 y}{\partial x^2} + 2\eta \frac{\partial y}{\partial x} \right\} + y(1 - y)[s_1 y + s_2(1 - y)],$$

where
$$s_1 = \gamma_A - \gamma_B \quad \text{and} \quad s_2 = \gamma_B - \gamma_C.$$

As before
$$\eta = \frac{\partial}{\partial x} \log N.$$

When the diffusion component is written in the form

$$\frac{\partial y}{\partial t} = \frac{\sigma^2}{2} \frac{1}{N^2} \frac{\partial}{\partial x} \left(N^2 \frac{\partial y}{\partial x} \right),$$

an analogy can be drawn with heat conduction. At higher population densities both the "conductivity" and the "capacity" are greater. After all, it is the population which both carries and absorbs the genes.

The previous analysis throws light on the remarks of Hoem (1971) concerning formulae for period mortality rates. If, following Hoem, we define by $_n\mathcal{D}_x$ the number of deaths in $(0, T)$ with age between x and $x + n$ at death, then this is effectively written as

$$_n\mathcal{D}_x = \int_{u=x-T}^{x+n} \int_{t=\max(0,x-u)}^{\min(T,x+n-u)} f(u+t, t)\mu(u+t, t) \, du \, dt \qquad (4.1)$$

where Hoem sets $f(x + t, t) = p(x)[l(x + t)/l(x)]$ and $\mu(x + t, t) = \mu(x + t)$ both age dependent only. In this, $p(x)\delta x$ denotes the expected number of individuals between ages $(x, x + \delta x)$ in the population, and $l(t)$ is a mortality function.

The gist of Hoem's argument is that unless the population is stable, with age distribution density

$$p(x) = \sum_{k=0}^{\infty} A_k e^{-r_k x} l(x) \qquad (4.2)$$

and a birth frequency function

$$b(t) = \sum_{k=0}^{\infty} A_k e^{r_k t}, \qquad (4.3)$$

then the simplification usually introduced in the weighted average

$$\int_0^n w(x+t)\mu(x+t) \, dt \Big/ \int_0^n w(x+t) \, dt$$

for the n-year death rate by Keyfitz (1970) and others, who set
$$w(x + t) = p(x + t),$$

will not hold. What we show is that any formulation of the problem in a simple population of the type considered in Section 3 in which the birth and death rates $\lambda(x)$, $\mu(x)$ are purely age dependent is asymptotically of the type (4.2—4.3) for large t. The same applies to the analogous two-sex population. Where Hoem's warning remains valid is for more general birth and death rates $\lambda(x, t)$, $\mu(x, t)$ dependent on both time and age. For an illustration of the relevance of such age and time dependent rates to platelet kinetics, the reader is referred to Breny (1971).

For from (3.13) we see that in the population considered as $t \to \infty$, we may write

$$f(x+t, t) \sim Ce^{-Kx - \int_0^x \mu(v)dv} \frac{e^{-\int_0^{x+t} \mu(v)dv}}{e^{-\int_0^x \mu(v)dv}} = p(x) \frac{l(x+t)}{l(x)} \qquad (4.4)$$

Thus, asymptotically,

$$p(x) = Ce^{-Kx} l(x)$$

$$b(t) = f(0, r) = Ce^{Kt} ; \qquad (4.5)$$

these are precisely conditions of the type (4.2—3) necessary for the simplifications in weighted death rates to hold. It would thus appear that to avoid confusion in both discrete and continuous time population processes, it is essential to indicate the time-dependence of parameters governing them explicitly.

In this section the argument is given a mathematical formulation. Though the model is highly-simplified, it retains the main structure of, and bears some resemblance to reality. The changes in population size are described by a branching process in a random environment. A species breeds once a year. For simplicity it is assumed that a parent breeds only once then dies, and that a nestling takes less than a year to mature. Only counts of females are considered. In year i let $p_i(r)$ be the probability that a female produces r females that survive to breed in the following season. $\phi_i(s)$ is the corresponding probability generating function i.e.

$$\phi_i(s) = \sum_0^\infty p_i(r)s$$

Starting with 1 individual in year 0, the p.g.f. of females at the start of the nth breeding season is

$$\phi_1(\phi_2(\phi_3(\ldots \phi_n(s)\ldots)))$$

The ϕ_i vary randomly from year to year depending on the breeding conditions prevailing. For simplicity it is assumed that the environment varies between only three states, bad years, average years, and good years with equal probability 1/3 and with corresponding p.g.f's $\phi_\alpha(s)$, $\phi_B(s)$, and $\phi_\gamma(s)$. If in fact the environment is unvarying i.e. $\phi_\alpha(s) = \phi_B(s) = \phi_\gamma(s) = \phi(s)$ say, then the probability of the ultimate extinction of the population is that value q satisfying $q = \phi(q)$, a well-known result of the theory of the classical branching process.[56]

3.5 Geography

Another science that has recently found a deeper relationship with mathematics is the "new geography". What is "new" about the "new geography"? Instead of being largely descriptive in method with the region as its chief object of study, it attempts to use and apply mathematical terminology, techniques and models to social and economic factors rather than the historical or physical. The methodology of the new geography is analytic, using concept formation, modelling and data collection and representation as its main tools.

The new geography owes much of its impetus to a series of seminars (1963-66) held at Madingley Hall, Cambridge. Chorley and Haggett's "Models in geography" (Methuen, 1967) brought much of the current research to the notice of a wider audience at both school and university level. Cole and Beynon's brilliant "New ways in geography" (Blackwell, 1968) showed how these new ideas might be introduced into schools, and they blazed the trail which more writers are now following. The most interesting of these are the Walker and Wilson series "Location and links" (Blackwell, 1973), an excellent introduction to the new geography in Science in geography (Oxford University Press, 1974), Dalton's "Simulation games in geography" (Macmillan, 1972) and Walford's "Games in geography" (Longman, 1969).

The new geography has obvious significance for the mathematician, and many of the mathematical topics it uses are emphasised in "modern" mathematics at school and university: functions, transformations, probability and statistics, networks and numerical methods. The most exciting aspect of the new geography is the wealth of practical situations in which mathematics is relevant and useful: surveys and questionnaires to determine the siting of new supermarkets or factories, the concept of "distance" using different measures, topological ideas and networks for designing urban traffic systems or discussing human settlements. The development and application of mathematics in geography has reached a stage where initial communication and collaboration between geographers and mathematicians would be mutually beneficial. Mathematicians gain a fertile field of real-life situations to illustrate mathematical techniques, while there are substantial benefits for geographers in relating the applicable mathematics to their subject in an intelligible way. Two typical problems:

(1)   Consider a spatial system of N regions, $i = 1, 2, \ldots N$, and let $P_i(t)$ be the population of the ith region at time t. Let $b(t, t + T)$ and $d(t, t + T)$ be birth and death rates respectively for the period t to $t + T$, assumed to be uniform over the whole system. Let m_{ij} be fixed and unchanging rates of migration for each period of length T. Then we may suppose that

$$P_i(t+T) = (1 + b(t, t+T) - d(t, t+T))P_i(t)$$

$$+ \sum_{j=1} (m_{ji} - m_{ij})P_j(t) \tag{3.218}$$

This is an example of a recursive model: the value of some variables at time $t + T$ are calculated from the values of the variables for an earlier period. Then, for the next period for example, we would continue with

$$P_i(t+2T) = (1 + b(t+T, t+2T) - d(t+T, t+2T))P_i(t+T)$$

$$+ \sum_{j \neq i} (m_{ji} - m_{ij})P_j(t+T) \tag{3.219}$$

and so on . . . .

(2)   The development of a slope profile must closely follow the continuity equation, with conservation of mass as a necessary accounting procedure. In this case, in the absence of uplift, there is no accumulation of material from outside, so that $i = 0$, giving a simplification of the equation. In Figure 6.7, the transport rate S, is the rate of debris movement,

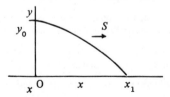

Fig. 6.7. Slope profile development

which is though to depend on slope gradient, $-(\partial y/\partial x)$, and on distance of overland flow, (x), so that a fairly general form for S is:

$$S = f(x)\left(\frac{-\partial y}{\partial x}\right) \tag{6.149}$$

The continuity equation then becomes,

$$\frac{\partial S}{\partial x} + \frac{\partial y}{\partial t} = \frac{\partial}{\partial x}\left[f(x)\left(-\frac{\partial y}{\partial x}\right)\right] + \frac{\partial y}{\partial t} = 0 \tag{6.150}$$

A variety of "initial" and "boundary" conditions might be suggested to obtain a solution to this equation, but a natural and simple set appears to be:

(a) Divide fixed at $x = 0$; that is:

$$S = 0 \text{ at } x = 0 \qquad (6.151)$$

(b) Base-level fixed at $x = x_1$, and base-level elevation specified over time; that is:

$$\text{at } x = x_1, y = y_1(t) \qquad (6.152)$$

The simplest case is of course a fixed base level elevation,

$$y = 0 \text{ at } x = x_1 \qquad (6.153)$$

(c) An "initial form" is specified at time $t = 0$, that is the profile from which development begins, is

$$y = y_0(x) \text{ at } t = 0 \qquad (6.154)$$

Inspection of the equations and consideration of the geomorphic literature suggest at least two types of solution to look for — a Davisian slope-decline; and a Penck/King parallel retreat (see, for example, Carson and Kirkby, 1972). These might be represented simply in the forms:

$$\text{Slope decline: } y = y(x)e^{kt} \qquad (6.155)$$

$$\text{Parallel retreat: } y = y(x - ct) \qquad (6.156)$$

A third type of simple solution can be seen for a base-level downcutting at a constant rate T; with elevation z measured above the (downcutting) basal point. In this case

$$z = y - Tt \qquad (6.157)$$

Substituting in equation 6.150

$$\frac{\partial S}{\partial x} + \frac{\partial z}{\partial t} - T = 0 \qquad (6.158)$$

and we can look for a *steady-state* solution.

$$\frac{\partial S}{\partial x} = T, \text{ or } S = Tx \qquad (6.159)^{57}$$

The mathematics relevant to geography includes elementary algebra, functions, graphs, coordinate geometry and equations, matrix algebra, calculus, differential and difference equations, probability and statistics, stochastic processes, maximisation and minimisation methods and problem-solving. Some interesting particular examples of mathematical modelling are given in Fletcher,[58] and in Andrews and McLone.[23 and 59]

3.6 Other Sciences

The interaction with mathematics is of increasing importance to Agriculture, Architecture, the Social Sciences (especially Economics) and Psychology. The case for architecture is nowhere argued more cogently than in March and Steadman [60] a fascinating and stimulating book that genuinely integrates mathematical ideas with architectural practice. [61] To some extent agriculture overlaps with biology but, in particular, uses statistical methods for analysis and modelling. [62] Economics is an enormously large subject which is now predominantly mathematically based, discussion of which is beyond the scope of this booklet. [23, 63, 64] In general the social sciences in America, Australia and India are emphatically and mathematically oriented (less so in Europe). The increasing emphasis on quantitative models, involving statistics and numerical analysis, is a significant factor for the future. [65, 66, 67]

4. Conclusions

What general opportunities and problems emerge from the interaction of mathematics and the sciences? Firstly the opportunities:

(1) Mathematics, almost by definition, provides a suitably abstract and general deductive structure of *models* which can be applied in a wide variety of sciences. Mathematics is both general in its structures and rich (plentiful) in the range of its structures.

(2) Contemporary mathematics is still not completely familiar to many scientists and considerable awareness is still needed of the full potential and applicability of vector methods, linear algebra and other modern topics. An increasing *communication* of mathematical ideas to scientists will reap rich rewards.

(3) Conversely, empirical investigation continues in all sciences and in some is opening out for the first time along quantitative lines. Mathematicians will benefit from information from scientists on their specialist studies and problems.

On the whole the relationship between mathematics and all sciences is now in a transition stage. Physics and Chemistry may revalue and transform themselves while Biology and Geography are developing a deeper and broader intercommunication with mathematics. The most likely sciences to see an explosion of mathematical applications are Biology, Geography and perhaps the Social Sciences, while the mathematical topics most likely to expand as a result are linear algebra, analysis, computing and numerical methods as well as probability/statistics.

5. The Problems

(1) A major international problem exists in the *teaching* of mathematics to undergraduate scientists. This crucial area for *mutual* communication is not always exploited as it might be:

> The big problem is finding sufficient teachers who are knowledgeable in both mathematics and the discipline in which it is to be applied. This is necessary in order to provide an abundance of elementary examples (especially in model-making) which can be used with many of the weaker students. The work of the Committee of the Undergraduate Program in Mathematics (USA) in collecting suitable examples was welcomed and the forthcoming publication of a collection is eagerly awaited. It was apparent in group discussion that participants from a number of European and Asian countries believed that mathematics was such an important subject that it should be taught in the same way to the mathematics specialist and to his engineering or scientist counterpart — indeed mathematics should be taught to all these in a common group. The respective science and engineering teachers would then be responsible for teaching applications of this mathematics. Such a system was certainly possible in some countries since the students admitted to these courses were highly "motivated" and, furthermore, selection procedures ensured that the students had a good mathematical training and background.
>
> The other school of thought, however, believed strongly that mathematics should be taught separately to engineering/science students and that the material should be strongly "motivated" all through their course. An essential part of this course was the inclusion of applications and a demonstration of the relevance of the mathematics taught. Additionally, the discussion of real problems, mathematical modelling and the solution of physical problems arising from their courses and from their experience was regarded as an important feature of such a course in mathematics.[68, 69]

This problem raises in turn the major difficulties of the training of lecturers, the provision of joint degrees and the breaking down of communication barriers between university departments.

At a deeper level it raises the difficulty that the "ideal" interaction between a science and mathematics presupposes *people* who have been trained, or partly trained in *both* disciplines. This is not always practical, economic or convenient to arrange and up to now has been true of only exceptional individuals. The argument is not met merely by the provision of joint degrees or integrated work at university (although, this helps of course).

"mathematical biology is not an elementary subject. Even the conceptually simplest parts of mathematical biology, which represent the application of physical principles to biological systems, are not yet part of elementary physics. Indeed, almost all of these applications presuppose the knowledge of a working physicist. The parts of mathematical biology that use the most elementary mathematics tend to use the deepest biology. Indeed, one of the difficulties of teaching mathematical biology in any broadly based way is the fact that one must spend so much time developing the tools before one ever gets to the specific content of applications."[70]

(2) Even if the teaching difficulties are solved or at least resolved a major problem remains in the variable level of ability in the students entering science courses. Some argue that this level of ability is in addition dropping overall at a time when the mathematical *content* of many science courses needs to be actually increased. The problem stated for biology applies to other sciences too:

The appreciation by the professional biologist of the value of mathematics produces a call from the "employment" area to "education" for more mathematics. The call is initially heard at tertiary level and is further backed by researchers at Universities and polytechnics. These same researchers are often also lecturers and are able to arrange for the introduction of mathematics courses in tertiary level biology. These courses are usually given in the first year so that use can be made of the mathematics in later years.

At many tertiary institutions mathematics for biologists is a crash course to be completed by the end of the first academic year along with other background courses such as physics and chemistry. The biologist is then free over the next 2 years to get down to the main subject of interest — biology. If the level of mathematical ability required at the end of tertiary education is going to increase the only way that the steepness of the shock front can be prevented from increasing, and may perhaps even be decreased, is to spread the acquiring of this mathematical ability over a longer period. This could be accomplished entirely within the tertiary level by putting further mathematical topics into the second year. This will of course squeeze out something else.[71]

This general problem for all sciences poses questions about *school* work in science and mathematics.

(3) *Pre-University*

The relation of mathematics and statistics in science at school has recently attracted increasing and constructive attention. This particularly applies to attempts to increase communication between mathematicians and scientists. Some helpful articles stating the problems [72, 73, 74] have been followed by classroom materials in the U.K.[75] The pre-University stage is important in as much as many scientists have only the equivalent of O or A level Mathematics to relate to their science in University. Hence the relevance of three joint Royal Society reports on Physics, Chemistry and Biology which have been followed by more international cooperation.[76, 77] This has resulted in 1977 in a joint CTS/ICMI/UNESCO programme of cooperation between mathematics and science teachers to culminate in the publication of a series of booklets in 1978/9 outlining the major problems and opportunities for mathematics and science at school level.* Communication often presupposes the *willingness* to communicate and it is this spirit of cooperation which must be stimulated and practised at school level for todays pupils — who will be tomorrow's mathematicians and scientists.

REFERENCES

[1] A.G. Howson (ed.), *Developments in Mathematical Education*, C.U.P., 1973, p. 38.

[2] *Bulletin of the Institute of Mathematics and its Applications*, vol. 13, 314, 1977, pp. 96, 100.

[3] *Bulletin of the Institute of Mathematics and its Applications*, vol. 10, 3, 1974, 1973.

[4] *Routes to Qualifications in Mathematics.* A Report of the Institute of Mathematics and its Applications which gives a helpful overview of U.K. degree courses, p. 33, *et seq.*

[5] *Ibid.*, p. 33, *et seq.*

[6] *Bulletin of the Institute of Mathematics and its Applications*, vol. 13, 2, 1977, p. 55.

[7] Sir James Lighthill in *Bulletin of the Institute of Mathematics and its Applications*, vol. 13, 7/8, 1977, p. 178.

[8] R.R. McLone, *The Training of Mathematicians*, S.S.R.C. Report, 1973, p. 20. In this survey of the educational qualities required and sought after by industry McLone discovered the increasing importance of computing and statistics (over pure mathematics) and numerical mathematics (over classical applied mathematics). At the same time there was a strong view that the *technique* of computing is best taught 'on the job'.

[9] L. Fox and D.F. Mayers, *Computing Methods for Scientists and Engineers*, O.U.P., 1968.

[10] B.L. Van der Waerdon, Modern Algebra, vols. I, II, Unger, 1949, gives a complete and detailed survey.

* Edited by A.T. Rogerson.

[11] R.R. McLone, *op.cit.*, pp. 20, 21.

[12] *Bulletin of the Institute of Mathematics and its Applications*, vol. 13, 5. May 1977, p. 117.

[13] T.J. Fletcher, *Linear Algebra Through its Applications*, Van Nostrand, 1972, pp. 100, 158, 159, 160.

[14] I.M. Yaglom, *Geometric Transformations*, vols. 1, 2, Random House, 1962, 1968, describes the revolution in geometry, see also reference [15].

[15] Max Jaeger, *Transformation Geometry*, Allen & Unwin, 1966.

[16] E.A. Maxwell, *Geometry by Transformations*, C.U.P., 1975, gives brief but clear introduction.

[17] G.H. Hardy, *A Course of Pure Mathematics*, C.U.P., 1958, gives a definitive classic account.

[18] *Bulletin of the Institute of Mathematics and its Applications*, vol. 10, 4, 1974, gives the applications of *functional analysis.*

[19] B.R. Russell and A.N. Whitehead, *Principia Mathematica*, C.U.P., 1910.

[20] L. Wittgenstein, *Remarks on the Foundations of Mathematics*, Blackwell, 1967.

[21] P.G.T. Lewis (ed.), *Vectors and Mechanics*, S.M.P. Further Mathematics Draft Texts, C.U.P., 1971, gives introduction of vector analysis through physical situations.

[22] Sir James Lighthill in A.G. Howson, *Developments in Mathematical Education*, C.U.P., 1973, p. 95.

[23] *Ibid.*, pp. 96, 97.

[23a] J.G. Andrews and R.R. McLone (ed.), *Mathematical Modelling*, Butterworths, 1976.

[24] W. Weaver, *Lady Luck, The Theory of Probability*, Heinemann, 1963. An entertaining and readable introduction to probability.

[25] R.R. McLone, *The Training of Mathematicians*, S.S.R.C. Report, 1973, pp. 1, 17, 20, 21.

[26] *Routes to Qualifications in Mathematics*. A report of the Institute of Mathematics and its Applications, 1976, p. 30.

[27] H.B. Griffiths and A.G. Howson, *Mathematics, Society and Curricula*, C.U.P., 1974, for a brief overview of mathematics.

[28] K.P. Beltzuer, A.J. Coleman and G.D. Edwards, *Mathematical Sciences in Canada*, Science Council of Canada, 1976, p. 76.

[29] G. Polya, *Induction and Analogy in Mathematics*, O.U.P., 1954.

[30] A.G. Howson (ed.), *Developments in Mathematical Education*, C.U.P., 1973, pp. 32, 33, 69.

[31] *Bulletin of the Institute of Mathematics and its Applications II,* 6/7, 1973.

[32] *The Bulletin of the Institute of Mathematics and its Applications,* vol. 13, 2, 1977, p. 34; 13.3/4. 1977, p. 77.

[33] P.J. Black, Trend Paper No. 2. *Physics curricula and courses at the undergraduate level,* I.C.P.E., Edinburgh, 1975, p. 2. Black estimates that U.K. students at 18 are about 1 year ahead in specialised knowledge of the U.S.A. and Europe.

[34] K. Maurin, Trend Paper No. 116. *The Interface between physics and mathematics at university level,* I.C.P.E., Edinburgh, 1975, pp. 4, 5. Gives a detailed list of the mathematical content of physics courses.

[35] P.J. Black, *op.cit.,* p. 3.

[36] K. Maurin, *op.cit.,* pp. 1, 2.

[37] Joan Bliss and J. Ogborn, *Students Reactions to Undergraduate Science,* H.E.L.P.(P); Heinemann 1977, p. 76.

[38] P.J. Black, *op.cit.,* for a detailed and thorough discussion of physics courses internationally.

[39] F. Noble, *Applications of Undergraduate Mathematics in Engineering,* Macmillan, 1967.

[40] G. Stephenson, *Mathematical Methods for Science Students,* Longman, 1961.

[41] F.E. Rogers, *Topology and Matrices in the Solution of Networks,* Illiffe, 1965.

[42] P. Hlawiczlka, *Matrix Algebra for Electronic Engineers,* Illiffe, 1965.

[43] G. Merlane (ed.), *Differential Equations and Circuits,* S.M.P. Further Mathematics Draft Texts, C.U.P., 1971. An elementary introduction to mathematical ideas.

[44] *Individual Study in Undergraduate Science,* H.E.L.P.(P), Heinemann, 1977, pp. 51, 52.

[45] E.A. Barton, *A Report on the Prerequisite Skills required for the Engineering Tripos at Cambridge,* 1969.

[46] T.J. Fletcher, *Linear Algebra Through its Applications,* Van Nostrand, 1972, pp. 198-9, 200, 223.

[47] G.G. Hall, 'Molecular Models', pp. 56-70, in J.G. Andrews and R.R. McLone (ed), *Mathematical Modelling,* Butterworths, 1976.

[48] Institute of Biology Series, *Studies in Biology,* vols. 23 and 43.

[49] D. Machin, *Biomathematics, An Introduction,* Macmillan, 1976.

[50] M.S. Bartlett and R.W. Hiornes (ed.), *The Mathematical Theory of the Dynamics of Biological Populations,* Academic Press, 1973.

[51] *The Mathematical Needs of School Leavers Entering Employment II,* I.M.A. Report, 1976, p. 22.

[52] R. Rosen (ed.), *Foundations of Mathematical Biology Vol. 1.* Academic Press, 1972.

[53] M.S. Bartlett and R.W. Hiornes (ed.), *op.cit.*

[54] J.G. Andrews and R.R. McLone (ed.), *op.cit.,* pp. 98-115.

[55] *Mathematics for biologists,* Journal of Biological Education (1974), 8 (5), pp. 267-276.

[56] M.S. Bartlett and R.W. Hiornes (ed.), *op.cit.,* pp. 82, 83, 300, 301, 316, 317.

[57] A.G. Wilson and M.J. Kirkby, *Mathematics for Geographers and Planners,* O.U.P., 1975, pp. 91, 206-7.

[58] T.J. Fletcher, *Linear Algebra Through its Applications,* Van Nostrand, 1972, pp. 134-5, 250-1.

[59] M.G. Bradford and W.A. Kent, *Human Geography,* O.U.P., 1977.

[60] L. March and P. Steadman, *The Geometry of Environment,* Methuen, 1971.

[61] L. March and P. Steadman, *op.cit.,* pp. 336-350.

[62] *Mathematical Gazette 31.* 293, 1974, pp. 21-30.

[63] T.J. Fletcher, *op.cit.,* p. 230.

[64] R.R. McLone, *op.cit.,* p. 21.

[65] R. Stone, *Mathematics in the Social Sciences and other Essays,* Chapman and Hall, 1966.

[66] J.R. Newman (ed.), *The World of Mathematics Vols. 1-4,* Allen and Unwin, 1956, pp. 1148-1294.

[67] T.J. Fletcher, *op.cit.,* pp. 230-1, 260-1.

[68] A.G. Howson (ed.), *op.cit.,* pp. 34, 35.

[69] P.J. Black, *op.cit.,* p. 22.

[70] R. Rosen (ed.) *op.cit.,* p. 19.

[71] *The Mathematical Needs of School Leavers Entering Employment II,* I.M.A. Report, 1976, pp. 24, 29.

[72] J. Bauser, *Mathematics and Science: Uneasy truce or open hostilities,* Mathematics Teaching 1974, 68.

[73] N.G.G. Webb, *Correlating the Teaching of Mathematics and Science,* Inst. J. Math. Educ. Sci. Technol. 1975, vol. 6, No. 1.

[74] A. Maplas,. *Mathematics and Science in the Secondary School,* Education in Science, April 1973.

[75] *Modern Mathematics and its Implications for Physics Teaching,* Scottish
      Centre for Maths/Science and Technical Education, Dundee; and A.T.
      Rogerson *et al., Modern Mathematics in the Science Lesson,* C.U.P., 1977.

[76] W.U. Walton, Trend Paper No. 11a, *The Interface between physics and
      mathematics at school level,* I.C.P.E., Edinburgh, 1975.

[77] P.J. Black, *op.cit.,* pp. 77-82.

Adapting Instructional Method to Class Size

Paul G. Bamberg

1. Introduction

The purpose of this text is to describe some of the wide variety of alternatives which are available to the college teacher who is searching for the most appropriate teaching strategy for his course and to provide a basis for choosing among these alternatives. I have focused on two aspects of the problem of selecting a method of instruction: first, the comparative advantages and disadvantages of group instruction as contrasted with individualized instruction, second, the suitability of various methods for classes which range in enrolment from one student to several hundred. While space does not permit a detailed description of every possible style of teaching, I have tried, in the case of methods which are not widely known, to provide a model by describing the structure of specific courses which I have taught by using these methods.

At most institutions, some form of group instruction is the norm for all courses. The precise method varies, but whatever it may be, it is frequently adopted uncritically by most of the faculty, who tend to perpetuate the methods by which they were taught. In consequence, at one institution, one may find lecture courses in which a professor lectures to an audience of three students for an entire term without pausing to entertain a single question. Elsewhere, perhaps at a law school, courses with enrolments of two hundred may be taught by the Socratic method. Still elsewhere, at an institution which prides itself on its small classes, many different faculty members may all be working independently of one another, each preparing his own complete version of the same introductory course in economics or calculus for a section of twenty-five students.

These examples illustrate how group instruction can be used inappropriately or inefficiently. While the available data on effectiveness of instruction indicate that none of these teaching methods can be judged generally superior to any other[1], a good case can be made for trying to choose the method which is best suited to the size of the class.

During the past decade, a different sort of teaching/learning strategy, based upon carefully prepared learning modules and individual interaction between teacher and student, has been growing in popularity. Originally called "Keller plan" or "self-paced instruction", this method of teaching is now generally known as "personalized systems of instruction" or "PSI". A wealth of information on how to prepare learning modules[2] and how to organize PSI courses[3] is now readily available. While it is not clear whether or not PSI is more effective than conventional group instruction, it is certainly a well-established alternative which merits serious consideration.

Many of the features of PSI—careful specification of instructional objectives, for example, or the use of repeatable mastery tests—are in no way incompatible with group instruction. I, like many other teachers who use PSI routinely, have tried to combine PSI with group instruction and thereby to obtain the best of both worlds. In my attempts at creating such hybrid courses, I have found that the larger the course, the better the mixture of methods works. Indeed, for courses of several hundred students, which pose difficulties no matter whether they are taught by means of large lectures, or divided into many independent discussion sections, or taught on a strictly individual basis by conventional PSI methods, a course structure which combines individual and group instruction offers distinct advantages over either group instruction alone or individual instruction alone.

In the next section of this article I have attempted to summarize, without specific reference to course size, the comparative advantages and disadvantages of group instructional activities and individual instructional activities. Section 3 reviews the preparation of learning modules for use either in a PSI course or in conjunction with group instruction. Section 4 describes forms of group instruction appropriate for classes of various sizes and discusses the effect of class size on the operation of a PSI course. Section 5 presents a brief description of two simple but effective combinations of PSI and small-group instruction which I have employed, followed by a detailed description of a rather complex but very effective system for using group instruction in a large course while retaining all the flexibility of PSI.

2. Selecting Instructional Activities

The most important decision to be made in organizing a course is whether the activities in which students interact with the teaching staff are to be primarily group activities or individual activities. At one extreme is a lecture course, in which the activities might consist simply of three weekly lectures and final examination; at the other extreme is a PSI course in which each student interacts solely with a tutor or proctor on a one-to-one basis. Clearly the activities will be governed to some extent by course enrolment; a course with only one student cannot have group activities, while a course with hundreds of students, taught by one instructor with no assistants, could hardly be built around individual activities. Frequently, though, either type of approach is possible, and the advantages and disadvantages of the two approaches must be weighed. These advantages and disadvantages may be considered under the headings of *flexibility, teacher-student interaction,* and *efficiency.*

Flexibility

A course built around individual activities permits considerably more flexibility, both in terms of content and scheduling, than one based on group activities. In a lecture course, all students must usually study exactly the same material and must attend class, whether prepared or not, at exactly the same time. In contrast to this, a PSI approach, in which many learning modules are available, permits each individual student to build his own course out of the available modules. Even in cases where the curriculum is prescribed in advance, so that all students will study the same modules, an individualized approach allows each student to learn at whatever rate permits him to master the course material, possibly going quickly over familiar topics, while taking extra time for modules which prove exceptionally difficult.

As many teachers have discovered while using a PSI approach, flexibility and self-pacing are not unmixed blessings. Many students freely admit that they lack the self-discipline to keep themselves working steadily in a course in which there are no regularly scheduled classes to provide a timetable for learning. Sitting in the back row of a lecture hall by no means guarantees learning, but it is undeniable that students are less inclined to procrastinate when doing so involves missing regularly scheduled classes. Classes which are not merely lectures, but which require preparation on the part of students, are likely to be even more effective in discouraging procrastination.

Of course, there is no reason why individual activities cannot be structured in a manner which provides a strong inducement for students to keep up with their work. The same student who skips half the lectures in one course would very likely be present and prepared every week for an individual tutorial, and activities which make much less lavish use of faculty time than individual tutorial can still be arranged to provide a strong incentive for students to "keep up". The literature of PSI abounds with descriptions of schemes to replace the lecture as an antiprocrastination measure.

One might be tempted to conclude that flexibility and self-pacing are incompatible with group activities, but it is possible, in very large courses, to have both. Such an approach will be described in section 5.

Teacher-Student Interaction

Since the total number of hours which an instructor can devote to his course is limited, it is tempting to maximize the "exposure" of students to the instructor by gathering everyone together for lectures. All too frequently the result is much exposure but little interaction, with the lecturer functioning almost as a videotape recording of the lecture might have done. On the other hand, if the instructor attempts to divide his available time equally among the students, interacting with them only on a one-to-one basis, then instructional time is likely to be severely limited, and the instructor must take great pains to assure that he is not spending this precious time on functions which could equally well have been carried out by printed materials or student assistants.

Whether the overall teacher-student interaction is most beneficial if the teacher interacts with students on a group basis or an individual basis depends heavily upon the nature of the course. Lecture demonstrations, which may be difficult to set up and require experience and skill to perform, are an example of a group instruction activity which can hardly be modified to fit into a course built solely around individual activites. On the other hand, a student might well find a half-hour conference to discuss his term paper with a professor to be more rewarding than attending a month of lectures on material which is fully presented in print.

In addition to teacher-student interaction, one must consider also the interaction among students in a course. This is not especially fostered either by lectures or by individual tutorial, yet suitably designed small-group activities may encourage students to learn from one another.

Efficiency

Group activities are highly efficient in dealing with problems which are common to all students. For presenting facts or ideas which are nowhere available in print, or for demonstrating phenomena which cannot be adequately described in words, the large lecture is hard to surpass in efficiency. The traditional "conference section" of fifteen to twenty students is equally well suited to the teaching of methods of analysis which all students can be expected to find difficult.

From the student's point of view, of course, the most efficient instruction is that which makes best use of the student's time. By this criterion, group activities, inevitably addressed to the average needs of the group, are considerably less efficient than individual activities in which the student's specific problems can be addressed directly.

3. Preparation of Materials for Flexible Use

Through careful planning, it is possible to prepare written materials which can be used in teaching a given subject efficiently to one student or to a class of several hundred students. My own experience is that the time invested in this preparation is recovered the third time that the materials are used. A sound policy is to prepare learning modules which are sufficiently complete so that, by using them, it would be possible to teach an adequate course for a single student by spending one hour per week on tutorial discussion. This guideline assures that the modules will take care of routine transmission of information and enable students, working on their own, to meet the lower-level educational objectives of the course. Then, depending on the number of students in the course, suitable activities, either for individuals or for groups of students, can be developed to facilitate the mastery of higher-level objectives, to provide evaluation of student progress, and to offer as wide a variety of learning experiences as possible.

A typical module that I have used in my physics courses at Harvard consists of the following components:

1.   A careful statement of *objectives.* Defining these objectives clearly and explicitly is indispensable to the teacher[4]. Students frequently prefer an implicit statement of objectives such as might be provided by a problem set, a list of study questions, or a practice examination, but they also find it convenient also to have an explicit list of objectives.

2.   A list of *resources,* mostly written material but sometimes audiotapes, videotapes, or film loops.

3.   A suggested *procedure* for mastering the objectives. This consists usually of detailed reading assignments, with exercises (and their solutions) interspersed as appropriate, which is sufficient to permit students, *before* class, to learn the more straightforward aspects of the subject on their own. The procedure may include provision for one, two, or three classes for considering the more difficult aspects of the subject. Depending on the size and structure of the course, these classes could be individual tutorials, small group discussions, or large lectures, but they should address themselves to higher-level objectives, not to transmission of information.

4.   A group of *problems* more challenging than the routine exer-
      cises in the procedure. My own policy is usually to include
      solutions for these problems.

5.   A set of at least four equivalent *mastery tests*. One of these,
      chosen at random, is distributed to all students as a practice
      test; the others are used for evaluation.

6.   Frequently one or two questions about a module are of such
      overriding importance that they ought to appear on each of
      the mastery tests. Such questions are best framed as *"mini-
      lecture topics"*—subjects for five or ten-minute lectures
      which students will present to a member of the teaching staff
      or to a classmate as part of demonstrating their mastery of
      the module.

4. Organizing a course—Group and Individualized Methods

By using learning modules prepared as described above, it
becomes possible to deal efficiently with a class of any size from
one to five hundred, using group instruction, individualized
instruction, or a mixture of the two forms. Depending on the
number of students, the nature of the subject, and the constraints
of time and teaching space, at least a dozen different types of
courses can be distinguished, as follows:

Methods built around regularly scheduled group instruction:

1.   Regularly scheduled tutorial (1-3 students)
2.   Classes in which the students share the lecturing responsi-
      bility (4-12 students)
3.   Informally structured discussion classes. (8-30 students)
4.   "Socratic method" classes, possibly supplemented by small-
      group discussion sections. (20-120 students)
5.   Autolecture-seminar method. (20-50 students)
6.   Lectures, possibly supplemented by small-group dis-
      cussions. (40-500 students).

*Methods built around self-paced personalized instruction
(conventional PSI). Here the number of students influences the role
of the instructor and thus affects the character of the course.*

7.   Independent study, supervised by one instructor alone.
      (1-10 students)
8.   Course meeting on a regular schedule, with instructor and one
      assistant doing all the teaching. (10-35 students)
9.   Students assigned to proctors, with instructor acting mainly
      as a supervisor. (35 to 100 students)
10.   Completely decentralized course, with instructor exerting
      very little direct personal influence on students. (100-500
      students)

*Methods built around a combination of group and self-paced
instruction.*

11.   PSI course with discussion at start of each class. (10 to 30
      students)
12.   PSI course with optional regularly scheduled discussion
      classes. (30-100 students)
13.   PSI course with discussion classes scheduled according to
      student interests. (100-400 students)

Some of these methods are familiar to all teachers; others, such
as the PSI approach, are described in great detail in the literature. I
shall comment briefly on the more familiar approaches, principally
in order to point out how learning modules may be employed.
Methods 2, 4, 5, 11, 12 and 13, which deserve to be better known,
will be discussed in more detail.

4.1   Regularly scheduled tutorial

In conjunction with a regularly scheduled tutorial, learning
modules provide a means of defining what preparation is required
of the student and of taking care of the routine aspects of
instruction, thereby assuring that the tutorial itself can be used for
activities which exploit fully the opportunity for one-to-one
interaction between student and tutor. This approach has been used
successfully at Harvard in an advanced classical mechanics course,
taught only in the fall term, which one student wished to take in the
spring. The student was asked simply to work through one module
per week in preparation for the one-hour tutorial, at which he was
expected to present at the blackboard his solutions to three
"discussion problems" assigned in the module. Use of the
materials which had been developed for a class of fifty students

made it possible for a faculty member to spare enough time to offer a well-organized tutorial for a single student.

4.2 Lecturing by students

For a class of four to twelve students, I have found it useful to supplement existing modules with lists of "study questions" whose answers, taken together, form a well-organized lecture on the material covered in the module. Each study question should require less than ten minutes to answer, so that six students can have an opportunity to lecture during a one-hour class, with time left over for discussion and comments by the instructor.

This approach requires very careful preparation on the part of the students. I doubt that students would feel it worthwhile to prepare all the questions unless they have the opportunity to lecture at least once every two classes.

4.3 Discussion classes

The discussion class, probably the most common form of instruction apart from the lecture, requires no detailed description here. Frequently, in my experience, such classes degenerate into lectures because the students are too unfamiliar with the subject to participate. Use of modules alleviates this problem in two ways. First, the students have a clear idea of what preparation is required, Second, in cases where a large course is divided into many small sections, the modules provide a well-defined common curriculum and eliminate the need for each section instructor to do the work of organizing his own complete course. Thus it becomes possible for a group of teachers working together to devote more of their time to classroom teaching, less to preparation.

4.4 Socratic method

The "Socratic method" is common in professional schools, especially in law or business schools which use the case study method, but it is little used at the undergraduate level. Its principal advantage is that it permits class time to be used to help students in mastering higher-level objectives such as application and analysis, rather than for routine transmission of facts.

In contrast to discussion sections, which frequently are built around students' questions, the Socratic method requires a carefully planned sequence of questions posed by the instructor, which are designed to bring out the important points which he wishes to make. A Socratic method class serves much the same function as a lecture, but it has several advantages. First, since the students have come to class prepared to answer questions about the module which they have studied, there is no need to spend class time reviewing matters which students can just as well learn on their own. Second, since any student may be called on to answer the next question, the class can usually be relied upon to remain alert. Third, the instructor receives immediate feedback as to how well students are understanding the subject.

In conducting a Socratic method class, it is advisable to begin by selecting one student at random and asking enough questions of that one student to introduce the subject of the day's discussion. These questions should be ones which require just sound preparation, not great analytical powers, to answer. As the class proceeds and the questions become more difficult, one should more and more call upon volunteers for answers. This approach, in my experience, assures a generally adequate level of preparation. Having required students to prepare, one must respect that preparation by not dwelling upon topics which students were supposed to have mastered before class. It is especially important **not** to fall into the trap of lecturing on the material that students were to have prepared. If you appear to be assuming that students are not preparing adequately, you will soon find that assumption to be correct!

4.5 Autolecture-seminar method

The autolecture-seminar method, developed by Alfred Bork and Albert Baez, makes use of tape recordings to structure a discussion. The tape, accompanied by projection transparencies or slides, contains the basic information for the class. Its running time should be no more than half the available class time. The tape recording is then "moderated" by its author or by a teaching assistant, who can answer students' questions, pose questions for students to answer, and clarify the presentation made on the tape.

When an autolecture tape is moderated by its author, it needs to be little more than a straightforward lecture, which can be recorded without interruption. In using this approach in teaching statistical mechanics, I found that interaction with the students proceeded much better than when I had tried to lecture on the same material. Not surprisingly, students are considerably more willing to interrupt a tape recorder than a lecturer.

When an autolecture tape is to be moderated by a teaching assistant who has not heard the tape before, then it must be considerably more than just a short lecture. As a general rule, the moderator cannot pose his own questions, because he runs a significant risk of asking a question about precisely what the tape is going to discuss next. It therefore becomes necessary to include questions every couple of minutes on the tape itself. A consistent policy must be followed with regard to the answers to these questions. After students have discussed them, either the tape or the moderator, but not both, should summarize the correct answer. A tape which has been carefully prepared can sometimes be successfully moderated even by a student, but to produce a half-hour tape of this quality may require several hours of work.

At its best, the autolecture approach combines many of the advantages of the lecture method and the Socratic method. If enough teaching assistants, even comparatively inexperienced ones, are available, it permits a large course to be divided into sections which are small enough so that each student has the opportunity to participate regularly and actively in discussion. At the same time, it assures that a common core of information, that on the tape, will be presented in all sections.

In contrast to the methods presented earlier, the autolecture does not assume prior preparation on the part of the student. In fact, the alternation of presentation of basic information with questions closely resembles the written procedure of a typical learning module. For this reason, it is advisable to follow each autolecture with a "seminar" or discussion class in which the issues raised by the autolecture can be discussed in greater depth.

4.6 Lectures

After learning modules have been prepared, the lecture loses its role as a primary medium of information transmission. For certain restricted purposes, however, the lecture continues to be useful. A lecture can be used to introduce each module, for example. In science courses, certain demonstrations can only be presented once to a large lecture audience. Finally, for presentation of information or viewpoints which cannot be found in print, there is really no alternative to the lecture.

Keller and others[3] have advocated use of lectures for entertainment and motivation in courses where most instruction is on an individual basis. The idea is that lectures should function as a reward for students who have kept up with their work. Attendance at such lectures is usually disappointingly small, but the students who have chosen to attend such lectures enjoy them. Such lectures do not make sense in a moderate-sized course, where the expected turnout scarcely can justify the effort of reserving a lecture hall and preparing a showmanlike lecture. In an extremely large course, on the other hand, where a thirty-per cent turnout represents a large audience, optional lectures can be a worthwhile addition to a course.

No matter what the size of the class, individualized instruction is built around the process which Bloom[4] calls "formative evaluation"—the grading and discussion of the mastery tests which accompany each module. Nonetheless, the administration of an individualized course depends strongly upon the number of students enrolled and the amount of time which the instructor can devote to each of them, as follows:

4.7 Supervised independent study

With only a very small number of students, the instructor is likely not to be kept busy for even the two two-hour meetings per week which are typically a minimum for a PSI course. Under these circumstances, it sometimes makes sense to treat a course as supervised independent study, with each student contacting the instructor to discuss each module as he completes it.

Given a well-designed set of modules, it requires comparatively little time for an instructor to supervise a few students working on a PSI course. If the instructor is already teaching a larger PSI course, so that a procedure for administering tests is already established, then it requires scarcely more time to teach a student doing a different course than to teach one more student in the larger course. I have taken advantage of this feature of individualized instruction, for example, to make it possible for a handful of students in the Harvard extension program to take advanced courses in physics in conjunction with a large introductory course taught by individualized methods.

4.8   Regularly scheduled PSI course

When the enrolment in a PSI course reaches ten students, then the instructor's time will be almost fully occupied during four hours per week of regularly scheduled class meetings. With more than fifteen students, an assistant becomes a desirable addition. In a course of this size there is frequent personal interaction between the instructor and each student, and, with some effort, the instructor can usually induce the students to help with teaching one another. If the instruction is completely individualized, it makes little difference whether all students are studying the same set of modules or whether each is taking a different course.

4.9   PSI with many proctors

When the enrolment in a PSI course exceeds thirty, it becomes difficult for one instructor to remain in close contact with each student. Under such circumstances the usual solution is for each student to have his own "proctor", an undergraduate assistant who answers his questions and administers his mastery tests, with the instructor on hand to provide additional assistance and supervision as needed. As enrolment grows, the instructor is faced with a choice among a number of alternatives: either to tolerate crowding in the classroom, or to give up more of his own time in order to extend the class hours, or to delegate responsibility for supervising the course to one of the proctors for part of the time.

Even when students are urged strongly to proceed at their own pace, in a group of more than fifty students there are likely to be ten or more who are all studying the same topic at the same time and who could benefit from a group discussion of it. In other words, as PSI courses become larger, possibilities arise for group instruction which do not interfere with any of the advantages of individualized instruction.

4.10 Very large PSI course

In a completely individualized course with an enrolment of more than a hundred students, the instructor frequently finds himself unable to maintain regular contact with a majority of the class. At the same time, natural opportunities for efficient use of group instruction become more and more frequent. Under these circumstances, it makes sense for the instructor to try to interact with small groups of students, rather than with individuals. A detailed strategy for achieving this goal will be presented later.

> *Since group instruction typically takes place early in the learning process, while individualized instruction centers around mastery testing, the two are by no means mutually exclusive. In particular, repeatable mastery tests can be used with any of the methods of group instruction described earlier. Or, looking at the same possibility from the other side, group instruction may be added to a PSI course. The advantages of this group instruction must be weighed against two disadvantages: first, the time which the instructor has available for individual interaction with students is diminished; second, the possibilities of self-pacing and flexibility in choice of topics are diminished. As a general rule, the larger the course, the more the advantages of group instruction outweigh these disadvantages. Here are three models for courses which combine group and individualized methods, each suitable for a different number of students.*

4.11   PSI with discussion at start of class

With a comparatively small number of students, between ten and twenty-five, group instruction makes sense only if one is willing to forego flexibility and self-pacing almost completely. Under those circumstances, it makes sense to schedule two classes, each two hours in length, each week, using the first half of each class for discussion, the second half for mastery testing and assistance with individual problems.

I have been using such an approach in teaching an intensive calculus course in which students complete an entire year's work in one semester. All of the twenty students in the course have had some previous exposure to calculus, so that, of the seventeen learning modules, the first nine are partially familiar to many students, while the last eight cover entirely new material.

For the first third of the course, while students are solidifying their mastery of the first nine modules, I use individualized methods exclusively. A diagnostic test, administered during the first week of the course, reveals which of the first nine modules each student has already mastered. Each student then works through the modules which he has not yet mastered until he has passed a test on each. During this phase of the course, group methods would be inappropriate, since each student has a different background, and on a given day as many as six different modules are being studied.

The last eight modules are covered at the rate of one per week. Students work through the first half of the week's module in preparation for the first class, the second half for the second class. The first hour of each class is spent in a group discussion of applications of the theory and techniques presented in the module, while the remaining time is used for taking and discussing mastery tests. Because the students have previously become used to learning from the modules alone, they come to class well-prepared, with the result that discussion can focus on the difficult aspects of the material rather than the routine aspects.

This course is a good example of a situation in which the introduction of group activities into what is otherwise a standard PSI course costs nothing. Because the calculus curriculum is fixed and strictly sequential, there is no scope for flexibility, and because every student has to complete the entire course by the end of the term in order to receive credit, there is really no scope for self-pacing. Yet because all the lower-level objectives are dealt with thoroughly before class as the students work through the modules, class time can be used very efficiently.

4.12   PSI with scheduled and self-paced examinations

In cases where self-paced and flexibility are real advantages of an individualized approach, it requires a larger enrolment, usually at least fifty students, before it makes sense to introduce group instruction into a PSI course. With this large an enrolment it begins to make sense to include a series of optional regularly scheduled discussions into the course structure. Students who find these discussions compatible with their schedules can attend them, while others can feel free to ignore them while proceeding either very quickly or very slowly through the course.

An example of this sort of course is an adult-education course in introductory physics which I have taught. In this course thirty-six learning modules were available, each including a tape-recorded lecture. Students were permitted to select any sequence of modules and to work through them at any rate that they chose, receiving course credit for each six modules which they mastered. Some students found time during a year to complete only six modules, while others completed as many as twelve in a single month. Under these circumstances, to constrain all students to follow the same schedule would have been too high a price to pay for the benefits of group instruction, yet there were a substantial number of students who were inclined to study the modules in strict numerical order at the rate of one per week. The enrolment in the course was large enough (about sixty) so that a choice could be offered. Weekly discussions of the modules were offered for those who found the schedule convenient, while others were free to proceed at their own pace. Because I had two assistants and an extra classroom, the discussion classes did not interfere with the learning activities of the students following the self-paced option.

In this same course an attempt was made to arrange a second series of discussions following a schedule of one module every two weeks. It turned out that the number of students who found this pace appropriate was insufficient to justify the use of my time for this purpose, and so these classes were discontinued. As a general rule, the larger the enrolment, the greater the variety of group-instructional activities which can be maintained, and in this case the enrolment was just too small.

4.13   Large PSI course with demand-scheduled classes

For small or medium-sized courses, either group instruction or individualized instruction can be used, but it is usually inefficient to try to obtain all the advantages of both types in a single course. When enrolments exceed 100 students, both types of instruction begin to encounter problems. Large lecture courses are notoriously impersonal, while large PSI courses are difficult to manage because the instructor loses visibility. As the preceding discussion indicates, large enrolments do have one advantage: they make it possible efficiently to introduce group activities into an individualized course. In the limiting case of very large enrolments, it becomes possible to realize the full potential of both types of instruction. I shall illustrate this point by describing in detail a course in which, by taking advantage of the large enrolment, it was possible to combine the flexibility of individual instruction with the efficiency and liveliness of group instruction.

The course was an elementary physics course, populated mainly by life science and premedical students, which I taught at Harvard in the summer of 1974 and 1975. With an enrolment of 150 students, all working full time at physics in order to compress a year's work into eight weeks, the course was equivalent, in terms of the hours spent daily at teaching and the size of the staff, to an academic-year course with an enrolment of 600. The teaching staff consisted of myself, one other faculty member teaching half-time, twelve graduate students teaching half-time or full-time, and eight undergraduate assistants. This staff was at the same time also teaching six other modularized physics courses, with enrolments ranging from two to nine.

Forty different modules, covering virtually all of introductory physics, were available. Students were expected to master between 20 and 30 of these modules, depending on the mark which they hoped to receive. The median number of modules completed was 28. Students were encouraged not simply to study the modules in numerical order but to put together a course based on their own interests and needs. To aid in this process, a flow chart showing the interrelationships among the modules was distributed at the start of the course. To a certain extent each student's plan of study was governed by his choice of laboratory program; students who elected the laboratory which stressed optics and holography, for example, were expected to complete the module on geometric optics early in the second week of the course and to move as quickly as possible to the modules on waves and interference effects.

The individualized instruction in the course was built around the repeatable mastery tests and minilectures which formed part of each module. The mastery tests were administered in a testing center which was open for thirty-five hours each week, with two graduate students and two undergraduates on hand to mark tests and provide on-the-spot tutorial assistance to students who had been unable to pass a mastery test. There was no penalty for failing a mastery test; only a student's best attempt on each module counted in the grading.

Because of the large number of hours that the testing center was open, a student could not have all his tests graded by a single proctor, as is usually done in small PSI courses. To insure that one member of the staff would assume responsibility for monitoring the progress of each student, an advisor was assigned to each student. Completed mastery tests were delivered to a student's advisor, who could then identify and remedy recurrent problems. Advisors met individually for at least half an hour each week with each of their advisees. These meetings were used for reviewing completed tests, for planning what modules the student would study next, and for presentation of minilectures. Typically, a student would have to present eight five-minute minilectures (two for each of four modules) per week. Three or four of these would be given for the advisor, the remainder at a weekly one-hour "minilecture session" consisting of one graduate student, one undergraduate assistant, and four to six students.

For a small class of twelve students, the program of modules, unit tests, and minilectures would have constituted the entire course. In all probability, no more than two students would ever be studying the same module on the same day; so group activities could not have been introduced without sacrificing flexibility. With 150 students this was not the case, and it became possible to introduce a variety of group instructional activities.

Each day, fourteen different two-hour discussion classes, one taught by each faculty member and teaching fellow, were offered. A room and meeting time were assigned to each staff member, but the module to be discussed was usually not selected until two or three days in advance. Forms listing the times and places for classes were posted on a notice board approximately a week ahead of time. As instructors chose the subjects of their classes, they wrote the number of the module which they had selected on the form; students then signed up for the classes which they planned to attend. If fewer than four students signed up for a class, it was automatically cancelled, and the instructor provided extra help in grading mastery tests instead. If more than sixteen students signed up for a class, a second instructor usually offered another class on the same module. By watching the notice board, it was easy for instructors to anticipate what modules they ought to be offering.

To provide an incentive for students to come prepared to class, a set of worked problems for the module being discussed was required as a ticket of admission. Instructors could therefore confidently assume that students had already learned the rudiments of the subject being considered and could concentrate on those aspects which students find difficult to learn on their own. Students were, of course, free to attempt a mastery test before attending class in order to determine whether a class on that particular module was necessary at all for them. Some students attended a class for every module which they studied, while others attended practically none. Because there were no fixed assignments of students either to meeting times or to specific instructors, there was none of the discontent with section assignments which frequently arises when a large course is divided into small sections. By and large, the more experienced teachers attracted larger audiences, but every member of the staff eventually attracted a following of students who liked his teaching style.

In addition to the regular modules, students could receive course credit for participating in "seminars" organized by members of the teaching staff. These seminars explored applications of physics to varied fields such as music, photography, baseball and medieval weaponry. A dozen students typically prepared reports for a seminar, and the best four reports were then presented to the group. Again, advantage was being taken of the large enrolment; in order to find twelve students who are interested in the physics of medieval weaponry, one must have a large pool from which to draw.

For each module, a one-hour tape-recorded lecture was made available in the library. (One of the advantages of having the order in which the modules were studied to be flexible was that four copies of each tape were adequate to meet the demand.) In addition, optional demonstration or guest lectures, usually designed to entertain as much as to enlighten, were presented twice weekly. Attendance at these lectures ranged between 25 and 75 per cent of the course. In my opinion, the number of students attending was always sufficient to justify the effort of setting up all the demonstrations, especially since there was no "captive audience"; the students who came to a lecture were all interested in the subject.

The lectures, did, however, make apparent one of the disadvantages of introducing group instruction into an individualized course. Because they were held in the same lecture hall which functioned as a testing centre, mastery tests could not be taken on afternoons when lectures were being held, and some students came to regard this as a serious inconvenience toward the end of the summer. Furthermore, it proved impossible to schedule the demonstration lecture to everyone's satisfaction. For example, some students had completed the module on rotational motion by the time the demonstration lecture on tops and gyroscopes was given, while others had not even glanced at that module. As a result, it was impossible for the lecturer to assume any common level of preparation on the part of the audience.

Student response to this course was strongly favourable. By a majority of more than five to one, students reported that they would favour the format of the course over a conventional lecture format if they were to take another science course in summer school. For the most part, the activities which were judged most valuable were the individual activities, especially taking and discussing the mastery tests, while the discussion sections were rated moderately valuable. The only activities which were felt not to be worth the time invested were listening to other students' seminar reports and minilectures.

REFERENCES

[1] Dubin, Robert and Taveggia, Thomas C. *The Teaching-Learning Paradox.* Center for the Advanced Study of Educational Administration, University of Oregon, Eugene (1968)

[2] Russell, James D. *Modular Instruction* Burgess (1974)

[3] Keller, Fred and Sherman, J. Gilmour *The Keller Plan Handbook* Benjamin (1974)

[4] Burns, Richard W. *New Approaches to Behavioural Objectives* Brown (1972)

[5] Bloom, Benjamin, "Mastery Learning", in *Mastery Learning: Theory and Practice,* edited by James H. Block, Holt, Rinehart, and Winston (1971)

Group Methods in University Science Teaching

B. Eckstein

University education—in science as well as in most other disciplines—is still essentially based on the lecture. Even though problem-solving classes, laboratory courses, and project work gain importance towards the students' last year, lecture and lecturer represent the basic philosophy and spirit of the institution. Like the examination, which is strongly correlated to it, the lecture has become an institution in itself, an end rather than a means. Printing was invented centuries ago, paperback and Xerox are available, and students are able to read. But still the spoken word emanating from some lecturer remains the main source of University instruction. The main source of students' information however, frequently are the students' lecture notes, known to be fairly imperfect and deficient.

The doubts about the efficiency of the lecture for transferring information are serious and well founded. The misfit between the rate of lecturer's information output and students' rate of information intake causes a poor and unreliable information transfer. The transfer by suitably processed written information is much more reliable. Objection to the lecturer as a central means of students' instruction arises from its implicitly conveyed philosophy: the importance assigned to the lecture-method (rather than the lecture in itself) suggests the learner's inability for self-instruction, and makes him dependent on an expert teacher. By attending lectures the student may become conditioned to consume passively the lecturer's wisdom, rather than to think on his own, to question, let alone to contradict the lecturer.

Until some decades ago, the knowledge and skills acquired by a scientist-to-be during his University training essentially provided him with all professional needs throughout his career. Sciences, now however, are not only expanding acceleratedly, they are changing in their fundamental tools, in the way of representation and handling of problems, in their basic paradigms. His ability for efficient self-instruction, and for adapting to new ways of thought and new insight, thus become most important for the scientist. Again, in order to produce results, much science is now carried out by (generally interdisciplinary) teams. Professional scientific education ought, therefore, to include some training for teamwork as well as for self-instruction. The lecture, which has the effect of isolating the student and fostering intellectual dependence rather than originality, and which induces convergent rather than divergent thinking, hence ought to be supplemented by other teaching strategies.

During the last decades, techniques and possible advantages of the "learning group" and of group teaching were extensively explored. We now know for sure, that every and any topic can in principle be learned effectively by group methods, generally following a phase of self-instruction or of any other form of acquiring information, to provide a common basis for the group discussion. The group discussion is not to replace the phase of information acquisition, but to add to it.

Learning groups can have an immensely stimulating and motivating effect and thus increase willingness and hence ability to learn. Among the chief cognitive aims of learning groups are the classifying, understanding, handling, and questioning of incorporated facts, while simultaneously by a group discussion, retention and availability of the memorized facts dealt with are improved. In addition, group discussions offer a training in general and in scientific communication, in questioning and proving statements, in group decision making and conflict solving—all important for a modern scientist.

Group teaching may become a most helpful tool to make the scientist-to-be professionally competent and socially responsible.

However, it ought not to be overburdened by exaggerated expectations. As an educational technique, it demands involvement, knowledge, and skills on the part of the teacher. To be successful, group teaching has to be taken seriously, and—to do it competently—most teachers first ought to undergo some related training. Altogether, however, group teaching might bring a new impetus and even a new dimension to University science education.

1. On the background of group methods

This section gives some theoretical background on the necessity, psychology, and possible problems of group teaching applied in science, to make the following sections more easily understood.

1.1 The expanding sciences and new goals of science teaching

The accelerated development in the sciences and in technology lead to the most outstanding feature of our age: the quick changes in general conditions and way of life. The sciences themselves are expanding rapidly. The expansion leads, or is leading, to disintegration, and brings about the dilemma either to prolong unpracticably the scientist's vocational training, or to narrow down the scientist to the merest specialist, a "scientific technologist" on a limited research topic rather than a scientist. To overcome this problem, the very concepts and goals of University science teaching—beyond the mere methods and ways of tuition—have to be redefined and re-established.

Evidently, the future scientist can no longer be provided by the University with all possible professional needs. The first goal of University science education hence will be to enable the student to achieve effective self- and peer-instruction about the facts, methods, and skills of his science. The present teacher-oriented systems of instruction then have henceforth to be modified into learner-oriented ones, and the examination systems into instruments of effective self-assessment for rationally controlling their own learning progress, rather than a tool for selection and for coercing the students to work. The role and function of the teacher will change. From the former source of information and wisdom, from a domineering guardian, the

University teacher will become a facilitator of learning processes for increasingly autonomous and self-responsible learners.

Two approaches to new teaching strategies are fairly well explored. Individualized systems of instruction, such as "PSI", * improve cognitive learning, but they don't offer a training for future teamwork. Group methods however simultaneously improve cognitive learning, and offer a training for teamwork. Dealing with information in a multitude of connections and aspects, group discussions additionally improve availability as well as retention of the memorized content. The stored information is within call under a multitude of headings, in contrast to most information conveyed by conventional instruction, which generally favours convergent and compartmentalized thinking, and stresses mere "content" rather than the diversity of connections and interrelations.

Eventually, when group methods focus attention on the "process" of a group discussion as well as on its content, the participants can be made aware of the way they act and react to each other. Thus social attitudes and interactions can be improved or corrected, and social virtues such as tolerance, concern for the fellow-man, and awareness of one's own tendencies to prejudice may be developed. Improving a scientist's perception and reasoning by making him aware of possible prejudice is always worth while. Again, by favouring co-operation, group work may counteract the traits of excessive competetiveness, which increasingly become a threat to our whole culture.

A common prejudice against the applicability of group teaching is the hypothesis of its immense expenditure in students' and teachers' time. However, in the long run, adequate group teaching proved to be not more time-consuming than other well accepted teaching strategies (Abercrombie 1974). On the other hand, the effectiveness of the lecture generally is largely overestimated. Actually, it always was the teacher rather than the learner, who "covered the syllabus" in conventional teaching, and an unprejudiced test of the actual effectiveness of the lecture—information intake vs. information output—might come as a bad shock to many lecturers. Competent group teaching is not unreasonably time-expensive. With the further development of the sciences, and the related shifting of the goals in science teaching, group methods will become an essential part of the scientist's vocational training.

*See "Adapting Instructional Method to Class Size" by P.G. Bamberg, page 97.

1.2 A bit of applied educational and group psychology

In contrast to all the evidence for "social" (biographical) factors controlling the so-called "giftedness" of man, Universities and University teachers mostly cling to the concept of an essentially hereditary, fateful, and unchangeable "giftedness". However, the learning results achievable by some individual, are controlled broadly by his former learning experiences, and by affective factors, mainly by the relation to self and teacher. Self-confidence and the feeling of being accepted by the teachers, improves the willingness, courage, and ability to learn. The teacher's doubt of the learner's ability, however, inevitably transfers to the learner, and impedes his learning efforts and results. To foster "giftedness", a learning climate of mutual confidence and esteem, trust in the learner's ability, and the teacher's intrinsic interest in student and topic, are of central importance.

The assumption of an essentially hereditary "giftedness" provides teacher and learner with the very best excuse in the case of under-achievement. They both abandon further efforts, rather than increase their shared endeavour. With sufficient effort and time invested by teacher and learner, nearly any learner can achieve astonishingly high learning standards (in some cases, however, the effort might surpass the advantages gained). The different effort and time needed for a certain learning result by different learners, however, make teacher-centered tuition with its fixed teaching rate a fairly inappropriate approach. Actually, the rate of information intake varies from one individual to the next, and for any given learner with his momentary condition, his pre-knowledge, and his interest in the subject. A combination of self-instruction and group discussion allows for an appropriate learning rate for any individual learner, without unduly isolating him.

"Group" here is defined by the essentially symmetric, multilateral pattern of communication (Fig. 1). Mistaking lecturing to a small audience (one-way communication!) for "group teaching" is a common misunderstanding, and slipping back into lecturing a constant temptation of the inexperienced group teacher. Another problem of group teaching is the possible loss of balance between task and "group process", the mutual interactions and emotional relations among the group members. Competition among group members—inevitable in a competitive culture like ours—impedes the necessary cooperation. The strong competition is mostly

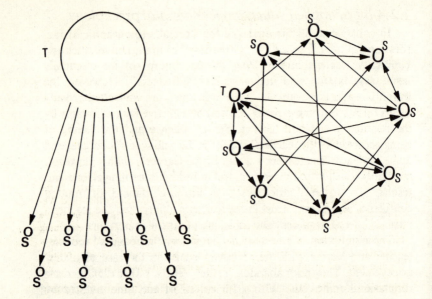

Fig. 1 Communication pattern in lecture and group discussion.

In contrast to the one-way communication of the lecture, the "group discussion" is defined by the multilateral, essentially symmetric communication pattern. An adequate and symmetric seating pattern facilitates the establishing of multilateral discussion in the presence of a teacher: Sitting in front of the students or at the "top of the table" automatically keeps you in a dominating role.

T teacher
S student

masked as a technical argument, though with strong emotional undercurrents. Underachieving working or learning groups generally fail by internal competition and rivalry, i.e. for emotional reasons, rather than for task-based difficulties.

The proceedings in a working or learning group are regulated by the "task", by the single participants and their individual concern for the task, and by the group process—the mutual relations and interactions. Ruth Cohn (1969/70) hence suggested a system of triangular co-ordinates, the so-called "Cohn-triangle", to describe the group's proceedings within the "components" of "it" (task/theme), of "I" (the single learners with their individual concerns, hopes, and fears), and of "we" (the group process). As learning, even of the most "ego-distant" facts, is strongly influenced by emotional factors, strict

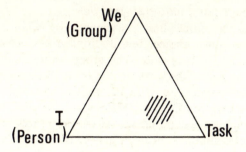

Fig. 2 The "Cohn-triangle"

A description of the group proceedings in a system of triangular co-ordinates. In the "normal" academic discussion, human relations and emotionality (the I- and We-corner of the triangle) are ignored, causing the discussion mostly to remain sterile and tedious. Allowing for human emotional needs by not strictly confining discussion to the task, but by admitting personal and mutual feelings, creates a favourable group climate and thus actually promotes even the "factual" results. The discussion essentially ought to be kept to the indicated (shaded) region.

limitation to the "theme" by no means offers optimum learning results. The learning person has got feelings and emotions as well as an intellect, and he is involved in learning as a whole person. In science teaching, best learning results are gained by groups staying in the region of the Cohn-triangle indicated in Fig. 2. This region may be left temporarily, but should be kept by a science learning group.

When aims such as communicative and co-operative skills are valued higher, the group must be run somewhat farther from the "task"-corner, devoting more interest and more time to persons and process. A less experienced group leader however, safely keeps somewhat closer to the task, to avoid the members entangling in mutual fights and the process possibly getting out of hand. Any decision to be made by the group offers cause and opportunity for fights, and thus reinforces the group process. By offering a choice among alternatives, the leader thus always can direct the group proceedings towards the "we"-corner of the Cohn-triangle. When, on the other hand, the group pays too much interest to persons or process, it is generally brought back to the task by a question "what are we dealing with now"? or "is that our intended task?". When a group discussion becomes purely academic and sterile, the leader by referring to his own feelings of boredom and tediousness shifts the attention back to the neglected non-intellectual aspects.

1.3 Group phases and leadership style

Especially in the initial phases, a group never must be over-burdened by too much choice, lest it disintegrates before ever reaching the actual working state. The group leader has to state clearly the task as well as the working procedure. Successively, the group can be accustomed to efficient decision making, and to handling its internal conflicts. Offering too little guidance and "structure" (running a group "laissez-faire-style") forwards insec-urity and promotes mutual fighting; it may cause the process to get out of hand, and in the extreme it leads to group anarchy, disinte-gration, and the members' aversion against future group exper-iences.

In contrast to the laissez-faire-style leader, the "autocratic" leader cuts off mutual fighting among the members by his dominance and control of the group (the members however may ally to fight him). The group thus autocratically led generally achieves working results, but stays far below its possible standards, as the members hardly identify with the group and its task, and tend to leave the group altogether. As maturity and social skills of the members are hardly promoted, the autocratic leader always has to stay with his group, and never becomes superseded. In case of doubt, however, autocratic group leading still implies less risks than laissez-faire-style leading.

The most successful way to run a group is the so-called "social-integrative" ("democratic") style: The leader is "primus inter pares" rather than a "boss", his authority—stemming from superior knowledge, insight, and maturity—is consented to by the group. He increasingly shares responsibility and decision-making with the group, without overburdening it (see e.g. "Cohn-rules", p. 129). He gives as much guidance as is necessary, but sparingly to forward the group's development towards autonomy, self-regulation, and maturity.

In the initial stages, groups need extra guidance and reassurance, as rules and conditions are sought for, and the members feel uncertain about the role and the influence they can achieve. It is the phase of self-representation of the members, of orientation, of defining their own identity under the conditions of the group. If the leader does not offer enough guidance, this phase of orientation develops into a mutual fight for power, status, and leadership in the group (Bernstein and Lowy 1965), and the members temporarily are mainly interested in their mutual relations rather than in the subject task. Blocked by an autocratic leader, this phase of mutual fight is but delayed, and on some occasion or another, sudden outbursts of hostility and aggressiveness occur. A skilful social-integrative leader knows how to make the members aware of the process, its background, and its functions. He thus keeps the level of frustration, hostility, and anxiety low, and overcomes this phase fairly soon and keeps fighting and irritation to a minimum.

When the phase of fights for power is well pronounced, it generally is followed by a stage of overidentification of the members with the group. Individual traits and goals are strongly suppressed, and the group strives for strict conformity, lest the so laboriously achieved norms be risked. Eventually, however, the members realize that the group cohesion is not unduely stressed by their diversity. They have found their identity, including the status assigned to them and now are free to concentrate on the task rather than on self or group: The group has reached the "working stage", and no longer depends on presence and skills of a formal group leader.

The time needed to reach the working stage varies with the urgency of the task, with external conditions (such as the overall climate of the faculty), with personal traits of the members (ambitious and eccentric personalities enhance and prolong the fighting phase) and with aims, skills, and leadership style of the facilitator. The working stage is reached the sooner, the more task-centered and structured the group is run. However, the sooner it is reached, the lesser are the opportunities for social and emotional experiences, and hence the members' acquired skills of conflict handling and decision making. Led by a skilful, social-integrative facilitator, a group generally experiences a less pronounced fighting stage, followed directly by the working stage. This phase can be reached in the second or third session (a session lasting 60 to 90 minutes). However, the group then has not yet become altogether independent of the leader, who still has to stay with the group (and later to be available on demand) for quite a number of additional sessions.

In the working stage, the roles no longer are fixed to a certain member, but shift among the members according to the momentary needs. Such shifting roles are the momentary (factual, in contrast to the "formal") leader, the experts, and the sceptic, who has the important function to focus on aspects neglected by the group. With a group climate of overall hostility, the sceptic may become an outsider and even the scapegoat of the group. The role of the scapegoat generally is fixed to one member, who is mostly the spokesman for the group's denied troubles and anxieties (hence it is well worth while to take him very seriously). To expel him from the group is mostly a bad mistake and may start the group's disintegration—generally another member follows in the role. The scapegoat par excellence is any non-member who wants to share a group session. If there is any frustration among the members, it turns into hostility towards the "intruder", who generally is speedily turned out again. The attitude of the group towards outside guests is thus a sensitive indicator for the group climate, and for repressed mutual hostility, indicating that the working stage has not really been achieved.

In case of poor group cohesion—internal tensions among members—the "shared adversary, shared joy, shared work, shared success" may prove a remedy. The cohesion gained by sharing an "adversary" ("the establishment", "the Faculty", some individual teacher) however has but little duration, being based on a scapegoat mechanism and not really promoting the group's and its members' autonomy and maturity. Shared work and success however actually improve the group cohesion, and increase the group's ability to handle its internal conflicts successfully.

A very effective tool for making members aware of and understanding the group process, is videotaping the sessions (never without the consent of the group!), and analysing the tapes with the group. Thus the group and individual members are confronted with their behaviour and attitudes. The tape especially helps the leader to recognise and control his own share in the group's behaviour. By threatening or ridiculing a member (worst of all!) he may have intimidated the group, thus causing it to become passive and silent. "They just sit tight staring at me!" is a most common complaint and fear of inexperienced group leaders. The leader however unknowingly may have impeded the members' contributions by talking himself too soon, too often, too long. He may have struggled with the group, or given too little guidance and information. The tape generally clearly exhibits the cause of the group's withdrawal or refusal, and thus helps to overcome it. Lacking a videorecorder (a taperecorder is but a poor substitute, as all non-verbal traits are missing), a questionnaire (see p. 158) may help to elucidate and to overcome the difficulties.

Confronting a group with its videotaped sessions, however, demands an experienced group facilitator. In a few years, a time-saving approach for less experienced group leaders will be available in the form of (at present non-existent) multi-media demonstration material. By films on typical group situations, related instruction for observation, some theoretical explanations, and highly structured group dynamical exercises, this material would offer a basic introduction for groups as well as for their inexperienced leaders. The groups thus would get a quick and safe start, avoiding most of the irritations of the initial group phases.

With a good group climate, and the proceedings kept sufficiently close to the task, even a "dull" topic gains the learner's interest, as he can approach it from and deal with the aspects meaningful to him. Learning motivation and thus learning results are improved. The extra time needed in the initial stages is more than compensated for by the higher learning intensity and progress, and the better retention and availability of the "covered" content. However, it is quite a major change in role and self-conception from the former lecturer to the facilitator of a largely autonomous learning group. The facilitator in particular gets thorough feed-back about the actual learning results, and thus unexpectedly may be confronted with vast gaps in the learners' assumed knowledge, which might come to him as a shock. However, group teaching as well has its own and special rewards in interacting with persons, rather than merely instructing people.

1.4 Some problems connected with group teachings

Actually, group teaching does not imply any more or any more serious problems than conventional tuition. However, a teacher favouring group methods usually feels himself under a special stress to succeed, lest he brings discredit to the method, which — being highly innovative — is regarded much more critically than any conventional teaching strategy. The teacher may be afraid that his students by group methods achieve poorer results in the exams than with conventional teaching (the examination system being adapted to conventional rather than group teaching), or he may feel that he brings the learners — while preparing them better for their future vocation — into contradiction with the institution and with the educational system. Being offered just one group seminar within an otherwise teacher-centered, rigid institution, actually might confuse the students, and bring irritation rather than advantages.

The teacher's stress in starting group work, can be largely reduced by beginning with "simple tasks and small groups for short periods" (Bligh 1971), by offering the students a free choice between conventional and group teaching (any experiment is more easily run with volunteers), and by running the first group seminars declaredly as "an experiment" with a small number of participants and a less important course. Not that group teaching any longer *IS* an experiment, but Faculties' and colleagues' suspicions and hence the teacher's stress thus are lessened, and, anyway, innovations are best done in small steps.

Faculties and professionals frequently object to group teaching because of the implications for examinations and grades. How can one grade the share of any single student, when students produce their work in a team? This, however, actually is an objection against an unrealistic system of examinations rather than against group work. Science now *IS* done in and by teams, and the examination ought to correspond to an actual working situation. Meanwhile, in assessing teamwork, the single members' grades may be discussed and decided on with the group. This method is somewhat demanding on teacher's time, but it offers the additional advantage to train the students in efficient self- and peer-assessment, which is badly neglected by our present educational system (Rogers 1969). To save teacher's time, the group's statement on the single members' share in the results might be demanded along with the work.

The "problems of group teaching" in grading and assessing are as much pretences as the alleged "ineffectiveness" of group work in subject teaching. The true reasons of most objections to group teaching are connected with the implied variations in role and attitude of teacher and learner. Any uncertainty of role and expected behaviour, any necessity of change, is experienced by most persons as irritating. In addition, group teaching confronts teachers and system with some denied parts of reality in education, and thus causes extra anxieties. Altogether, the challenge of group teaching easily activates "neophobia" ("terror novi") on the part of teachers and students, which explains most of the reserve and even hostility group work sometimes is met with.

Trying to force group work on a reluctant Faculty might prove an unwise approach. If your Faculty actually is hostile to the method, better wait till you may ally with at least one other convinced colleague. If however you have decided in favour of group teaching, don't be timid about it. In the long run, your colleagues will become accustomed to and convinced by group methods in teaching and learning, and eventually group methods will develop into an essential part of University teaching.

2. Some useful hints for small group work

To prepare for more detailed group methods in University science teaching, this section offers some hints and techniques generally useful in practical small group work. It is however, not intended to replace a proper training in group techniques, if ever available.

2.1 The "Cohn-rules" for communication in groups

Some most useful rules on communication in learning and working groups have been formulated by Ruth Cohn (1969/70). For science learning groups we especially need the first three. The rules are best offered to the group at the beginning of the first session, and the group leader looks to their being observed. The first and central rule is

— Be your own Chairman:

decide yourself, what to get from and what to invest in the group, when to speak and what to say, balancing your personal interest and the needs of the group. This rule implies "just one person is to speak at a time". If several persons wish to speak simultaneously, they have to settle the sequence. First just stating what everybody wants to speak about, generally indicates a logical sequence of speaking. (If however a group disintegrates into informal chatting subgroups, offer three minutes' "informal discussion" rather than trying to force the group back to "order"; then ask for a report on the results of these discussions!)

Another important rule is

— Distractions have got priority:

If a member feels distracted and hence is unable to participate in the discussion, this is to be settled before going on with the task. A trivial distraction such as "anybody got a cigarette for me?" or "may we open the window?" is quickly settled; a conflict between members—"I become infuriated by hearing your very voice!"—may be more time-consuming. A member unable to concentrate on the common task not only misses the progress of the group, but at least temporarily is lost to the group. Again, temporary distractions are a part of human existence and reality and hence ought to be accepted and dealt with rather than just denied.

— Avoid saying "we", "one", "everybody", if you mean "I" or "me"

is another important rule, as nobody actually can speak for anybody else, and by saying "we" frequently a non-existent consensus is feigned, or a personal statement and involvement avoided. Additionally try to avoid masking statements as questions—"are you sure?" frequently just meaning "I disagree!". This rule is seemingly concerned with formalities of speaking, but the way of speaking indicates the general attitude towards self and others. Thus such a "verbal" training implies a training of social attitudes.

The Cohn-rules define role and responsibility of the leader, when the group is agreed on them. "Being one's own Chairman" implies that the members themselves are responsible for their participation and their learning results and thus can't blame (at least not exclusively) the leader for any group's or individual's failure. The leader provides the necessary facilities, looks for observation of the rules, and keeps the group in the intended region of the Cohn-triangle. He may intervene when a member evidently wants to speak, but is hindered by the more eloquent ones, or if a member seems acutely disinterested. The leader then may address him, but being careful not to press him to answer or to contribute. If the group feels irritated by a not-participating or not-contributing member, it is up to the participants to state this fact. The leader does better to avoid being the spokesman for what he thinks to be the group's wishes.

2.2 Fishbowl

By means of the "fishbowl" a small-group discussion can be implemented into a plenary session too large for a formal round-table-discussion. It has got features of the panel-discussion, allowing however for any interested party temporarily to join the panel, or to replace one of the initial members. The "bowl" contains about eight participants—either a group of less timid or of better informed volunteers, or (in a controversy) representatives of the different opinions, or delegates of small groups reporting to the plenary session. The discussion is best run according to the Cohn-rules, or lead by a skilful chairman; a formal list of speakers is incompatible with the fishbowl as with any other sensible group discussion.

One or two extra seats may be provided in the "bowl", to be occupied temporarily by any interested member from the plenary session, and to be vacated again once he has made his contribution and got his answer. The plenary session is more intensely involved, when a member wishing to join the bowl may replace one of the existing participants. He approaches one of the members in the bowl with the request to replace him. If the existing member wishes to stay and refuses the request, at least the third debater thus addressed has to vacate his seat; he may come back later by the same procedure. Thus not too big an audience, by turns, may actively participate in the discussion, and the disintegration into an actively discussing panel and a more or less disinterested audience is avoided.

Fishbowl may help to start a discussion in a plenary session by overcoming the restraints due to the larger number of participants; it may lead to general buzz-groups (see p. 138) and a subsequent new fishbowl to bring back the small groups' results. Students mostly contribute more easily and willingly in smaller groups, e.g. in the bowl; a change between larger and smaller groups—down to three members—is thus frequently useful. To avoid a possible disintegration into stationary small groups, unwilling to participate in plenary sessions, a fishbowl at the end of the sessions offers opportunity for a quick report and exchange of results among the diverse subgroups.

2.3 Brain-storming

Abercrombie (1974) describes brain-storming as "a method for producing original ideas in groups"; besides that, it quickly provides a survey of a group's level of pre-knowledge on a given topic, or on the range of standpoints towards and interest in a certain problem, or as a basis for establishing an agenda, or splitting a plenary session into smaller working groups. In a brain-storming the participants spontaneously contribute any idea they connect with a given problem or key-word. Even with possibly wild contributions offered, all criticism is withheld till later on, and first all contributions are collected on the blackboard. Only if the participants, due to the lack of criticism, feel absolutely free, do they dare to offer unusual contributions, which might prove most valuable. A brain-storming can be run for quite a while, till new and unusual connections are offered, allowing for new approaches to the given problem.

When no more contributions are offered, the results are classified, selected, and ordered. The evident variety of possible and plausible schemes for ordering and classifying, may offer different approaches to be tried by various working groups. Brain-storming thus generally reveals the arbitrariness and ambiguity of any classification, and thus in a way counteracts possible narrowmindedness.

With confabulatory groups chains of consecutive associations may be offered rather than a collection of different associations concerning the actual key-word. In this case, the brain-storming ought to be stopped then and there, rather than criticising the single associations. To avoid chain-forming of associations, the brain-storming can be first run for several minutes "individually", every single member noting down his associations, which will be collected on the blackboard later on. Generally, a brain-storming produces many more ideas than can be used by the group, which might cause a feeling of frustration. "Putting the extra ideas aside for possible later use" may help to avoid ill humour.

2.4 Snapshot

"Snapshot" serves quickly to make evident the overall opinion concerning a special topic, or to elucidate the momentary condition of a group. The members are asked to speak in the sequence of the seating, and strictly (!) to limit to one single sentence, making their statement, but not giving any reasons. It is essential to stick strictly to these rules and to postpone any extras till afterwards! Thus very quickly an impression is formed as a basis for a decision, or for realising the present trouble of a group. Before running the snapshot, make sure that all members know what it is about, and that it is to give an impression, not a vote.

In decision-making, snapshot takes a bit more time than voting, but it offers the opportunity of finding a compromise, rather than just out-voting a minority. It thus markedly improves the group climate, helps the members to identify with the group, and thus markedly enhances the group's effectiveness. If, for example, a snapshot exhibits a minority disagreeing with a proposition favoured by the rest of the group, these members may be asked under what conditions they still might consent. Generally an acceptable compromise is found, and snapshot—if carried out according to the rules—in the long run actually proves time-saving in decision-making.

Suitable topics to be clarified by snapshot are "what do you think our next step ought to be?", "under what conditions might we handle this topic?", "would you prefer to split up into smaller groups now?", "what were you actually concerned with during the last minutes?" (if the leader gets the impression that too many of the members are absentminded).

2.5 On composing groups

There are special exercises in group dynamics to demonstrate that the mutual choice of members for forming subgroups goes by liking and sympathy rather than by rational considerations based on greatest competence for the intended task. A group brought together at random generally — assuming a skilful facilitator — soon develops a feeling of "we" as contrasted to non-members. In favourable cases this feeling even develops to mutual esteem and sympathy. Even an initial non-ideal combination, as long as not too fervent antagonists are included, does not really matter. Thus, if the groups have to be formed in advance, they may, to save time, be composed just at random. If possible, however, the formation of the groups ought to be left to the members in the first plenary session, offering, preferably, different tasks for the various groups to be formed. Any person feels more motivated to try and come to terms and identify with a group of his own choice, rather than with a group he just has been assigned to.

A later re-distribution of members occasionally may become necessary, for example, when several members are unmanageable and support each other in their resistance to group and/or leader. Rather than exchanging just some members among several groups, a total redistribution of the whole class then is preferable, so as not to give a special importance to the members exchanged.

Teachers sometimes feel tempted to combine participants according to their performance—i.e. the performance as perceived by the teacher, which might markedly differ from the students' opinion.

They thus form groups of (supposedly) "bright" and others of (supposedly) "dull" students. A possible advantage of group work is then abandoned, i.e. overcoming a fixed self perception of the student as being "bright" or "dull". By group work, a student may learn that he—as well as anybody else—has got his strengths and his weaknesses and that, by co-operation, he can compensate his weakness and make best advantage for himself and his peers of his strengths. In contrast to conventional education, which tends to make the "bright" students brighter, and the "dull" students duller, group work—if the groups are accordingly composed and run—may demonstrate that "bright" or "dull" performance is not a fate, and that the "dull" learner may develop into a "bright" one. A certain heterogenity is desirable for any group. Trying to collect the "brightest" students in an elite group might have painful consequences.

A fairly common question is that of the "optimum size" of a group. This "optimum size" largely depends on the aims and on certain details of the task of the group. For a group mainly concerned with experimental work, the optimum size is given by the apparatus, and rarely exceeds four members. For group discussions, a sufficient variety among the members is desirable, suggesting an optimum size of about twelve participants. The upper limit for a discussion group is about twenty; if possible, a group of twenty however ought to be split—at least temporarily—into two subgroups. While a large group demands a more skilful and experienced group leader, it offers better opportunity for social and personal experiences. A strictly task-centered working group with few members will, generally, get working results sooner.

2.6 "In case of emergency"—handling fights, refusal, and disintegration

Group and leader sometimes experience an open fight among implacable adversaries as an "emergency". Such a fight may be overcome by the so-called "alter-ego-technique": two volunteer substitutes act as "auxiliary egos" for the quarrelsome ones, carrying on a dispute in their place. They articulate what they think to be the concealed or unconscious mutual feelings, fears, notions, and reproaches, and especially the assumed suppressed thoughts which unspokenly would accompany the actual discussion.

Meanwhile the debaters themselves just have to listen without breaking in. They are asked later on to state and correct where they feel misrepresented by the representatives. Thus the concealed subcurrents of the conflict become evident and thus lose much of their threatening quality. They can be worked through and either be settled or accepted as a stated dissent. (Groups frequently feel obliged to always reach consensus, instead of just accepting a dissent they easily may live with).

In a variant of this technique, the debaters carry on their own dispute, giving, however, ample opportunity to the substitutes to fill in the assumed unspoken thoughts of the adversaries. Subsequently, the adversaries again state where they feel misrepresented. The method can be intensified by taperecording, thus the debaters are more intensely confronted with their attitudes and behaviour and with possible mutual misperceptions.

An inexperienced group leader ought to be careful about using the alter-ego-technique, as it involves the risk of emotional outbursts, which easily might get out of hand. If a group is impeded by an internal conflict, which the leader does not dare or not succeed to settle, professional help—e.g. the students' counsellor or a suitable psychologist—ought to be sought.

Another "emergency" might arise with the taciturn and reluctant group, which refuses all co-operation with the leader. In the beginning of the group's work, the leader might remedy this situation by increased guidance and structure, by simpler tasks, and amply offered interspersed buzz-groups (p. 138). Later on, he may use a questionnaire (p. 158), which offers a choice of possible reasons for the group's refusal. The members tick the reasons they think most important. The number of ticks gained by any item is counted subsequently and noted down (best using a transparency and the overhead projector). Generally one or two peaks are clearly distinguished in the whole distribution, indicating the group's present difficulties, which then can be worked through and overcome.

If a group has more than the usual difficulties in finding a special decision or any decision, similar questionnaires make evident the repressed fears and problems involved. If the leader feels uncertain about possible motives, he may try to find them by an appropriate brain-storming, or he may discuss the matter with an experienced facilitator. He thus will be provided with the necessary material for preparing the questionnaire.

Trouble in a group is caused sometimes by some eloquent members monopolising the discussion (and inevitably later on complaining about their taciturn peers). As a last resort, too persistent speakers may be asked to take notes and run a report of the session, or given another special task keeping them busy (Beard 1972). Again a questionnaire (p. 159) is helpful, and ought to be adapted according to the special needs of the group. This questionnaire simultaneously develops the mutual empathy of the members. It is limited to items with possible answers "yes" or "no", and the members are requested to estimate the number of "yes"-answers to come from the group. The questionnaire filled in, the "yes"-answers of any question are counted and noted down. Members tend to take a long time to estimate the respective numbers of positive votes, hence the number of questions ought to be small (about five). "Do you agree with the present progress of the group?", and "Could you contribute as you wanted to?" are always important questions. "Did you experience the proceedings as dominated by single members?" makes evident undue dominance by the leader or other members. The subsequent discussion of the questionnaire's results with the group reveals the cause of discontent in the group, and ways to overcome it.

A questionnaire of the same type may be used regularly at the end of the group sessions, to provide feed-back to leader and group, and thus to avoid developing trouble. Useful questions are "Did you learn something about task / groups / communication?"—"Could you / the facilitator / other members have done more for the progress of the group?". These questionnaires ought not to take more than five minutes' time, and they focus unobtrusively the members' attention on items which otherwise might go unrealised. To quantify the results, the items may be graded by scales, running from (-2) for "nothing / not at all" to (+2) for "extremely / very much". At the end of a session, the questionnaire is filled in, and the group's mean value for any item stated. Another type of concluding question at the end of a session, giving feed-back, and drawing off any established ill-feelings, is "what do you regard as the present problem of highest priority for the group?". The answers are written down individually and exhibited on a notice-board, the whole procedure again taking just some few minutes.

If a group is troubled by splitting into distinct or even hostile subgroups (junior vs. senior, coloured vs. white, female vs. male), a "segregation exercise" may help. During a session, the group is subdivided successively according to varying criteria, to discuss in each of these combinations for some minutes (maximum ten) a question like "what do you regard the most urgent problem of the group?". Within one session the participants thus undergo a multitude of different subdivisions. An interdisciplinary group which lacks integration of the different disciplines, may be divided temporarily into "smokers vs. non-smokers", "first term vs. senior students", "catholics vs. protestants, "female vs. male", "chemists vs. physicists". The last split is always that of the initially hostile subgroups. Subsequently, the whole group discusses the experience, generally agreeing that all of these criteria and subdivisions are fairly meaningless, including the formerly disturbing one. The exercise thus generally results in the integration of the formerly distinct subgroups.

3. Some types of group teaching applicable to the sciences

In this section, we will deal with some applications of group methods in science teaching, to be adapted according to your own teaching needs and opportunities, as multilateral communication in instruction can be acquired and used in a variety of ways and for fairly different aims. For example, to avoid the otherwise inevitable fading of students' concentration in listening, a lecture may be interspersed with active passages of group discussions. Or the lecture may partly or altogether be replaced by self-paced reading of a given text, with subsequent group discussions to clarify, to improve the understanding, increase the retention, and train the application of the memorized content. "Skill sessions" may supplement a lecture, or partly replace a problem-solving class. "Abercrombie-sessions" improve unbiased perception, reasoning, and communication. Group discussions as well are useful for interlinking related—perhaps interdisciplinary—courses, to compare the approaches of different disciplines to a given topic, or to connnect problems of science and education in the training of science teachers.

3.1 Small group phases within lecture or problem-solving classes

A fairly common defence against all forms of group teaching (mainly based on prejudice) is its assumed limitation to small numbers of students. However, special group methods are applicable even within a lecture and with some hundred students. Until now lecturers hardly ever offer problems, open questions, or controversial points to the audience for discussion, which would markedly increase the student interest and willingness to listen further. Even with the unmovable seats in most lecture halls, students can easily turn round to face the next row and thus temporarily form groups of four to six members. The discussions cause an increase in noise level; the "humming" due to this technique lead to the name of "buzz-groups". A lecturer using this technique prepares suitable items for some minutes' discussion at adequate intervals of about 20 to 30 minutes. To find items which can be dealt with in some few minutes, fitting well in the progress of the lecture, is a challenging but gratifying task for a teacher.

They are easily found for a lecture combined with demonstrations. e.g. in physics, after the basic demonstration of the pendulum: "What do you expect to happen when coupling two identical pendula / two pendula slightly differing in length?". For momentum exchange: "What happens when a hard sphere is reflected by a retreating wall? Any singularities?"—In chemistry: "Concluding from the compounds of F, Cl, Br—what do you expect for the compounds of iodine?"/"What do you expect for subsequent homologues / branched chains / closed rings / certain substitutes?"—In biology: "What consequences do you expect to follow a certain variation in nutrition / humidity / climate?" / "What variations in outer conditions might cause a certain variation in the organism?" If available, "trigger" films or video tapes (perhaps produced locally) of some 1-3 minutes duration, may be used to initiate discussion.

After some three to five minutes' small group discussion the results are reported to the plenary session. The groups may offer their solution including the reasons, while the teacher collects the different suggestions on the blackboard and possibly confirms the right one(s). Or he may invite advocates of different opinions to participate in a "fishbowl" discussion (p. 130). The whole procedure—small groups and finishing—may take about 12 minutes, generally markedly refreshing the students' interest and attention. The transition from a passively consuming to an actively participating audience in the long run well makes up for the "loss" of lecture time.

To invest less time, the lecturer just may list the most common results and give a short comment, verbally or by a hand-out (this additionally avoids the time wasted by the students' taking notes). By use of hand-outs and prepared transparencies for the overhead projector, the procedure can be shortened down to hardly more than five minutes. The lecturer may or may not indicate the "right" answer; leaving it open might stimulate the students to go on to discuss the topic, to think, and even to read about it after the lecture. Then, however, the lecturer ought to ask the students at the beginning of the next lecture which solution they meanwhile decided on, and for what reasons. Thus science learning might acquire some of the exciting and fascinating quality of puzzle solving.

To avoid a "loss" of lecture time by interspersing it with group discussions, the lecturer may integrate part of a connected problem-solving course. Combined courses of four hours' lectures and two hours' problem-solving class every week are fairly common in Germany in science teaching. By reorganizing the whole course, time may be gained to invest in group discussions; the problems to be dealt with are at least partly taken from the connected problem-solving class. At present, in many of the so-called problem-solving courses, the teacher does the problems on the blackboard, and the students again are passive consumers. To activate the students, small-group problem solving might prove convenient. The problems offered, however, ought not to be too lengthy and complicated, lest one out of many possible mistakes makes the whole work in vain. Lengthy problems generally have several simultaneous (and sometimes mutually incompatible) objectives, and they are better replaced by a series of shorter ones, each dedicated to one single, clearly defined objective.

Small group work in problem solving is considerably time-saving. While the "single learner" wastes much time with approaches leading to dead ends, or finds no workable approach at all, in a group usually somebody comes up with a workable suggestion, or realises the inadequacy of an approach. The more crammed the students' schedule, the more important is the replacement of time-consuming single-learner problem solving by adequate small working groups. University teachers however frequently fear that by officially allowing, let alone encouraging group work, students might become lazy and take advantage of the endeavours of their more industrious or more "gifted" peers. Actually, groups are mostly fairly well self-regulated, and find a sensible sharing of the work, hardly ever allowing a member to be totally lazy—if so, then generally but temporarily and for good and acceptable reasons. The rare actual abuse of group work ought not to be a reason against group work as a whole.

Integrating group discussions into a lecture initially takes some teacher's extra time for preparing the problems and restructuring the lecture. As it provides feed-back on the teaching results, it unexpectedly may reveal inadequacies of the lecture, and the lecturer may feel obliged to invest some more extra time to make major changes in the lecture. Replacing a problem-solving class partly or altogether by group work generally, in the beginning, takes some more time, as the whole course has to be restructured, and new problems to be found. The extra time and work needed by the students—if any—is optional rather than compulsory, intrinsically motivated, and rewarded by extra fun and fascination.

3.2 Skill sessions

Some years ago, Paul Black (Black et al. 1974) devised a special type of small group seminar, designed to develop certain scientific "skills" (hence the name "skill sessions"). They are intended to supplement lectures, problem-solving classes, or laboratory courses, or even partly to replace them. In a skill session, a "menu" of problems is offered to the participants, who form groups of four to six, working on one of the problems. The groups are left to themselves for an appointed time of 20 to 30 minutes. A teacher may or may not be available on demand, or he may visit the groups to make sure that none gets stuck. After the appointed time the groups reunite, to present, substantiate, and discuss their solutions, and the approaches and arguments used. Thus every group, beyond its "own" problem, learns something about the other problems as well. In the plenary discussion, the teacher indicates neglected aspects and implicitly made assumptions, and adds further and on-leading questions.

To design a menu of problems, the teacher has to consider objectives, pre-knowledge of the participants, directions of interest, and time available. Open-ended questions are just as suitable as closed ones, and reference books may or may not be available and used (a skill session can be used to make students familiar with certain reference books). To allow for the different time needed by different groups, additional supplementary questions are provided for groups finishing well in advance.

An important aim for the beginner in all sciences is a familiarity with orders of magnitude, giving the ability to estimate the possible influence of various factors on a given process, and developing a sense for what may be neglected and what not. For physics, Black suggests the following order-of-magnitude "menu", easily to adapt to other disciplines: (1) Estimate the rate of growth of your hair in metres per second (supplementary question: in atomic layers / atoms/grams per second). / (2) Estimate the total daily income of a town bus. / (3) Estimate the number of atoms lost from your sleeve when you rub it across a table. / (4) Estimate the number of grains of salt in a salt cellar. The questions ask for a lot of implicit reasoning, and make use of everyday-life experiences. The student can handle them fairly easily, and still they are not at all trivial. They thus improve the learner's self-confidence, and mostly are experienced as exciting, and generally markedly increase the motivation for further learning efforts. Following these everyday-life problems, further problems are offered which arise in laboratory experiments and thus emphasize the relevance of these considerations to the work of the scientist.

Other typical skill session topics are the translation of information between table, graph, formula, and verbal description (implicitly a training for optimum presentation of scientific results); the planning and design of apparatus, single experiments, and whole research topics; the handling and application of special methods; the estimation of reliability, and the interpretation of one's own and others' experimental results.

Black suggests questions like "What problems arise by varying the linear dimensions of a given device by a factor of two?" / "Given a phenomenon to investigate experimentally, what would one look for and what measurements might be most useful?" / "What physical effects happen in closing a circuit of source, resistance and switch?" Questions from my own collection are "What problems arise in increasing a special engine's (a chemical plant's) capacity by a factor of ten?" / "What parallels and diversities exist in relaxation phenomena in mechanics, thermodynamics, electro-magnetism?" / "Varying the wavelength of electromagnetic (mechanical) waves from the largest to increasingly low values, what variations in what phenomena will happen?" / "Varying the molecular weight of an organic substance from monomer to the highest possible values—what differences in the properties do you expect?" / "List all expected differences between a "normal" crystal and one free of dislocations—any differences for ionic, metal, and homopolar crystals?" / "To improve the world's supply of cereals, new and improved types are bred. List the properties desirable in a new cultivation, and give and substantiate your priorities among them." / "List all chemical reactions able to cause polymerisation, and consider their characteristics and their technical applicability." / "What types of intermediately ordered structures between ideal monocrystalline order and gas-like disorder can you imagine? Are any of them realised by material systems? Are special properties of materials connected with special types of order?" / "Assuming the transparency of the atmosphere would increase (decrease) by 20%—what consequences for the climate of the continents would you expect? Additional consequences?"

Sessions on basic scientific vocabulary (originally part of the "Abercrombie course") have special importance: "What do you call in science 'evident', 'plausible', 'probable', 'certain', 'proved'?" / "What do you mean by 'statistically homogeneous', 'random', 'normal', 'average' 'mean value'?"—Another skill session may be dedicated to the demonstration of implicit assumptions in perception and reasoning (see p. 147).

A course of lectures or a laboratory course may be supplemented by an occasional skill session, to refresh interest and learning motivation. Skill sessions as well may be offered as a whole course of one session every fortnight or every week, connected with one or with some courses of lectures or laboratories. The extra expenditure in students' time is hardly relevant, and in the long run well compensated for. For example, advanced laboratory courses with preparatory skill sessions avoid the otherwise inevitable waste of students' and consulting teacher's time, and of other facilities. In addition, skill sessions increase the students' ability of problem handling and solving, of expressing and substantiating their ideas, of scientific argument and fluent speech, and of understanding and judging other peoples' reasons.

Preparing a course of skill sessions for the first time demands some teacher's time and endeavour. In a few years, an extended literature on skill session topics will exist, offering "menus" suitable for diverse disciplines, levels, objectives, and conditions. When the "menu" is settled and tested, the session itself may be run by a junior staff member or even an advanced student. To test a (course of) skill session(s) for the first time or with a varied population of students, a more experienced teacher is desirable, in order to check for necessary changes or possible improvement. Appropriate skill sessions allow one to test a new or newly changed course or syllabus, or to retest it after a variation in the student population (e.g. in the selection of admitted students, or in highschool education) and for this purpose again ought to be run by an experienced teacher. Actually, the feed-back provided by skill sessions is a most valuable extra and allows for testing of assumptions about student capabilities and progress in higher education research.

Black worked with one teacher for 16 students—four groups of four. With groups up to seven members (that is larger than the optimum), a teacher in a skill session can attend to up to about 60 students. This may be more sensible, but for many faculties with large numbers of students still a dream teacher/student-ratio. By somewhat varying the concept, and using the buzz-group technique (p. 138), something similar to skill sessions may be run by only one teacher for several hundred students. Then the final report of the groups in the plenary session has to be abandoned and replaced by written information (giving and substantiating the most common and important approaches, solutions and mistakes) and/or a final report by the teacher, or by a panel report given by representatives for each topic on the "menu". This approach, even less satisfactory than an original skill session, is still much better than leaving the students altogether as silent consumers.

Additionally, skill sessions may help markedly to improve student communication and co-operation. Besides, skill sessions counteract the isolation and alienation of students by establishing peer-contacts. At large Universities and especially in the first term, students' feelings of "being lost" may cause a marked decrease in the students' ability to learn, possibly with long-lasting consequences for the students' performance. Students rated skill sessions more highly than other forms of tutorial classes on the criterion of "getting to know other students" (Black l.c.). Skill sessions, especially in the first term, thus help to overcome learning barriers and thus may improve the students' performance beyond expectations, while simultaneously diminishing the need and costs of students' mental health care.

3.3 Tutorial groups

The availability of facilitators for small group work becomes a problem with large numbers of students. In Germany good results were obtained by employing advanced students after a short training as group facilitators. That they hardly "master" many of the topics dealt with in the groups, proved an advantage rather than a disadvantage. With but a small difference in knowledge and status between the group members and the facilitator he feels less tempted to run the group session as a "mini-lecture", and the students are more willing to admit learning deficiencies and lack of understanding.

"Tutorial groups" (groups facilitated by trained advanced students) are suitable for accompanying a course of lectures or the syllabus in general, to give the students an opportunity to clarify uncomprehended points left over from a lecture. In Britain "single consultee tutorials" frequently serve the same purpose. They are very demanding on teacher's time, and frequently experienced as ineffective. "Small group tutoring" (with about ten participants) is much more time effective and more suited to the task.

Additionally, an effective interview with a single student is not easy to run.

A good lecturer easily gives his audience a comforting but deceptive feeling of complete understanding. By trying to reconstruct the lecture in a group session, the students generally become aware of any gaps in understanding. However, admitting to the lecturer defective or lack of understanding, may be construed, by him, as implicit criticism, and he may feel tempted just to blame the student. Again hence a junior staff member or an advanced student is a more suitable facilitator for such a group.

On the other hand, a student facilitator generally is afraid of making a fool of himself by not knowing the answer to questions, or how to solve problems offered by the group. This fear easily leads him to defensive and hence authoritarian behaviour and might entangle him in fights with the group. With an adequate training he learns to accept his own defectiveness, to handle his own and the members' emotions, to avoid fights in and with the group, to keep the group to the task, and not to feel ridiculed by not knowing all the answers.

This type of group is most reasonably run with about a dozen participants and one session of 45 to 90 minutes (according to the number of lectures it is connected with) every week. The tutor best starts the sessions by asking the students to report on the lecture(s) given since the last session. Generally a group reconstructs fairly precisely the progress and content of the lecture. By observing the contributions and behaviour of the members, the tutor becomes aware of individual gaps in understanding, and suggests a suitable textbook, or asks another group member to help, before a gap becomes "self-amplifying" and cumulative. By making the students actively reproduce the content of a lecture or a laboratory experiment, the understanding can best be tested, and the retention and accessibility of the acquired content improved. A tutorial of this type might be run as a remedial course. Integrated into the syllabus and offered from the very beginning, it might make remedial courses unnecessary.

Again, tutorials connected with a lecture give quick and efficient feed-back on the teaching results, provided the results are experienced as teaching rather than exclusively learning results. If a whole group (or even several groups) are unable to reconstruct a lecture, a deficiency of the lecture is probable, and the fact ought to be reported immediately to the lecturer for remedy.

Tutorials of another type replace rather than add to a lecture. Some years ago, a German University offered a course on wave mechanics either as a course of lectures, or as a tutorial run at the same time. The students had free choice between both courses. The tutorial was based on an appropriate textbook, and the students had to prepare for the sessions by reading appointed texts. Most remarkably, the students in spite of their crammed schedule were regularly and sufficiently prepared, and thus successfully worked through the text during the sessions. The common examination for lecture and tutorial gave no significant differences among the participants of both methods. In the long run, however, the participants of the tutorial exhibited a marked advantage, being accustomed to more independent, self-directed, and autonomous work—the main pay-off became evident about three terms later on.

If self-instructing material (e.g. "PSI") is available, a course of lectures may be replaced by a tutorial course using this material. To help with the conduct of the group discussions, Hill's "Learning Thru Discussion" ("LTD") method (Hill 1969) offers material to structure and understand the group process, namely a "group cognitive map" as a guide through the logical progress of a discussion, a list of Group Roles and Members' Skills, and a list of Criteria. In a German approach (Bernd Schmid), well applicable to the sciences (devised originally for economics and Business Schools), factual course material is proportioned adequately for group sessions, and supplemented by highly structured group dynamical exercises (including instructions for the tutor) and basic information on the group process. This "pre-fabricated" material, where available, makes these courses rather easy and safe to run.

Tutors working with this "pre-fabricated" material need less group dynamical training. A weekend seminar, run by a more experienced tutor, will do. For less structured courses, based, for example, on a textbook and thus leaving more decisions on procedure to group and tutor, tutors ought to have a seminar lasting a few days, or two connected weekend seminars, run by an experienced group facilitator. The same training—to be run perhaps by the Department of Psychology—is desirable for any teacher starting group work. If an experienced facilitator additionally is available as a consultant, either running regular group sessions for the tutors, or giving individual counselling, the tutors feel safer and thus get less difficulties in running the groups.

If tutors are not available, smaller leaderless groups — up to about six members — may work on appointed texts, using the "Student Manual for *E*ducation *T*hrough *S*tudent *I*nteraction" ("ETSI-method", Kitchener and Hurst 1972). ETSI is similar to Hill's LTD-method, using, however, additional questionnaires to be filled in by every group member. One questionnaire acts as a reading guide to the appointed text and is to be filled in in advance of each session ("admission ticket"). The other — to be filled in at the end of the session — asks for an assessment of the group's proceedings, and provides group and teacher with information on the group's progress. With the guidance provided by ETSI, leaderless groups may be run without risk; but they do offer less opportunity for social learning than tutorial groups.

3.4 The Abercrombie course

Unbiased perception, reasoning, and communication ought to be basic abilities for any scientist, they are however badly neglected in the present science education. Jane Abercrombie, a biologist, who originally specialised in psychology of perception, designed and tested a special course to demonstrate and overcome the far-spread distortion of perception and reasoning, which is due to the individual "frame of mind"—habits, "experience", expectations, fears, and hopes: the whole apparatus of the human psyche. Many "misconceptions" are based on a masked deduction, on a mistaken interpretation of the perception according to the individual frame of reference, and "experience" individually is shaped to fit into the frame of expectations and notions of the individual. Abercrombie demonstrates the share of implicit assumptions in perception, deduction, and "experience".

During the first ten minutes of an Abercrombie session the participants individually write down their perception of the offered "material"—e.g. a radiograph or a verbal statement. Then the session is opened for unstructured discussion. The original course, designed for students of biology and medicine, is described in detail in her book "Anatomy of Judgement" (Abercrombie 1969). For other sciences, the material may be adapted, using graphs, tables,

X-ray diffraction patterns, and the like. An example, suitable for scientists of all disciplines, is given in Fig. 3. A first implicit assumption generally made here is the linearity of the scales, which actually—lacking further indication—might be logarithmic, making quite a difference with respect to errors of measurement and reliability of results. Again, the points of Fig. 3 generally are assumed to scatter around a single "true" curve; they might however, be assigned to two slightly different curves (due e.g. to two similar elements, or two different isotopes). They even might not scatter statistically, but represent true values not connected to a smooth curve. Missing these possibilities may mean missing a possible scientific discovery, and even experienced scientists, conditioned by their expectations, sometimes fail to recognise implicit assumptions (compare Kuhn 1970).

Another important topic of Abercrombie sessions is the ambiguity of words and language. Sessions are dedicated to explore the range of meanings associated by different scientists to terms like "average", "normal", "plausible", "probable", "random", "mean". Becoming aware of the ambiguity of language is a first step towards more precise language and understanding, improved communication, and more differentiated thinking.

The students responded to the courses with a mixture of irritation and fascination, due partly to the "content" (confrontation with ignored or even denied parts of reality), partly to the structure of the course—the unusual and unexpected amount of autonomy and responsibility offered to them. To run an Abercrombie session, a facilitator has to command considerable experience in unstructured group work—this is no domain for the inexperienced! A less experienced teacher is advised to agree with the group on the "Cohn rules" (p. 129) for regulating the communication, and to initiate and markedly to structure the discussion.

With the present crammed schedules and lack of suitable facilitators, Abercrombie courses—desirable as they are—will hardly become common in the near future. However, at least the ambiguity of perception and of language are suitable topics to incorporate in a skill session course or any other group seminar. By the way, these topics ought also to be dealt with in the training and retraining of University staff and tutors, generally emphasising a

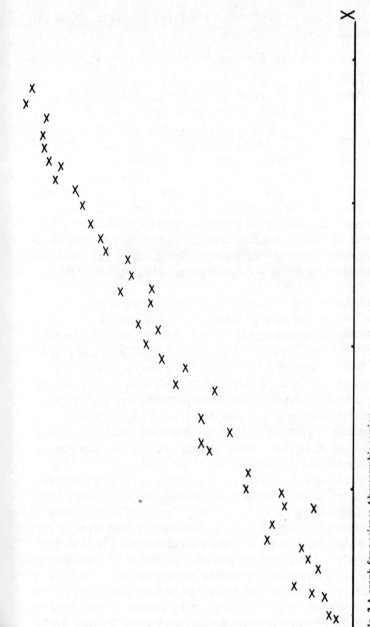

Fig. 3 A graph for a science Abercrombie session

The discussion of this graph generally reveals implicit assumptions and reasoning concerning particularly the interpretation of the pattern by one single smooth curve.

possible misperception of students and their behaviour on the part of the staff.

3.5 Small groups for teaching subsidiary subjects in science

In teaching subsidiary subjects, a fairly common complaint on the part of the teacher is "the students' lack of interest". On the part of the students, however, it is the lack of relevance to the main subject. Most teachers teaching, for example, physics for chemists, make only poor allowance for the students' main subject and hence main interest. They chose a content they think appropriate or indispensible, generally without consulting their colleagues from the other discipline. They thus offer the topic with hardly any interest and concern for the students. From the connections among interest, learning motivation, and learning results, we thus hardly can expect an outstanding learning performance, and the scarce knowledge acquired is mostly forgotten when the examination is passed.

A syllabus, better in accordance with basic learning psychology, might bring better results. Mathematics, for example is generally taught well in advance of and in poor connection with the problems it is needed for. The students thus learn it unwillingly and forget it long before they actually need it. Integrated courses and team-teaching might help, giving the "tools" not in advance and separately, but in handling the actual problems they are needed for. These integrated and team-taught courses however mostly prove "unfeasible", formally for administrative reasons, actually because of a certain rivalry among the various departments.

Even without the opportunity of integrated courses and team-teaching, a teacher teaching, for example, physics to chemists could use lecture and interspersed group phases, starting perhaps with a brain-storming (p. 131) to get a list of physical problems of immediate interest to the students. Dealing first with these, he may succeed, gradually in establishing a genuine interest in other topics of physics and in physics in general. He may offer small groups, each working on one of the problems, using textbooks or handouts, or attended to by a tutor, till the groups present their results in the plenary session, in short lectures or in demonstrations (students are mostly fervently interested in lectures given by their peers).

With a larger audience, the teacher may prefer to structure the results of the brain-storming, thus developing a scheme of the subsidiary subject and its connections with the main subject. Using this scheme as a thread, he may go on essentially lecturing, with interspersed group phases *ad libitum*.

Or an initial brain-storming serves to collect problems shared by the main and subsidiary subject, and the audience then is asked to compare and differentiate what they expect to be the approaches of both disciplines to the topic, thus establishing a close connection between both disciplines. Any such opening, establishing connection between main and subsidiary subject is favourable, especially when leading to self- and peer-instruction and to active participation by the students. Once intrinsic interest of the students is established, any teaching strategy may be used.

Beyond interdisciplinary team-TEACHING, interdisciplinary team-LEARNING would be plausible—e.g. mixed groups of physicists and chemists for the learning of subsidiary physics (for the chemists) and chemistry (for the physicists). Interdisciplinary team and group offer the best conditions for engaged and fruitful discussions and learning, and correspond to a later interdisciplinary teamwork. This approach however mostly meets departmental resistance, and administrative and organisational difficulties.

A special case of "subsidiary subject teaching" arises in the training of future science teachers. An integrated course combining science, science teaching, pedagogics, educational psychology, and educational technology in subsequent small group and plenary sessions is most plausible. Mostly, however, these topics are regarded and taught as strictly separated fields, hardly interrelated, even by the syllabus. In an integrated course, the basic knowledge of a scientific problem is to be acquired by the students, either in a lecture, or by PSI, laboratory sessions, or tutorial groups working on written information. Once the topic is mastered, it is subsequently prepared in small groups for tuition. The various groups have different tasks—different levels and forms, various context, varying time and teaching facilities, or even the production of multi-media self-teaching material. The approaches chosen by the groups then are tested by them in real teaching situations, which are videotaped. If real tuition is not feasible, the lessons at least are simulated by role-play. The tapes are presented and commented on in the plenary session with special regard for pedagogics and educational psychology implied. Based on the results of the plenary sessions, the groups revise or confirm their approach and, if no revision is necessary, try another approach to one of the other groups' topics.

3.6 Project work groups

By the generally rather vaguely used term "Project work" I denote a learning strategy in higher education based on the solving of "real-life" problems or at least problems sufficiently close to real life — in contrast to most laboratory problems solved long ago; a project in addition taking at least some days' work. Projects preferably are done in groups, as the group essentially increases the single member's reach and grip of the task, and "real science" actually is done by interdisciplinary teams rather than by single scientists.

A project group, as any other group, in its initial stages will have fights for status and power among the members. Mostly these fights go masked—e.g. as an argument concerning the best procedure for approaching the task—and stay unrecognised in their meaning and group dynamical context. The group may run aground by unrecognised and hence unsolved psychological problems. Attendence by an experienced facilitator, or at least a trained student tutor, avoids internal group trouble and frees the group to concentrate on the task, without first wasting too much time in the initial group phases.

A group facilitator may run the first sessions, till a favourable climate is established. A less experienced tutor ought to use structured material, including group dynamical exercises and connected basic information, in order to reach the working stage safely. The groups ought to be given their task, including detailed instructions on the procedure (at least for the beginning), by the teacher in charge of the project and group. Finding its own task would overburden an inexperienced group. A workable approach has been suggested and tested by Black and co-workers (Black et al. 1968) in physics. The groups worked for seven weeks of the final year in an honours degree course, fairly well simulating real research work. Students' response was generally favourable or even enthusiastic. However, these so-called "group studies" proved to be somehwat demanding on staff's time (20% increase in the teaching effort for the year as a whole).

With somewhat different types of project work, the demand on staff's time can be kept lower. The groups are left more to themselves. However, every group has to nominate a formal "chairman", staying in duty for about a week, and a "group reporter", also alternated about every week (preferably becoming the next chairman). The chairman regularly reports to the teacher-in-charge on the plans of the group, the reporter on the actual proceedings and results. The teacher ought not to participate at a group session unless directly invited by a group. With increasing experience of group and teacher, the groups may be charged with more of their own decisions, always keeping in mind that any decision may activate internal tensions and fights. Project groups thus guided fairly closely hardly run a risk of getting stuck, or investing too much time in the group process, and still are not too demanding on teacher's time.

3.7 First-term and preparatory courses

The first term frequently offers serious problems to many students. Mental trouble through experiences of isolation and alienation add to problems due to insufficient factual pre-knowledge and lack of studying techniques. Thus first-term or pre-paratory courses might be designed, combining some vocational guidance, "training how to study", refreshment or filling-in of factual knowledge, and reconciliation with the everyday-reality of the institution.

Faculties regularly offering courses on "How to study" have an adequate starting point and may just include some more aspects and aims. Good results were obtained with courses lasting some days and run essentially in tutorial groups during the beginners' first days or even in advance of the official start of the term. The groups started by exploring the members' hopes, expectations, notions, and fears connected with University, study, career, and future vocation. Simultaneously, the beginners were confronted with the time ahead of them, with the rewards, risks, and necessary endeavours. While exploring the members' notions of training and vocation, misconceptions and gaps in factual knowledge become evident. In overcoming them, the students are confronted with their learning attitudes and techniques and can be trained in autonomous learning. Information ought to be made available rather than spoon-fed into the groups, and the members challenged to try and find the best way to the missing information. Thus the use of library and textbooks, and the skills of making excerpts, stating and solving problems, establishing a working schedule, and finding priorities under limited time, are trained under "real-life conditions". The social contacts among participants avoid initial isolation and the connected effects of impeded learning.

These courses, especially when mainly run by supervised tutors (advanced students), do not demand too much staff time. Even the investment of a whole week in improving the learner's learning efficiency, pays off well for both student and staff.

4. A list of "don'ts"

Never, but never start group work, if you don't like it. If you feel happy with teacher-centered instruction, don't think you are obliged to change your tuition to group methods—you might easily end up in a fiasco and unduly blame the method. Better leave group work to colleagues who are eager to try it, as they dislike the role assigned to them in teacher-centered tuition.

Never ridicule, threaten, or punish a group member. If you want to establish a facilitating group climate, reward any contribution, even if it may seem stupid—the student tried to contribute, he may have had to overcome timidity and restraints, and this anyway ought to be met with approval. Don't fake appreciation, but at least appreciate his endeavours. Otherwise you might end up with a silent and reluctant group.

Don't fight a group or a member. Even if you—formally—win, you have fallen to the temptation of fighting, and thus may be diverted from the group's actual task. You safely may state your impression that you are offered a fight for power—but don't let yourself become entangled. If a member wants to demonstrate that he is able to lead the group, and he actually is, just stay back and be prepared to take over again as soon as the need arises. You thus will gain rather than lose status in the group.

Don't give way to possible emotions of anger, insult, disappointment, or frustration. Try to be aware of your feelings and emotions; state them, if you think it is useful or necessary—but don't act according to them. You safely may tell a member that you feel infuriated by him, but don't shout at him or try to ridicule him.

Don't feel responsible for the group. The members must take their own responsibility for their own learning. You provide the opportunity the best you can—it is up to the learners what advantage they take of it: you may lead the horse to the water, but it has to drink on its own. Don't feel irresponsible for the group. You have got at least some share in any failure of the group. Ask yourself, whether you might have dominated, patronised, over-burdened the group, whether you took the group and the single members seriously.

Don't feel obliged to be successful with every group, every member, every session. You can't win them all. A session you experienced as in vain may have been interesting and fruitful for the group or at least some members; if momentarily resultless, it still may and probably will bear results with some delay—group work frequently exhibits delayed results weeks or even months later on. Have confidence and don't be irritated by your momentary frustration. Just try again.

Don't refuse professional help if available. A training for group work, or supervision by an experienced facilitator, might make quite a difference. Try to organise co-operation with any interested colleague to share and overcome your troubles. Group work in the beginning is mostly tiresome, but in the long run it will reward you with the experience of new and fascinating ways of teaching and learning.

ACKNOWLEDGEMENTS
I am greatly indebted to my British colleagues, especially Jane Abercrombie, Paul Black, Brian Stace for critically reading the manuscript, for helpful comments, suggestions, and for polishing up the English.

REFERENCES

ABERCROMBIE, M. L. J., 1969: *"Anatomy of Judgement"*, Penguin Books, Harmondsworth.

ABERCROMBIE, M. L. J., 1974: *"Aims and Techniques of Group Teaching"*, 3rd ed., London SRHE Publications.

BEARD, R., 1972: *"Teaching and Learning in Higher Education"*, Penguin Books, Harmondsworth.

BERNSTEIN, S. and LOWY, L., 1965: *"Explorations in Group Work — Essays in Theory and Practice"*, Boston/Mass.

BLACK, P., et al., 1968: Group studies, Physics Educ. Vol. 3, p. 289.

BLACK, P., et al., 1974: Skill sessions, Physics Educ. Vol. 9, p. 18.

BLIGH, D.A., 1971: Techniques in Small Group Discussions, in *"Varieties of Group Discussion in University Teaching"*, report of the sixth conference organized by the University Teaching Methods Unit, University of London Institute of Education.

COHN, R.C., 1969/70: The theme-centered interactional method, Journ. Group Psychoanalysis and Process, Vol. 2, No. 2.

EPSTEIN, H.T., 1972: An experiment in education, Nature, Vol. 235, p. 203.

HILL, W.F., 1969: *"Learning Thru Discussion"*, London, Sage Publications 12.

KITCHENER, K.H. and HURST, J.C., 1972: *"The Student Manual for Education through Student Interactions"*, Fort Collins (Colerado), Rocky Mountains Behavioural Sciences Institute.

KUHN, T.S., 1970: *"The Structure of Scientific Revolutions"*, 2nd ed., Chicago/London.

OGBORN, J. (ed.), *"Small Group Teaching in Undergraduate Science"*, Heinemann Educational Books, in press.

ROGERS, C.R., 1969: *"Freedom to Learn"*, Columbus (Ohio).

Summary Table

	aims	class size	group size	staff time demanded	prepar. time	stud. time demanded	remarks
buzz-groups	interspersing lecture with students' active phases, refreshment of interest and concentration	up to several hundreds	3 to 5 +)	no additional teacher needed	moderate	no additional demand	takes about 10% of lecture's time
skill sessions	training vocational skills not or but poorly achievable by other methods	40 to 60, modified method up to some hundreds	4 to 7	up to 40: lecturer or junior staff member; beyond 40 some advanced students additionally	about the same as lecture	additional session or course, if not integrated into existing one	well liked by most students
tutorial groups	e.g. improving efficiency of lecture or laboratory, improving students' learning abilities	up to some hundreds	generally about 12	one advanced student per group, one supervising staff per 10 to 20 tutors, for 1 to 2 hours a week	moderate	about one session per week, compensated for by better efficiency in individual work	student tutors generally need some appropriate training
Abercrombie course	improving unbiased perception, reasoning, and communication		10 to 16	demands especially trained group facilitator		additional sessions or course	single A. sessions with more structure and guidance to be offered in a skill session course
project work	training for self-directed scientific and research work	up to about hundred	3 to 5 to 7	according to aims and method moderate to fairly demanding	moderate to fairly demanding	additional course	generally highly appreciated and enjoyed by students

+) 5 for small, 3 for large audience

QUESTIONNAIRE

Please tick the reasons (a maximum of five reasons you think important for the sluggish progress of the discussion in this group.

Number of participants . . . .

Number
of ticks

1) No concern for the topic.   ....

2) No concern for the group.   ....

3) Discussion too theoretical.   ....

4) Discussion too general.   ....

5) Level of discussion too low.   ....

6) Discussion runs in circles.   ....

7) Theme is exploited.   ....

8) Repeatedly in vain tried to speak.   ....

9) Other members too eloquent.   ....

10) Some members monopolise the group by running a fight.   ....

11) Hostile climate — people become attacked or ridiculed.   ....

12) Members interested in their personal status rather than in the task.   ....

13) Tiredness / headache / other causes not connected with group or topic.   ....

14) ....

15) ....

QUESTIONNAIRE

Number of participants . . . .

	Yes?	Yes-votes estim.	actual

1) i) Do you agree with the group's proceedings in this session (during the last minutes)?   . . . .

  ii) How many yes-votes do you expect to come from the group?   . . . .

2) i) Could you participate as you wanted to?   . . . .

  ii) How many yes-votes do you expect to come from the group?   . . . .

3) i) Was the group dominated by single members?   . . . .

  ii) How many yes-votes to you expect to come from the group?   . . . .

4) i) Do you feel accepted by the majority of the part- icipants?   . . . .

  ii) How many yes-votes do you expect to come from the group?   . . . .

5) i) Were you concerned by the proceedings of the group?   . . . .

  ii) How many yes-votes do you expect to come from the group?   . . . .

Date. . . . . .Session. . . . .

Laboratory Work in Undergraduate Teaching

P.J. Black and J. Ogborn

This article concerns varieties of practice and problems in university laboratory teaching. It attempts to give a picture of recent developments, mainly in biology, chemistry, and physics, and to set these both in a historical context and in one in which underlying similarities and differences between the subjects are explored.

It has two main sources. First, obviously, the relevant literature. We have looked fairly thoroughly at the major journals of biology, chemistry, and physics education, back to about 1970. The references are, however, relatively complete rather than critically selected: time did not permit the latter. The second source is work we have recently been engaged on, in surveying and investigating laboratory teaching in physics.[16] That work, while restricted to physics, will we hope prove to complement the necessarily superficial picture drawn from the literature by allowing some issues to be probed at greater depth.

Finally, we ought to declare our prejudices, the more so if we have successfully concealed them in what follows. We are inclined to be for laboratory work which emphasises individuality and choice as against that which emphasises carefully planned training. That does not necessarily mean that we are for 'freedom' against 'restriction' — that would be too easy. Nor are we necessarily for innovation as against tradition. We are for innovation in that it

161

expresses the desire of staff to do better and the will to try; but we recognise much that is rich and effective in traditional laboratory work, especially when taught with the same effort and devotion others give their innovations. If these prejudices have unbalanced our account too much, we apologise.

1. Historical Introduction

Laboratory work has not always been the self-evident part of university teaching that it now appears to be. Apart from demonstration experiments, which were an important part of the art of popularising science before and during the 19th century, elementary science was probably studied almost entirely from books until well after 1800. There are two early references to the idea that students might actually participate in experiments. At Rensselaer Polytechnic (U.S.A.) a student laboratory was introduced in 1825,[1] whilst the following account[2] by William Thomson explains the origin of student laboratories in Glasgow:

> 'When I entered on the professorship of Natural Philosophy at Glasgow (1846), I found apparatus of a very old-fashioned kind. Much of it was more than a hundred years old, little of it less than fifty, and most of it worm-eaten . . . There was absolutely no provision of any kind for experimental investigation, still less idea, even, for anything like students' practical work. Students' laboratories for physical science were not then thought of . . .
> 'I had occasion to undertake some investigations of electrodynamic properties of matter, to answer questions . . . which could only be answered by direct experiment. The labour of observing proved heavy; much of it could scarcely be carried on without two or more persons working together. I therefore invited students to aid in the work . . . Soon after, other students, hearing that their class-fellows had got experimental work to do, came to me and volunteered to assist in the investigation. I could not give them all work in the particular investigation which I had commenced . . . but I did all in my power to find work for them on allied subjects.'

Liebig was running a similar laboratory for chemistry students at Giessen in 1824.[3, 4]

A notable landmark was the publication in 1886 by the President of Harvard, of the 'Harvard Forty', a list of experiments that all students should have performed before entering Harvard (see Menzie).[1] The list was produced in an attempt to reduce the great diversity of experience of students entering the university. This problem has a familiar ring,[5-11] but what is more surprising is that the list itself could well have been accepted as a high-school or junior college inventory at least 70 years after its publication, although its use today might indicate that an institution was carrying the virtues of traditional treatment of classical physics rather too far.

As an aside, we may note that change in the content of teaching laboratories, as new research techniques filter down and syllabuses change, is a significant but not automatic process. On the one hand, there is often expressed a wish for students to become acquainted with important research tools, but on the other, a feeling that the art of experimentation is much the same whatever the hardware, and can as well be taught using a Wheatstone bridge as a digital voltmeter interfaced to a computer. Change of content is particularly notable in chemistry, where modern techniques keep research methods in a state of permanent revolution.[8, 22, 23] There is change in the content of physics laboratories, but it is still true that about half the experiments on offer in the Cavendish Laboratory Cambridge in 1933[24] could well be on offer today in a similar laboratory.

Menzie[1] has suggested that the traditional laboratory continued for so long without any apparent changes in method (and to a degree, in syllabus) because it provided a very flexible forum at a time when a typical department had only a handful of students looked after by three or four staff who could and did keep a continuing personal contact with them over the whole of their course. The system was not without its critics: there exist early complaints that physics laboratories imposed dull procedures on students who lacked any motive for interest in them,[12, 13] and there was serious discussion in the United States in the 1930's of the case for abandoning laboratory work for first-year chemistry students in times of financial stringency.[14, 15]

Continuing growth in student numbers over several decades has led to worries about the anonymity of large laboratory classes, whilst the growth in numbers of staff and in their research commitment has led to the delegation of laboratory demonstrating, first to junior staff, then to research students, and sometimes to senior undergraduates.[28] It may be that these changes removed the flesh and vital organs of the original flexible and personal system and left only the skeleton we know now as the 'traditional laboratory'. Whatever the reason, it seems broadly true that methods which suffered little change for almost a century have recently been questioned, researched into, modified and often replaced.[8, 16-21] Thus this review has to describe and appraise a variety of new approaches alongside the traditional methods which are still widely used.

2. Aims of Laboratory Work

2.1 Problems with Aims

It is not difficult to propose aims of laboratory work in terms which are generally acceptable to teachers. For example Chambers' list[19] contains such items as

> To train in handling data
> To train in writing reports
> To illustrate and drive home material taught in lectures
> To foster 'critical awareness'.

Similar lists are relatively frequent in the literature.[8, 17, 18, 21, 25] However, it is not clear how such lists should be assembled to give meaningful groups at appropriate levels of generality. A second problem is that of deciding whether or not aims have to be broken down into detailed objectives, so specified that there is no room for varying interpretations. A third problem is to find grounds for deciding upon priorities amongst different aims.[16, 21, 30]

2.2 Three Clusters of Aims

An approach to the first difficulty is to propose three clusters of aims; clusters which are implicit in much writing about laboratory work, and are explicit in several.[16, 26-29] The three clusters might be called:

> Training in techniques
> Learning the ideas of the subject
> Learning how to carry out experimental inquiries.

Techniques can be seen as belonging to three kinds: manipulative, observational and mental. The first are perhaps most strongly stressed in chemistry courses, and include not only such methods as fractional distillation or measurement of pH, but skill with glassware and, increasingly, with instruments such as infra-red spectroscopes which relate closely to physics. In physics, the oscilloscope is often mentioned at first-year level, electronic instrumentation at higher levels, and increasingly, use of computing facilities.[18, 27] Observational skill is frequently stressed in biology, especially in connection with fieldwork[31] but is also mentioned in chemistry.[6, 28]

The most obvious example of 'mental techniques' is the analysis of random errors. Others include aspects of report writing, systematic planning, methods of calculation, etc. A recent tendency has been to emphasise and train for such skills, with communication skills also frequently emphasised.[28, 32] Sometimes, the logical thought processes of scientific investigation are seen as trainable skills.[33-36]

The naturalness of such a grouping of disparate 'techniques' relies first on their being seen as suited for some kind of explicit training, sometimes detached from the whole (workshop techniques and computer programming are clear examples). It relies secondly on their being seen as component skills to be assembled into a complete performance in some other way, much as a factory worker may be taught to operate a machine, learning different operations one at a time. This has led many to a laboratory pattern of skills plus projects.

The second cluster of aims, learning ideas, is different. Few suppose (at the university level, by contrast with the primary school) that ideas are best learned first or mainly in the laboratory. The term 'illustrate' in statements of aims of this kind is significant. While most teachers would seem to agree that the laboratory can give ideas a certain 'reality', the nature of that offering is difficult to pin down. Some merely use the 'Doubting Thomas' argument, suggesting that to see is to believe, but this line of thought makes it hard to see what few ideas ought to be selected for added conviction out of the very much larger number taught in lectures and books. It is also open to the objection that theoretical ideas are usually sufficiently distant from the actuality of real experiments — so that they can be simple and general — that reality may confuse or disconcert as much as it convinces. Many, indeed, have moved towards reducing the emphasis on 'illustrating ideas' as an aim of the laboratory.[8, 11, 25, 28]

It may be useful to divide work serving this kind of aim into two kinds. Firstly demonstration, in which the apparatus and procedures are intentionally 'cleaned up' so that irrelevant but important side issues or complexities are avoided: choosing a reaction to show first order rate effects is a good example — most have to be rejected because of real complexities. Secondly, there is work intended to show the limitations of simple theory and to show the precautions needed to make it applicable to a real situation: work with a real inductor might be an example at a simple level, work on noise an example at a higher level.

It is perhaps in the second area that the laboratory can be argued to have the more important role of the two, if demonstration is made a part of other teaching. Little experimental work of a serious nature can be carried out without an acute idea of the difficulty of contriving that theoretical ideas apply with any exactness to a situation.

The last cluster, learning how to inquire, is at a different and more global level. Items appropriate to the first two can be specified with some exactness (carrying out a blood cell count; operating a scintillation counter), but no obvious analysis of the art of inquiry exists, any more than there exists much by way of analysis of the art of solving problems, or of designing houses. Here most rely more on the natural model of apprenticeship, of learning by contact with experts. The most obvious example of work intended to serve such ends is project work, by now well established in the sciences and in engineering as an important part of at least the final year of undergraduate studies. It can, however, be seen as implicated in experiments in earlier years, especially when they offer the student some need to choose.

2.3 Objectives

One teacher may interpret 'To train in handling data' as merely being able to compute a mean and standard deviation, where another may see it as involving selection of appropriate amounts and kinds of data to collect, relating the reliability of the data to the nature of the hypotheses to be tested, organising data in convenient forms and perhaps selecting from a battery of appropriate instruments.

This example illustrates the argument of a school of thought which would hold that the analysis of 2.2 above is quite adequate because it fails to specify the behavioural outcomes intended or implied by any aim. Those taking this view would wish to say, as exactly as possible, what the student should be able to do (in visible terms) as a result of various experiences in the laboratory (and elsewhere). Their position has the advantage that detecting the success or otherwise of work intended to serve some purpose becomes possible. It has the difficulty that it is by no means evident that everything one is clever enough to specify in such detail is what one really wants to specify. For example, 'being able to ask meaningful questions of nature' is turned by one writer[37] into:

> 'Given a particular phenomenon, the student should be able to state one hypothesis whose acceptance or rejection will contribute to the scientific understanding of the problem'.

Clearly even this is not totally precise (if one thinks of actually deciding in real instances whether or not a student has met the criterion); equally clearly, there is some kind of trade-off between precision and (save for definitions which would fill several books) the danger of trivialising an aim by making its achievement measurable. MacDonald Ross gives a long and careful critique of the value and limitations of this line of thought.[38] Bent gives a spirited account[39] of the educational trade-offs involved in specifying objectives:

> 'specify performance objectives exactly and students perform well on precisely those objectives; few go the extra mile. Specify objectives broadly, and many students, uncertain as to what is expected of them, do nothing; they go not even the first mile. The straight-crookedness of learning, like a good walking stick, is usually found, not contrived'.

No less pragmatically the chemist Clapp[43] poses awkward questions which have evident parallels in other subjects, such as, 'How many titrations equal mastery of titration?', and 'How many titrations can be abandoned to make room to learn (say) electronics?'.

2.4 Priorities

Clearly, neither analysis nor definition of aims solves the important question of choosing priorities amongst them.

The traditional approach to priorities is to think in terms of scale, with experiments getting longer and more complex (as well as involving more advanced ideas) as the years go by, but with each — even the smallest — in some way a microscosm of the whole art of experimenting.[8, 17, 19]

Another approach is to think in terms of sequence; often dealing first with component skills and ideas, and later with longer more complex experiments intended to weld the first into a whole.[27, 40, 41, 45]

Yet another way is to think functionally about the nature of laboratory tasks, dividing each into phases intended to emphasise one kind of aim more than another. An 'experiment' might then consist of a 'demonstration' phase, a 'skill' phase, and an 'investigation' phase.[28, 42, 44]

These matters cannot be detached from wider issues. For example, students new to the university in their first year are likely to have needs, such as building up confidence, which are not related to any set of aims in physics, but which are nevertheless crucial. Somehow the two have to be combined, an example in physics being the first term at Liverpool,[40, see also 16] where training in errors and techniques is combined with a tutorial format which makes it easy for students to communicate with staff and each other. Mellon[11] recognises the same need in chemistry:

> 'Many of the poorer students exhibit a desperate bravado under which is hidden a certain fear that chemistry will undo them. The situation is not totally bleak, however, since the average beginning student still brings a naive, but all too easily stifled, interest in chemistry'.

Those who teach service courses will often emphasise learning techniques and perhaps learning ideas, rather than learning to enquire. So, for example, Fraser Williams[29] rejects all but simple illustration of basic techniques, so far as microbiology for medical students is concerned. However, for those who teach a subject for itself, it is often the aim of learning to inquire which is paramount; other aims are a means to that end, not ends in themselves.

The main debate, therefore, ought to concern whether some kind of dissection into component aims is feasible, natural, helpful, and convenient, or whether development ought rather to be along the lines of slowly increasing the scope, difficulty, and complexity of tasks, each seen however as a whole. The latter is the basis of the traditional laboratory, except that there the development is made cruder and less effective by the requirement that all experiments in one year be roughly equivalent (because of the organisational pattern in which they are done in arbitrary rotating order).

Few, however, save only those committed wholly either to a view of teaching solely through work in 'project' style or to a view of the laboratory as a tightly designed piece of educational technology, will take to one view or the other alone. Most adopt some compromise, in which some things are treated as naturally best fitted to special training (such as computer programming) and other things as best suited to being learned along the way. What often matters is not so much the expressed intentions behind the work set, as the care with which its detail is worked out so as to realise aims to good effect. The student does not pursue aims; he does experimental work.

3. Approaches to Laboratory Teaching

3.1 Grouping the Various Approaches

It is a salutory experience to review papers describing approaches to laboratory teaching in journals of Biology, Chemistry, and Physics education. The same themes recur, the same worries are expressed, and the same solutions are proposed. There is of course variation too: field work in Biology, qualitative and quantitative analysis in Chemistry, or very high precision measurement in Physics, have little by way of counterparts in the other subjects. However, so far as the mainly educational aspects are concerned, the degree to which concerns and attitudes are common to all the subjects has led us to discuss in this section a number of different approaches to laboratory teaching under headings which reflect distinctive educational attitudes rather than differences in approach between the subjects.

Authors of scientific papers rarely differ markedly in their basic attitudes or styles of work, within a given field. If they do, the differences are well known in the field and easily describable. By contrast, papers about laboratory teaching can differ fundamentally in aims and assumptions, in ways that are not easy to capture. We have therefore divided them, and the approaches they reflect, into groups which we find useful and natural, but which need explaining.

Papers in the first two groups are concerned with individual experiments; the authors take for granted the general definition and purpose of such experiments and the context into which they are to be fitted. The first group (3.2) is of those concerned with good ideas for a traditional laboratory, the second (3.3) of those which introduce new technologies such as computers or video-taped materials.

The other three groups are about whole laboratories. Whilst those in the third group (3.4) reorganise the laboratory to achieve the clearly defined objectives called for by educational technology, those in the fourth (3.5) take a different stand characterised by 'open-ended', 'integration' and particularly 'reality'. Projects often feature in this last group, but discussion of the literature on these is put in a separate section (3.6).

All of the papers considered in these sections emphasise the content of laboratory work. There are others, concerned with such matters as organisation and structure, or the training or supervision of teachers or teaching assistants. These form part of the subject matter of section 4 and are considered there.

The division adopted is rough and ready, and not entirely clear-cut. It does, however, provide — or so we think — a reasonable framework within which to discuss the main approaches to laboratory work. It does not accommodate certain ideas which we judge to have more entertainment value than anything else — there exists for example a report of research on the effect of students' diet on performance in the laboratory, and several on methods of automatic computing of grades for experiments based solely on numerical results obtained.

The framework at least distinguishes those who see innovation as change within a fixed pattern from those who want to break the mould, and amongst the latter, those whose new mould is cast in the tradition of programmed learning and behavioural objectives from those who see learning as involving the whole 'real' task from near the outset. Finally, it raises one of the most crucial questions about laboratory work: what makes it 'real'? Answers vary from investigating the properties of the local plastic coffee cups to sending students out into industry.

3.2 Good Ideas for the Traditional Laboratory

The great majority of teaching laboratories follow (at least for the first few years of the undergraduate course) the traditional pattern of a menu of experiments, done more or less in any sequence, each often existing as a single copy with permanently dedicated apparatus, and each with more or less detailed instructions. Similarly, the greatest part of innovative effort expended in laboratories seems to be devoted to devising and implementing novel experiments of this type. Since developing an experiment requires several tens of man-hours of work, a rate of one or two new experiments per laboratory per year represents a very large investment in innovation.

It follows that the papers in the literature describing new experiments are a resource of considerable value. We have no data on the extent to which this resource is used; we would guess it to be uneven. Experience, and the inspection of citations, supports the further view that specialists in one discipline rarely use the educational journals belonging to other disciplines. So far as experiments are concerned, this seems a pity. Experiments with interdisciplinary aspects are by no means uncommon, and are becoming more frequent. A few examples may help make the point. Thus the *Journal of Chemical Education,* 54 (1977), 125, has an experiment on the application of nuclear magnetic resonance to biochemical kinetics, which could obviously interest biologists and could be useful to physicists, and another (page 130) on determining dipole moments using cheap equipment; *American Journal of Physics,* 45, (1977), 497, has a note on black box electronic 'unknowns' and on biological scaling models; the *Journal of Biological Education,* 10, (1976), 303, has an exercise on determining protein structures which uses both chromatography (of interest to chemists) and Schlieren methods (of interest to some physicists). These are just a few examples, culled more or less at random and without extensive search. Many like them exist.

Reasons for introducing such new experiments are varied. One may be paraphrased as, 'in view of recent developments (in the subject/in techniques) it would be nice if students could see . . .'. These are often allied to recent commercial availability of reasonably priced equipment or specimens. A related reason might be called, 'Now it can be shown . . .'; experiments which use new equipment to show effects which have hitherto been lecture topics alone. Rather different are experiments along the lines of 'Here's a simpler/cheaper way to . . .', many of which use modern electronics to bypass difficulties of traditional methods.

One thing that strikes us, however, is that it is rare for such experiments to be motivated in any detailed way by an analysis of what activities would be good for students — such things as being encouraged to be systematic, deciding between alternatives, confronting a puzzle or contradiction, and so on. It is also rare for the place a new experiment is intended to fill in a laboratory to be described, saying for example what qualities it has that others lack, or vice versa. The absence of such an analysis is, however, just what one would expect, given the nature of the traditional laboratory, and, within traditional terms, is not obviously a defect. Experiments are independent, are rarely individually compulsory, and generally each of them serve most of the aims of the laboratory, being roughly equivalent in difficulty, scope, and demands.

The last paragraph raises a peculiar difficulty for this review. The nature of the traditional laboratory is very much a matter of common experience, and very little the subject of description, analysis, or investigation. Accounts of innovations in the whole laboratory (see 3.3 below), and conferences or symposia on laboratory teaching [e.g. 8, 17, 18] generally assume that there is something wrong with it — dullness, the routine or 'cookbook' nature of tasks — but rarely pick out the virtues it almost certainly must have, if only to have survived unchanged for so long. The only substantial attempt to describe traditional patterns of laboratory work in a detailed way, paying attention to their structure and variations, of which we are aware is that undertaken in the United Kingdom by the Higher Education Learning Project (Physics) in which the present authors were both involved, [16] (referred to below as the H.E.L.P. study), though Chambers' survey [19] and an unpublished survey by Donald et al., [46] contain much factual information about organisation and content. All these studies concern physics, and their findings will not all be applicable to other subjects.

Chambers found, for example,[19] that experiments became longer and that more choice was allowed, with the years. First-year experiments could be described in terms such as, 'introducing basic equipment' and 'providing simple exercises in data handling'. Second-year experiments were generally regarded as more demanding, and more comprehensive in their range of demands.

Moves towards project work in the final year encouraged staff to think of second year experiments as projects in miniature in some sense, albeit constrained. Chambers also comments adversely on the literature:

'. . . the problems (posed for students by experiments) should be neither too simple nor too difficult; neither too obvious nor too subtly concealed . . . Unfortunately, when undergraduate experiments are described in the literature, emphasis is more often placed on the elegance and clarity with which they illustrate the theory than on the problems they offer the student. Consequently, it takes a good deal of time and effort to build up a reasonably wide selection of suitable experiments, and a good deal of care to produce a lab. manual which gives the student just the right amount of help.'

It would be wrong to suppose, however, that there are no departures in traditional laboratories from the pattern of set experiments. Those directing such laboratories in physics have frequently introduced sequences of brief experiments in electronics, often tied closely to lecture courses. In several sciences, students learn computer programming, often using specially prepared teaching materials. Teachers who would not ordinarily interest themselves in programmed learning or audio-visual instruction nevertheless use such means in these special cases, where they seem natural.

It would also be wrong to suppose that the traditional pattern is not subject to significant variation. Donald[46] found much variation in detailed organisation. The H.E.L.P. study[16] (chapter 5) looked in part at five laboratories, all in some measure 'traditional', but all also with important modifications. One, for example, gave first-year students rather easy tasks for the first term, harder and longer ones after that, and included miniature projects at the end of the year. Another consisted in effect of a number of small laboratories each with perhaps half a dozen experiments, each under the charge of a different member of staff, so permitting more variation within the laboratory than is usual (one teacher used no scripts at all, for instance). Two others retained the notion of equivalent experiments, but both made them all rather more like projects, by requiring the students to find the theory for themselves, to design parts of the experiment, to choose what to measure, and so on. Yet another had moved, by way of streamlining experiments, writing detailed teaching manuals, producing tape-slide sequences, and in-training demonstration, a long way in a direction which might have been, but was not in fact, called 'audio-visual programmed instruction'.

It should by now be clear that 'the traditional laboratory' is an elusive concept. If one defines it as the organisational system of a 'circus' of equivalent experiments, one finds laboratories that do not at all fit the definition, but which are in no sense innovative or remarkable. If one defines it (as the innovative literature tends to do) as that which is sterile in the past tradition, one finds laboratories which could without difficulty have existed one or more generations ago but in which students visibly find pleasure and profit today. If anything defines it, it is perhaps that it is evolutionary rather than revolutionary, ad hoc rather than systematically designed, and unreflective rather than highly conscious so far as detailed aims or objectives are concerned.

Two charges can however be brought against the traditional laboratory. One frequently brought is that of stereotyping. A laboratory with relatively permanent experiments as its basis is in obvious danger of going 'dead', just because the experiments are fixed and not fluid or subject to decision. Good intentions and existing ideas may, as time goes by, become tedious and repetitious. What, on the face of it, could be more modern and motivating than the now widely despised system of presenting students with 'unknowns' in analytical chemistry?

The second charge is more subtle and can be brought against other than traditional laboratories. It is that of having an ideology forced by circumstances. In an ideal world, one might decide what to ask for student by student and task by task — so must Thomson and Liebig have conducted matters (section 1) — and so do we with research students. But, with many students and many other matters to attend to, things have to be better defined. The trouble arises when what is convenient (or necessary) becomes seen as principled. There is nothing inherently meritorious in students repeating the same exercises, but the fact of it can lead to their being seen as 'standard', even 'basic'; there is arguably much that is valuable in students talking to one another, but it can easily come to be thought of as 'cheating'. So there can — perhaps must — grow up a whole set of conventions about what is right, which have more to do with how things are than with how they ought to be.[47]

3.3 Experiments using Novel Technology

A parallel can rather easily be drawn between some modern ideas about teaching and traditional experiments. Typically, a whole class of modern approaches result in work having the following features:

— a specially designated working place (often a 'carrell')
— special dedicated hardware for the student to use
— specially prepared software, often in the form of detailed step by step procedures (often 'programmed learning')
— well defined short term goals
— immediate checks on progress.

What, on the face of it, could be more like the traditional experiment, despite its quite different origins?

It may well be that the similarity, at least so far as the organisation of work into well defined and finite tasks is concerned, has made it rather natural for educational ideas influenced by programmed learning to infiltrate the laboratory (as opposed to the lecture room, for example). At all events, a considerable number of papers report the introduction of experiments using programmed manuals, audio-visual instruction, and aid from a computer.

Developments of this kind are often associated with a critique of the aims of laboratory work that wants them made more precise, and in doing so, tends to focus on techniques and concepts (see section 2). Consistent with such a view, experiments tend to be streamlined; to be shorn of features which are seen as confusing or distracting — valuable though they might seem to others. In physics, for example, Goldberg[48] makes a strong case for focussing experiments on learning ideas, and paring away technical difficulties, error analysis, etc., for lack of time to do more than one aspect effectively.

The focus can be on techniques in physics,[16 (chapter 6), 27] but seems more often to be on concepts.[49-54] In chemistry, the emphasis is perhaps more often on techniques, though it must be remembered that something like electron spin resonance or infrared spectroscopy is likely to be called a 'technique' by chemists and a whole experiment by physicists. In biology in particular, but also in chemistry, the influence of Postlethwait[55] who pioneered the so-called audio-tutorial method, is strong.

The audio-tutorial method replaces, or supplements, written programmed teaching material by audio tape and slide presentations (closed-circuit television is also used by some). It is not necessarily linked to laboratory work, but many have used it in conjunction with experiments, or to replace parts of them.

Some use audio-visual material to replace the laboratory demonstrator,[56] arguing that it saves time and performs more consistently. It does seem arguable that where complex instructions have to be given and followed, but are not in themselves things to be learned, tape may have advantages. Unlike written instructions, instructions on tape have to be attended to one at a time, without the distracting presence of previous or future instructions.[57, 58]

Some use audio-visual material to supplement or replace some experimental work. To replace it all and still call the result a laboratory[59] is rare; more common is to use it in support for such roles as introducing experiments, giving background theory, or showing techniques.[8, 28, 36, 49, 60-67] Some such uses, especially in biology and medicine, aim to make accessible to the student situations which would otherwise be beyond the scope of the laboratory — remote ecologies, difficult or dangerous operations, or things which change too slowly for student investigation. Some chemists report using slides, film or television to show dangerous or expensive experiments, and industrial processes, but few physicists seem to exercise this last kind of option. Other uses, as mentioned, emphasise the economy and efficiency of having small 'canned' pieces of teaching available to students at will.

Those with any experience of preparing audio-visual material often emphasise the very considerable time and effort that has to go into it.[68]

In the last decade, the computer has made its presence felt in the laboratory, in three main distinct roles: as a computational aid; as a 'simulator' of experiments; and as a tutorial device. In terms of investment and of papers produced, this is a very substantial field indeed. The American Journal of Physics carries a section on uses of the computer in every issue; papers in journals of physics and chemistry education are frequent (less so in biology). In 1970 the Commission on College Physics held a conference on computers in undergraduate science education the report of which[69] surveys a wide variety of such uses. In the United Kingdom, the National Development Programme in Computer Assisted Learning[70, 71] has funded some 25 studies, several in the area of undergraduate science, including one in physics, one in chemistry, and one on computers in the undergraduate science curriculum. The International Federation for Information Processing held a conference on computers in education whose proceedings give an international overview of recent developments,[72] while in the United States CONDUIT[73] offers a forum for the exchange of ideas, and there are regular conferences on computers in undergraduate curricula.[e.g. 74]

Perhaps the most obvious and most widespread use of the computer in the laboratory is for analysing data. It is now possibly the exception rather than the rule for there not to be an undergraduate course in programming in BASIC, FORTRAN, or other similar languages. In consequence students can deal routinely with much more data than was possible a decade ago, and can make more sophisticated analyses as well. Uses in physics and chemistry commonly include error analysis, curve fitting, and statistical testing.[75, 76] Programmes can often be adapted from those in use in research, but attention may have to be given to getting the level of the programme right for students.[76, 77] The computer programme may be integrated into the planning and analysis of the experiment, for instance in the determination of reaction kinetics,[78] for predicting molecular spectra,[79] or for on-line experimenting.[80] Such integration is likely to develop in the future, particularly with the increasing use of microprocessors.

The use of the computer to 'simulate' experiments is related to its use in research to model complex systems. Examples include the numerical simulation of genetic experiments,[81] of titration,[82] of reaction kinetics[83, 84] and the deflection of charged particles,[85] amongst many others. Sometimes simulation replaces all actual experimenting (on grounds of cost, time, danger, and so on). More reasonably, perhaps, it can usefully extend the range over which variables can be studied, thereby adding to the experience got from apparatus[86] and so perhaps help develop a more critical attitude to hypotheses.[87]

Simulation programmes can usefully be divided into those in which the model of the situation is fixed, and the student can just vary the 'data' fed in, and those in which the student can vary the model, so as to explore consequences of changing it. The first can be in danger of reinforcing the heresy that theory is true, and experiment a pale and error-prone reflection of that truth.

With simulation, we border on tutorial uses of the computer, which range from teaching about simulated systems, through using the computer for such things as 'dry lab' or 'armchair' chemical analysis,[88] to full-blown interactive question and answer tutorial systems. One of the most widely used and reported tutorial systems used in higher education in science is PLATO at Illinois,[89-91] a system which allows data-processing, simulation, and tutorial mode. Others have devised their own systems, exploiting languages such as APL which are flexible, and integrating the computer in all its modes into the laboratory,[86, 92] with the student sometimes programming as well as being taught via a programme. [93, 94, 95]

It is difficult to evaluate the vast flurry of activity in all these uses of the computer in connection with the laboratory. To say that the computer (in education as elsewhere) is a good servant and a bad master is to state the obvious: what is difficult is to detect the point at which a sophisticated system is developed more for the interest and challenge of doing so than for any realistic expectation of value for students in return.

In the modest aim of increasing students' power to calculate, the computer has proved a considerable success in the laboratory. However, for the most ambitious aim of replacing the teacher in dialogue with the student, our view is that there are many serious difficulties. All too many of the systems which attempt this are inflexible and naive in their responses to students' statements or questions, as would be expected by anybody who tried to write down an algorithm for teaching a topic. In between these extremes many exciting things have been done in the simulation mode, but they range from those with rather obvious value to others with more entertainment value than anything else.

3.4 The laboratory as planned educational technology

In the context of this booklet, we use 'educational technology' to refer to the detailed previous planning of educational experiences, starting with well-defined objectives and using materials, whether written, on film, slide, tape, videotape, or in a computer programme, explicitly designed to attain those objectives and test their attainment.

As the previous section showed, individual experiments have frequently been recast in this mould. The success of such changes raises the question whether the whole laboratory ought not to be thought through in the same way, and this section describes various attempts to do so. One outcome is what we have elsewhere [16 (chapter 4)] called 'singleminded' laboratories; that is, laboratories with a rather clear and narrow purpose pursued to the relative exclusion of other objectives. Another result, forming a bridge to section 3.5 on 'open-ended' laboratories, is an attempt to plan a varied and balanced menu, which may include small projects, seminars, experiments in techniques and so on.

A typical example of the first kind might be the programmed-learning laboratory in biology described by Diamond and Benton.[96] Programmed booklets were provided for experiments, together with 8 mm films, slides, and apparatus — there being 27 booklets covering 13 areas of study. Two hoped-for effects of this kind of planned teaching were claimed: slow students could and did spend longer and learn as much as fast ones, and the teaching materials did operate independently of staff, so saving faculty time (apart from that invested in developing materials). Students reported feeling that they had made definite achievements ('I actually learned something') — an outcome possibly linked to the well-defined nature of objectives presented to them. An assessment of something rather similar, but in plant physiology,[97] makes the point however that it is not easy to link the slow pace of much experimental work in biology with prepared teaching packages. Another, though, points out[98] that it is easier to use such materials to link 'lecture' and laboratory work, if theoretical ideas are taught by the material along with experiments, and another[99] that more students can more easily be put through such a system.

In such cases, the 'singlemindedness' is a focus on learning the subject through experiment and associated teaching materials. Related to them are laboratories which focus on reinforcing ideas taught elsewhere; examples being a laboratory concerned with the ideas of mechanics,[48] laboratories of demonstrations in introductory physics[49, 54] and a chemistry laboratory.[62] In order to focus on showing ideas, the apparatus is designed and instructions arranged so that the experiments always 'work' — often in something like push-button mode. Objectives need not always be exclusively of the 'learning ideas' family but can be varied from experiment to experiment, perhaps allowing the student some choice of objectives.[100]

A different focus can be a set of objectives to do with the processes of scientific investigation. There are those who hold that these can be identified and specified, or at least that there is value in the attempt. One rather thorough example is offered by Nedelsky,[26] whose experiments fall into a pattern in which the student is told that he will have to predict some (unspecified) values of parameters in an experiment yet to be performed, experiments and collects data until he thinks he can do so, and is then tested by seeing if the actual experiment yields his predicted values. A different slant is taken by Richards,[36] who sees the scientific process as one of identifying potential functional relationships between variables (often using dimensional analysis), and devising systematic means of identifying the functional relationships that actually hold. He, and Nedelsky, both show the singleminded trait, in designing apparatus which limits the student deliberately to desired courses of action, and which, for example, gives rather precise measurements in order not to confuse or confound the relationships which are to be identified.

There are a number of reports of laboratories designed to go with self-paced courses (Keller Plan[101, 102]), or themselves to work in a self-paced mode. Here again, experiments often have programmed instructions, with the addition of some kind of test of attainment of objectives before the student can pass to the next. Examples in physics,[16] (chapter 2) and in chemistry[103] both use a mixture of experimental and theoretical study units, an arrangement which provides a useful timing buffer to allow flexibility of pace to be realised more easily (especially where it involves changing apparatus as the course progresses).

Another chemistry laboratory (also associated with a Keller Plan theory course)[104] has its focus on techniques rather than on ideas. Indeed, the author (Palma) reveals a different kind of singlemindedness when he says,

'Laboratory time is too precious to be spent on teaching concepts that could be taught as effectively elsewhere.'

It is worth contrasting this with almost its contrary, from a physicist (Goldberg),[48]

> 'Since our emphasis is to be on the theory and ideas learned in the classroom, we have made what some instructors might consider a radical decision: we have removed all attempts to train students in the arts of experimental techniques . . . We believe that all that (these) aspects succeed in doing is to divert the student's attention from what he needs most: a better understanding of the basic concepts.'

However, what Palma means by 'techniques' is titimetric analysis, chromatography, distillation, spectrophotometry, etc.; a list which certainly contains some things which Goldberg would reject but contains others which to a physicist would look more like 'basic ideas' — spectrophotometry, for example. The examples do suggest, though, that 'singlemindedness' is a genuine trait which does distinguish some laboratories from others, even though they are by no means singleminded about the same things. One of its advantages is a certain sharpness of focus, so that students can more easily mark and note their progress. One disadvantage (as Palma notes) is a tendency to dullness and sterility.

One example is a laboratory which focusses for a whole term on data analysis and error calculations, removing all other aspects to the extent of avoiding interesting or novel apparatus.[16 (chapter 8), 40] On the face of it this is an invitation to boredom and pointlessness, but it seems to avoid this unfortunate tendency by having students work in groups with a member of staff teaching them as a group all the time, so that students report feelings of security and confidence. It seems to us that the clear-cut simple success offered by a singleminded laboratory is likely to have its greatest appeal when students are new, confused, and unsure of themselves. For just this reason, some first year laboratories progress during the year from an initially well-defined set of objectives to do with techniques or ideas or both, to small scale projects or other open ended work.[e.g. 16 (chapter 6), 27]

3.5 'Integration'; 'Reality'; 'Openendedness'

Innovations have a habit of clustering around slogans. Those of the previous two sections cluster around such items as 'techniques', 'concepts', 'demonstration', and 'training' — all having to do with precision and limitation of purpose. The slogans of the present section move in the opposite direction, towards openness, variety, and reality, at the price of some uncertainty (which may be redefined now as a good thing). As one would expect there is great variety in what these moves mean in practice. They may mean no more than a few options at the end of an experiment, or they may mean free project work. They may mean using ceiling tiles to investigate thermal conductivity, or they may mean a laboratory geared towards solving a related set of industrial or ecological problems. They may mean just abandoning the written instructions for experiments, or students working in 'research teams' to define, plan and conduct investigations.

In this area there are important differences between the sciences. In chemistry, the tradition has been laboratories devoted to types of technique or process: qualitative analysis and quantitative analysis, both inorganic and organic, and synthesis (mainly organic), together with physical chemistry and, recently, instrumentation. This pattern built on a tradition of experiments in descriptive chemistry (e.g. the properties of salts of transition metals) in school or introductory courses, a tradition which some feel is dying out.[6] Criticism has been centred on the lack of relation between experiments in this pattern,[105] the lack of context when techniques are learned,[25] and, in general, the artificiality of the traditional divisions and the consequent triteness of experiments. The answer has often been seen as integration: as devising a laboratory in which methods of 'different' kinds are learned and used as appropriate to a problem.

By contrast, physics has traditionally been more integrated, at least in the simple sense that laboratories were divided by large divisions of subject matter (properties of matter, heat, electricity, etc., for example) and not into such divisions as data analysis or standardisation on the one hand and such things as measurement of time on the other (though electrical measurements have sometimes found a place of their own). A recent exception is electronics, where specialised techniques (e.g. digital methods) not met elsewhere have often been taught apart from other things. Criticism here has nevertheless picked out the artificiality of many exercises and the way they do not necessarily lead to a rounded performance, to learning the whole art of experimentation.[1, 45] King, in an influential paper,[106] helped to set part of the tone of the response as being the development of project work at all stages of the undergraduate course; Soules and Bennett[107] contributed the much-used notion of the 'instrumented laboratory' filled with instruments to be used in a whole variety of ways, at the initiative and choice of students. Thus, in physics, the debate has been in terms of 'open-ending' experiments or laboratory.[44, 45, 108, 109, 110] This is not to say that all those using such terms agree with one another; Ivany and Parlett nicely trace deep differences of opinion and approach underlying a superficial agreement.[111]

Biology, unlike physics and chemistry has long had a robust tradition of practical work which deserves both the labels 'integrated' and 'open-ended'. We refer to field work. In consequence, biologists debate in the literature not whether or why to expand the range of challenges presented by practical work, but how to do it better, and how to meet the very real problems of the complex and contingent nature of the environment.

Because of the lessons that might be drawn for other subjects, it is useful to consider biology first. One problem addressed by some is the question of sheer scale: students may have to travel large distances in large numbers to a suitable location. For example, one Russian account[112] cites a case of spending 50 days travelling in tarpaulin covered trucks (eight students to each), covering 5,000 km, and stopping at seven field stations. Work done is correspondingly varied, including team work, excursions, keeping field diaries etc. One very important problem is that of taking the laboratory, as well as the students, into the field. With modern instrumentation and techniques, this is increasingly difficult:[113] a pH meter can without much trouble be added to specimen box and hand lens, but provisions for, say, gas chromatography is another matter. One (expensive) solution is to equip trucks as mobile laboratories.

None of this is to claim that laboratory work in biology is an uninhibited free investigation of the whole environment. One survey[114] estimated that of 53 first year American biology courses, the percentage of laboratory work that could be called 'investigative', while more than 90 per cent in six places, was 0 per cent in seven. At the same time, except in the case of 'sandwich courses' involving industrial experience, few physics or chemistry courses have gone far in the direction of taking the laboratory out of the campus, and into the field — to industry or elsewhere.

Returning now to chemistry, integration has taken several forms. The most thoroughgoing is the development of a general integrated chemistry laboratory,[8] to replace all or most of the specialised laboratories. Such a laboratory is often organised around problems or projects; techniques may be taught within projects, or separately. Its aims are likely to be along the lines of,[25]

> 'to instruct in techniques, procedures, evaluation of results, and the planning, designing, and executing of laboratory projects'.

There may be introductory experiments as well as projects,[41] or experiments may be designed with introductory and project phases in each, as a compromise.[42] While some concentrate on integrating subject matter, some follow through the organisational consequences of integration rather a long way. An example is a laboratory described by Cochran:[115] experiments over the whole undergraduate programme are planned as a whole, with three levels of experiment — skills, standard experiments, and projects. Students are required to make a balanced choice, but can to some extent tailor their own programme of work. The laboratory has links with other departments, and, by including students at all levels, it can get some to teach others. An important feature is a programme of seminars which, with the option to work with staff on research, introduces a research flavour into the laboratory. Often, however, the development is more modest, perhaps to a core of experiments introducing a variety of chemical methods of all kinds,[116] sometimes with an attempt to simulate research in the experiments.[117] Another, less usual, focus is on such things as observation, deduction, and reportage, seen as skills to be developed by a variety of experiments.[118]

Innovations that sail under the flag of integration are not always attempts to integrate parts of the chemistry laboratory, but may rather be attempts to link the parts to the outside world. Thus several organic chemistry laboratories let students choose their own products to synthesise, either important real substances or substances the literature shows not to have been previously synthesised,[119, 120, 121] with more than one requiring the student to write up the work as a research paper. Similarly, substances used in quantitative analysis may be chosen for their relevance to students' actual planned careers.[122, 123] A related example is an introductory laboratory[124] in which aspirin is synthesised, its molecular weight is found, various conversions are effected, a commercial specimen is analysed, aspirin is recovered from the commercial mixture, and so on. Group work on projects can also be used, an example being in analytical chemistry, where the groups select projects, search the literature, do the analysis, and produce a joint report.[125] This last example is one, many of whose features could be adapted to other subjects. The projects offered are chosen to be real and relevant chemistry, and because of the use of groups, can be quite difficult and complex (analysis of tea, analysis of mercury in seafood, analysis of lead in petrol). Where many reports emphasise skill or knowledge, this one stresses initiative, ingenuity, and creativity, besides chemistry.

It is notable how in analytical chemistry, the notion of 'unknowns' (that is, ready made problem mixtures), once no doubt a bright, motivating, and effective idea, has gone stale on many ('an unknown is that which is known to everybody except the student' — [28]). This may especially be so where the division of kinds of analysis ('qual' and 'quant') leads to artificiality and to complaints that students do not use the techniques in new situations — a warning perhaps to those who see the potential of analysing and training skills as unlimited. This has led some[126] to provide unknowns, but to get students to analyse them by any means available, including NMR, IR spectroscopy, etc.

If chemists have sought an answer in reality — analysing vitamin E in lard, pyrogallol in hair dye, alkaloids in expectorants, and *E. coli* in dirty water,[63] physicists generally have not, at least not in the same sense. When they speak of 'opening up' laboratory work they are more likely to think of work which is more like 'real research' as opposed to 'real life'. The physicists' solutions vary most along the dimension of structure, from the open project laboratory,[106, 107] to laboratories containing set experiments with some flexibility in how they finally develop.[44] An interesting intermediate case is a laboratory in which the experiments are cumulative projects, each taken some distance by a group of students, who then move on to another, taking over and having their own taken over, by others.[110] This organisational device points to a problem not unique to physics: the problem of trading off intensity and variety in any kind of project work. Few dispute the considerably involvement of students in even modest project work, but the time needed for any substantial work to be done can rarely be held below a month. The price, if the time extends more, is a loss in the range of things students meet, and it is this which the last pattern attempts to preserve while not losing the other advantages.

Another approach to 'opening up' has been to extend the definition of what counts as an 'experiment'. So, for example, some increase the variety of work done by introducing paper planning exercises, computational work, the development of new laboratory exercises, small group projects or planning exercises, writing exercises, miniature investigations, and so on.[108, 109, 16 (chapter 8)] In some cases, the value of discussion is emphasised, with various kinds of seminars fitting into the pattern.[16 (chapter 8), 128]

In general, it is clear that in all the sciences, those concerned with the issues of the present section have not usually seen fit to abandon the laboratory to a free for all. Rather, they have tried to find organisational patterns, and ways of structuring work, which compromise between freedom and restriction, security and uncertainty, things to learn and chances to learn, planning and initiative.

It is appropriate therefore to mention here an organisational innovation, not within a laboratory, but in the pattern and division of responsibility for laboratories. The convenient neutral name adopted for the pattern was 'unit laboratories'.[16 (chapter 8), 129] It is common for the laboratory for a year in a large physics department to have to accommodate say 100 students attending on different days of the week in smaller numbers (perhaps 25), with a considerable number of different members of staff attending at different times. This arrangement obviously dilutes the staff sense of responsibility: they are more likely to operate the laboratory than to take much part in developing it. The overall direction tends to become an administrative rather than a creative responsibility, simply because of the scale of the job and the difficulty of persuading a number of 'part time' staff to collaborate in innovation ('Like getting blood out of a stone', said one such director).

The physics department of the University of Birmingham, England, following some such diagnosis, reorganised the responsibilities so that staff in ones or twos became responsible for briefer 'units' of laboratory work, lasting perhaps five weeks.

Groups of students then moved from unit to unit, the staff remaining to take on the next group.

Within this framework, it became possible for staff to plan a coherent programme of work, often developing from a simple introduction to something ambitious by the end of the five-week unit. They could schedule a variety of activities, no longer being constrained to the pattern of rotating equivalent experiments. One example may be worth giving. It is typical only in its individuality; in other units other staff devised quite different types of programme, a freedom the system gives them. The example is of a laboratory on electrical measurements.[16 (chapter 6), 129] Initially, students do a series of exercises intended to make them familiar with the range of instruments in the laboratory. Next they do a series of limited experiments, intended to show the instruments at work in typical situations. Then they are faced with the problem of instrumenting a prepared experiment, which might be to measure the melting point of a metal or to measure an inductance; this is discussed in seminars where students present their plans, and then they carry them out. Interleaved as required are demonstrations and other discussions. The point is not the actual work proposed, but the possibility of proposing a planned, developing, coherent and varied pattern of work appropriate to the topic.

It must be recognised that the unit laboratory concept is by no means novel, most notably in the teaching of electronics, where many have seen a brief laboratory course as the natural solution. At the same time, it may be worth recognising as a device which enables the large department to deploy the same staff in a healthier manner, and to escape the large-number trap of anonymity with its associated problems of boredom and routine.

3.6 Large Scale Projects

It is rare to find an innovation commanding wide and rapid acceptance; a proper sense of caution, reasonable scepticism, and the difficulty of making changes in large and complex institutions are sufficient causes. Project work, however, at least in the final year of undergraduate science, has been widely and rapidly adopted in all the sciences. The evidence of its spread in physics is documented by Chambers,[19] and is taken for granted in the report of the Rennsselaer Conference on Laboratory Instruction in Chemistry.[8] Thomas[154] provides an extensive bibliography.

In biology the long tradition of field work rather alters the picture, as discussed in the previous section. Whereas in physics and chemistry, project work is discussed as a possible option which may or may not be exercised, in biology field work is more often seen as a natural and necessary part of the course. The rather long time constant of laboratory biological investigations may also contribute to a shift in emphasis from laboratory to field. A comparison might be drawn here with 'sandwich' courses (as they are termed in the U.K.): that is, courses in science or engineering which include as an integral part a period of experience in industry.[141] It seems likely to us that in such courses the industrial experience will take over many of the roles otherwise attributed to project work, while projects within the course will be likely to be seen as preparation for that experience. Indeed, a study of the satisfaction felt by students in a (biology) 'sandwich' course[130] showed at the top of the list much the same things as might be expected from project work: getting experimental work done, consulting papers, and thinking through results with a supervisor.

It does seem to us that the industrial link approach to project work deserves serious consideration in all courses. It is by no means unknown in physics and chemistry for some project titles offered to relate to problems of local industry, and it is natural in engineering. But in physics and chemistry there is the competing ethos of research within the university, and very probably a built-in bias towards that ethos which may not always be desirable.

The most common form of project work is rather well known. Final-year laboratory work is replaced, in whole or in substantial part, by a single project undertaken individually under a supervising member of staff. A useful brief survey of this kind of project work and its problems in a wide range of academic subjects is offered in a booklet produced by a working party of the Society for Research in Higher Education.[131]

The general aims of such project work are equally well accepted, at least in general terms. A typical list[131] will include carrying through a problem to solution, using initiative, involvement in varied activities, the need to produce some end-product (usually a report or thesis), the pursuing of work over an extended period, and the value of working intimately with a member of staff. Some make large claims for projects, echoing Gull[132] writing of projects for young children:

'The project method is Nature's own method of education; it is the means whereby all civilisation has come about . . . .'

though few would adopt so romantic a tone. Many, however, point to the 'reality' of projects, and contrast that favourably with the artificiality of 'cook-book' experiments.[e.g. 106, 120, 133] There are doubts: about the effects of asking for too much too soon,[29] and about the need to think carefully through what a project is supposed to teach and not rely on its 'reality' to do the job automatically.[35, see also 16 (chapter 7)] Not much reflected in the literature, but surely present in much departmental thinking, is the trade-off involved between breadth of experience and depth and intensity in any move to project work.

A few are to be found urging a complete transfer of all laboratory work to projects,[134] but far more take a view of project work as a culmination of the undergraduate course. It may be worth noting in passing that this 'culminative' view is taken by teachers at all levels from primary school to university: do children and students really reach a series of stages at each of which they are just ready for projects, these stages neatly coinciding with the ages at which they are about to pass from one institution to another?

The literature reflects a very reasonable concern with problems of assessing projects, especially where the investment of time on the part of the student calls for a substantial weighting of the project in the final degree result. Problems include the relatively coarse grading which many feel to be all that is possible;[135] how to handle assessment if students work in groups;[125] relating assessment more carefully to aims;[131] the final weighting of project assessments;[131, 136] and questions of relationship between student and assessing supervisor.[131, 137]

It strikes us that, as compared with the attention given to problems of assessment, and to practical problems of finding topics, there is rather little attention given to trying to see whether the actual work done in project systems is or is not a promising reflection of the high hopes expressed for it. An attempt to discuss this issue is made in the H.E.L.P. book about laboratory work.[16] One question that can be raised, for example, is the extent to which the success of a project is to a degree assured, just because if it looks like failing, the supervisor often modifies it accordingly. If there is such a phenomenon, it clearly interacts with attempts to weigh up the value of the project. Another question might be the rather general assumption that, because what is good about projects is their 'reality', anything demanded by the 'reality' of the problem is necessarily good. Where this leads, as it can, to one student spending nearly all his time on routine data collection, another on fabricating apparatus, and a third on developing theoretical ideas, it cannot automatically be assumed that these very differently balanced activities are all equally good.

The concept of the undergraduate project has always owed a good deal to the related concept of research training. The project is frequently seen as 'research in miniature'. There are some who, rather than trying to devise miniature research problems,[142] see the solution in the direct involvement of undergraduates in research. One such example is the Undergraduate Research Opportunities Program at M.I.T. which embraces all subjects.[140] Another is the Undergraduate-Graduate Research Collaboration Program linking American graduate schools with colleges.[143] More modestly, a department can look for ways of involving its own students with research staff;[138, 139] this often being best arranged as an option for some students.[144] It is even possible for a whole undergraduate course to be a degree by thesis, exceptional though this is likely to remain.[145]

A variation on project work of some interest is group work, for which it can at least be argued that most research is done in groups and that much of the learning done after the degree is co-operative. One example in fact partly replaces individual project work by a group study of a topic leading to further projects, throughout which staff work closely with students in a fashion rather like that of a research group.[146] That example is in physics; there are others in biochemistry (though on a modest scale),[147-149] and in chemistry.[125]

It may be useful to speculate on the reasons why project work is so well-established in the form that it is. We think one reason is that projects in the form of small research projects seem immediately valid to teachers: they can easily be assimilated to activities which are highly valued, namely research and research training. They are also readily intelligible to teachers: the supervisor believes in his ability to handle such work by using his existing skills. Another reason, obviously, is that projects are popular with students, who value such features as independence and personal achievement.[150] Finally, we suspect that project work has succeeded by challenging just enough, but no more, accepted ideas of undergraduate teaching.

4. Evidence of what happens

In this section we enter upon difficult territory, difficult for two reasons. First the issues are decidedly problematic, with no assurance that any one approach is the right one. Secondly, they are issues with which we ourselves have recently been concerned and about which we know of little other similar work closely related to laboratory teaching. The reader should therefore be aware that the section reflects our personal views. Much of the material is drawn from the H.E.L.P. book on laboratory teaching in physics undergraduate courses[16] which was one product of a project concerned with undergraduate science.

The issue we wish to address is the question of the proper approach to collecting evidence on which to base judgements of success or failure in laboratory work, and with which to inform or support proposals for change.

We are not, however, here concerned with the construction of valid and reliable tests of student performance, important though that is. The problem is well and thoroughly treated in several books, one of the best being that by Nedelsky.[26] It would be simple and attractive to conceive the problem as one of collecting data on performance, under various conditions, and from that making inferences about which conditions lead to success. We hold, in fact, that only under very rare circumstances is any such thing imaginable as a practical policy. A real laboratory, with real students and real teachers, is influenced by so many interacting factors that no inference from data is remotely secure. Worse, one has little idea what the relevant factors are, and experience suggests that in teaching, as in life in general, rather minor changes can have rather gross consequences.

The problem as we see it is one of finding the right kind of description of laboratories, close enough to their daily reality to avoid falsifying it, but general enough to be a guide to action. It may be useful, to make the point, to contrast the way a scientist sees description with the way a literary critic sees it. A scientist who described the room in which he worked and his reactions to it would have his paper returned forthwith. A critic who merely listed the names of the characters in a novel, and their relationships would equally go unread. The problem can now be put: is a laboratory best described as a set of experiments on certain topics, done under certain rules and constraints, or as a web of interactions between people which must take account of how they react and what they think? We take something of the second to be essential.

Such a view has informed recent studies in higher education [155-157] and has been the point of departure for investigations of computer-aided instruction including laboratory work,[158] of a programme of concentrated study integrating theory and practical work,[159] and of attitudes of staff towards 'open-ended' laboratories.[111]

Rather than to offer further generalities, it may be better to give some examples. The examples come from material collected in a systematic study[16] of about eight different teaching laboratories in different universities. The material was collected by physicists acting as observers, watching work going on and questioning the teachers and students.

The first example concerns our attempt to trace the origin of the effectiveness of a very traditional second-year laboratory. It was not distinguished by the interest or originality of its experiments (many were traditional war-horses), by the quality of its apparatus (much was old and some decidedly tatty), by any special enthusiasm of its staff, or by any special attention to students. Seen in contrast to others, it was marked out by two related qualities which some had in less degree: consistency and realism.

By its consistency, we mean that an observer, asking what it was for and why, got the same answers from staff, students, and from inspection of experiments, instructions, and the actions of people. Each experiment was deliberately designed to force the student into making choices; consistent with this, the apparatus was rather simple and the instructions bare. Each was designed to require critical thinking towards improving the quality of the data; consistently each experiment had some component working near its limit of performance.

All this was explicit in the account given of the laboratory by those involved, the tone being well caught by the following from the written introduction to the laboratory:

> 'Good technique may be learned by overcoming the 'inadequacy' of some piece of apparatus, and our experiments have usually been designed this way, not out of pure malice, but because almost always at the research level some piece of the apparatus is working at its limit (it could hardly be research if it were not); that is, it is 'inadequate' for the job.'

By realism, we mean that demands were reasonably calculated to be within the reach of students, neither beyond them nor too easily attained. Problems were evident but not too evident; theory difficult but not too difficult; data analysis lengthy but not excessively so; requirements on written reports rigorous but not impossible of achievement. The evidence for this judgement is the acceptance by students of the situation, as for example in:

> 'I think it's better to leave the experiments with the difficulties there. I think you probably learn more. It's no use just going up to the equipment and being told to take this measurement. Anyone can do that.'

The point, it is important to insist, is not the policy but its consistency and realism. Looking at different laboratories, with very different policies, it seemed to us that success depended a good deal not on what they chose to do, but on the extent to which contradictions and obscurities had been faced and resolved.

The second example concerns a much debated point: the proper role of demonstrators, that is, graduate teaching assistants, in the laboratory. Some regard them as best fitted to give students practical advice, and unsuited to the job of marking work; others take exactly the opposite view. Some regard them as a regrettable necessity, forced on the laboratory by its economics; others think their closeness to and sympathy with students an essential and valuable contribution. Some regard the job as a gentle introduction to more demanding kinds of teaching; others see it as no less difficult and subtle than any other.

Comparing different laboratories, we were struck by the fact that every role reserved for post-graduate students in some could be found carefully denied them in another, and vice-versa. We could detect little if any consequences of these opposing policies.

Further, we were struck by the very widespread feeling of uncertainty and inadequacy amongst post-graduates about their role (whatever it was), coupled with the equally widespread belief that nothing could be done about it. Teaching, they generally held, is unteachable.

The lesson of the first observation seems to be that what many consider an important factor may not be one; post-graduates share the general adaptability of the human race. The lesson of the second is that there is scope to do something to help them at least feel more confident, and possibly even actually to be more effective. For example, many felt doubts about the reliability of their marking; a little time spent discussing sample reports and the marks they got could be repaid. It is convenient to mention here that training of laboratory demonstrators is not a totally neglected field. We found examples of teaching them at least about the apparatus [16] (chapter 5) and of annual planning and criticism sessions. [16] (chapter 8) The literature has examples of some systematic training, though it is worth noting that it is not an issue raised at all in typical analyses of the state of laboratory work and of directions for its improvement. [e.g. 11, 42] One such approach [151] attempted to observe different styles of teaching, and claims that a gentle, accepting, questioning style had advantages over a firmer, more directive style. Another [152, 153] provided seminars for teaching assistants using ways of analysing and observing behaviour, self-observation on videotape (micro-teaching), and practice in the art of asking students questions.

The third and last example starts from the obvious truth that it is not what is supposed to happen but what does happen that matters. Teachers may be supposed to discuss experiments with students in the laboratory: how much do they do it and what is the nature of the discussion? A piece of programmed instruction may be supposed to carry a student step by step through work: does it do so? A student may be supposed to be stimulated to thought and planning by an experiment: is there visible evidence that it happens?

To take one specific instance, we found very wide variations in the manner in which experiments were marked and in the way completed reports were discussed with students. In some places reports were marked and handed back without discussion; at the opposite extreme a mark was arrived at after an hour-long discussion with the student. Marking discussions varied a good deal in content. One phenomenon we felt we detected was the 'look at the errors' syndrome. This tended to arise where experiments had full instructions and fixed apparatus, so that the discussion of errors was in effect the only area which distinguished one student from another. Important though errors may be, having heard other marking discussions in which students had to defend their theoretical ideas, their experimental tactics, and their solutions for difficulties, it seemed to us that a discussion limited mainly to results and errors was unnecessarily limited. We also found that "discussion" between staff and students had its subtleties. One student rather acutely pointed to an obvious but perhaps too rarely admitted problem when he said:

> 'I tended to sit there and say, 'Yes, yes, yes' but half the time I was thinking, 'What on earth is he talking about?', and instead of pushing him, and getting it all out of him properly, I just didn't deal with it at all.'

It seems to us that these examples and others like them illustrate several general points. One point is that concrete knowledge of what is going on is an important ingredient in making decisions about laboratories: a point normally accepted in day-to-day discussion of problems but less often accepted in research into teaching. Another point is that judgements of the value of activities ought to be tied closely to what those activities actually are. Yet another is that laboratories are not well described by simple slogans — "open-ended", "skill-oriented", etc. — but are in fact complex systems in a state of delicate but stable balance. Finally, a teaching laboratory is a human system, not a mechanical one, so that understanding it requires an attention to and perception of the behaviour of people no less intensive than the scientist habitually gives to his research apparatus.

5. What next?

This article has described a very large variety of patterns of laboratory teaching in science, and a considerable number of very varied innovations.

It would be natural to ask at this point which are the best, or the worst. We do not think that this question has a simple answer.

One thing is very clear from a reading of the literature. The nature of institutions and their problems ranges extraordinarily widely. A large American State University teaching science to several hundred non-science majors is quite unlike a small British one teaching physics to a dozen specialists, and both have little resemblance to a French University with large numbers and high standards.

Another thing which emerges is the relative stability of the traditional pattern of laboratory work in science, with its set experiments done in rotation under the oversight of a shifting population of staff and teaching assistants. Almost every innovation is seen against this backdrop. It seems to us that the present time is one in which this traditional pattern is subject to a variety of kinds of questioning, in which many variations have been tried, but in which there is no clear consensus as to a way forward. This, in our view, makes it an interesting and exciting time, but one in which teachers need a high degree of tolerance of uncertainty.

Despite these remarks, the picture is not, we think, one simply of confusion. Definite trends are discernible.

One trend is towards closer definition of the objectives of laboratory work, and a corresponding attempt to design experiments in close and careful detail to serve those objectives. Those who find this view too narrow and restrictive can still gain something from it by asking whether their wider ranging experiments serve aims in some reasonable balance, or whether some aims are honoured more in the breach than in observance.

An opposite trend is to "open up" laboratory work: to place more decisions in the hands of students, and to encourage more by way of independence and initiative. Final-year project work has led the way here, but many have tried to introduce some such element into the work of previous years.

To write in this way of "trends" is to suggest too strongly that there is a general move away from the traditional pattern, and that would be quite wrong. There are large numbers of traditional laboratories in existence, and they vary in kind and quality no less than do innovations. Where they are good, we feel that it is often because care and thought has gone into the planning of work having sympathetic regard for the problems of students, and where equal care and thought has gone into the planning and functioning of the laboratory's human resources — its staff and teaching assistants.

Finally, another lesson to be learned, we feel, is that an important key to success is responsibility. It is those laboratories, traditional and innovative alike, where a person or a group of people have accepted it as their personal responsibility to see the thing through as well as they can, that do best. A weakness of the traditional pattern is that a laboratory can be — though it need not be — the personal charge of nobody, belonging to nobody and having no commitment (beyond the occasional call of duty) from anybody. Here the "unit laboratory" scheme described in 3.4 has potential advantages. The lesson is a simple, general, and obvious one: things in laboratories as in life go well when someone cares.

REFERENCES

[1] Menzie J.C. (1970) *Am J Phys*, 38, 1121-1127.
[2] Thomson W. (1885) Address at the opening of physics and chemistry laboratories, University College of N. Wales. N. Wales Chronicle, Feb 7th, 1885.
[3] Fife W.K. (1975) *J Chem Ed*, 52, 119-120.
[4] Ihde A.J. (1964) *The Development of Modern Chemistry*, Harper and Row, New York.
[5] Sutton R.A. (ed.) (1977) *Resource Booklet — Physics Interface Project*, University College Cardiff Press.
[6] Burke B.A. *et al.* (1977) *J Chem Ed*, 54, 360-361.
[7] Herron J.D. (1975) *J Chem Ed*, 52, 146-150.
[8] Report of the Conference on Laboratory Instruction in Chemistry, Rennsselaer (1974) *J Chem Ed*, 52, 27.
[9] Report of International Conference on Education in Chemistry, at Snowmass-at-Aspen (1970) *J Chem Ed*, 48, 3-38.
[10] Jevons F.R., Turner H.D. (1972) *What Kind of Graduates Do We Need?* Oxford University Press.
[11] Mellon E.K. (1977) *J Chem Ed*, 54, 115-118.
[12] Packard J. (1903) *Proceedings, N.E.A,* 881.
[13] Rosen S. (1954) *Am J Phys*, 22, 203.
[14] Reinmuth O.J. (1931) *J Chem Ed*, 9, 971.
[15] Hunt H.J. (1936) *J Chem Ed*, 13, 29.
[16] Ogborn J. (ed.) (1977) *Practical Work in Undergraduate Science, Higher Education Learning Project*, published for The Nuffield Foundation by Heinemann Educational Books, London.
[17] *The Role and Nature of Experimental Work in Chemistry Courses* (1972) Symposium Report, The Chemical Society, London.
[18] *Studies in Laboratory Innovation* (1974) Group for Research and Innovation in Higher Education, The Nuffield Foundation, London.

[19] Chambers R.G. (1970) Laboratory Teaching in the United Kingdom, in *New Trends in Physics Teaching*, Vol. II, UNESCO, Paris, 183-196.

[20] *New Trends in Physics Teaching*, Vol. III, UNESCO, Paris, 1977.

[21] Aspden P.J., Eardley R. (1974) *Teaching Practical Physics: The Open University and other approaches*. Occasional Paper, Faculty of Science, The Open University, Bletchley, England.

[22] Report of the Analytical Chemistry Sub-Committee of the Curriculum Committee of the American Chemical Society (1974) Part I *J Chem Ed*, 51, 472-473.

[23] Report of the Analytical Chemistry Sub-Committee of the Curriculum Committee of the American Chemical Society (1974) Part II *J Chem Ed*, 51, 657.

[24] *Notes on experiments for the Advanced Class* (Part II) (1933) Cavendich Laboratory, Cambridge, England.

[25] Aikens D.A. *et al.* (1975) *J Chem Ed*, 52, 232-235.

[26] Nedelsky L. (1965) *Science Teaching and Testing*, Harcourt Brace, New York.

[27] Squire P.T. (1974) *Physics Education*, 9, 45-47.

[28] Young J.A. (1975) *J Chem Ed*, 52, 41-42.

[29] Fraser Williams R. (1967) *J Biol Ed*, 1, 325-335.

[30] Boud D.J. (1973) *Higher Education*, 2, 81-94.

[31] Hambler D.J., Field D. (1969) *J Biol Ed*, 3, 75-90.

[32] Varnes A.W., Wetmore D.E. (1975) *J Chem Ed*, 52, 801-802.

[33] Lucas A.M. (1969) *J Biol Ed*, 3, 203-207.

[34] Hutchinson S.A., Martin E. (1967) *J Biol Ed*, 1, 261-272.

[35] Seel D.C. (1976) *J Biol Ed*, 10, 127-132.

[36] Richards M. (1974) in [18].

[37] Flansburg L. (1972) *Am J Phys*, 40, 1607-1615.

[38] MacDonald Ross (1973) *Instructional Science*, 2, 1-52, Elsevier, Holland.

[39] Bent H.A., Power J.D. (1975) *J Chem Ed*, 52, 448-450.

[40] Court G.R., Donald R.A., Fry J.R. (1976) Teaching Practical Physics I, II. *Physics Education*, 11, 397-450 and 488-492.

[41] Rose T.L., Seyse R.J. (1974) *J Chem Ed*, 51, 127-129.

[42] Venkatachelam C., Rudolph R.W. (1974) *J Chem Ed*, 51, 479-482.

[43] Clapp L.B. (1973) *J Chem Ed*, 50, 248-249.

[44] Shonle J.I. (1970) *Am J Phys*, 38, 450-456.

[45] Beun J.A. (1971) *Am J Phys*, 39, 1353-1356.

[46] Donald R.A. *et al.* Unpublished survey of several undergraduate laboratories in physics. Department of Physics, University of Liverpool, England.

[47] Ogborn J. (1976) *Am J Phys*, 44, 625-627.

[48] Goldberg H.S. (1973) *Am J Phys*, 41, 1319-1327.

[49] Price R.M., Brandt D. (1974) *Am J Phys*, 42, 126-130.

[50] Oppenheimer F., Correll M. (1964) *Am J Phys*, 32, 220-225.

[51] McCord W.M. (1968) *Am J Phys*, 36, 874-878.

[52] Long R. (1975) *Am J Phys*, 43, 340-342.

[53] King J.G. (1968) *Commission on College Physics Newsletter* No. 16, May 1968, U.S.A.

[54] White H.E. *et al.* (1966) *Am J Phys*, 34, 660-664.

[55] Postlethwait S.N., Hurst R.N. (1972) *Educational Technology* Sept. 1972, 35-37.

[56] Watson J.R. (1977) *Education in Chemistry*, 14, 84-86.

[57] Kempa R.F., Palmer C.R. (1974) *Brit J Ed Tech*, 5, 62-74.

[58] Neerinck D., Palmer C. (1977) *Brit J Ed Tech*, 8, 124-131.

[59] Poller R.C., Seeley M.E. (1977) *Education in Chemistry*, 14, 51-52.

[60] Buckingham D.J. (1974) *Brit J Ed Tech*, 5, 27-37.

[61] Pantaleo D.C. (1975) *J Chem Ed,* 52, 112-113.

[62] Thorne J.M. (1975) *J Chem Ed*, 52, 114-115.

[63] Meloan C.E. (1971) *J Chem Ed*, 48, 139-141.

[64] Nienhouse E.J., Nash E.G. (1971) *J Chem Ed*, 48, 141-142.

[65] Carré C.G. (1969) *J Biol Ed*, 3, 57-64.

[66] Ramsey H.P. (1973) *J Biol Ed*, 7, 19-24.

[67] Dowdeswell W.H., Potter I.C. (1975) *J Biol Ed*, 9, 247-250.

[68] Tressel G., Barnard W.R. (1971) *J Chem Ed*, 48, 143-146.

[69] Blum R. (ed.) (1971) *Computers in undergraduate science education,* Commission on College Physics, Maryland 1971, U.S.A.

[70] Hooper R. (ed.) (1975) *Two Years On: The National Development Programme in Computer Assisted Learning*, Council for Educational Technology, London.

[71] Hooper R., Toye I. (eds.) (1975) *Computer assisted learning in the United Kingdom*. Council for Educational Technology, London.

[72] Lecarme O., Lewis R. (eds.) (1975) *Computers in Education: Proceedings of the IFIP 2nd World Conference*. North Holland — Elsevier.

[73] CONDUIT (Computing ideas for higher education) P.O. Box 338, Iowa City, Iowa 52240 U.S.A.

[74] Proceedings of the Fourth Conference on Computers in Undergraduate Curricula, The Claremont Colleges, Claremont, California, U.S.A. June 1973.

[75] Burnstein R.A. *et al.* (1970) in [69].

[76] Milburn G.H.W. (1974) *Educ in Chem*, 11, 90-92.

[77] Seelig P.F., Blount H.N. (1975) *J Chem Ed*, 52, 469-473.

[78] Hogg J.L. (1974) *J Chem Ed*, 51, 109-112.

[79] Peterson D.L., Fuller M.E. (1971) *J Chem Ed*, 48, 314-316.

[80] Perone S.P., Eaglestone J.F. (1971) *J Chem Ed*, 48, 317-322.

[81] Mueller A.P. (1969) *J Biol Ed*, 3, 159-168.

[82] Jameson C.L. (1977) *J Chem Ed*, 54, 238-241.

[83] Cabrol D. *et al.* (1975) *J Chem Ed*, 52, 266-268.

[84] Merrill J.C. *et al.* (1975) *J Chem Ed*, 52, 528-529.

[85] Lindsay R.S. (1970) in [69].

[86] Davis L.N. *et al.* (1973) *J Chem Ed*, 50, 711-713.

[87] Craig N.C. *et al.* (1971) *J Chem Ed*, 48, 310-313.

[88] Venier C.G., Reinecke M.G. (1972) *J Chem Ed*, 49, 541-542.

[89] Bitzer D.L. *et al.* (1970) in [69].

[90] Alpert D. (1975) in [72].

[91] Smith S.G. *et al*, (1974) *J Chem Ed*, 51, 243-244.

[92] Herbert R.H., Hazony Y. (1974) *J Chem Ed*, 51, 245-249.

[93] Barrett J., Beezer A. (1977) *Educ in Chem*, 14, 42-43.

[94] McKenzie J. (1976) *Physics Education*, 11, 475-478.

[95] Whitaker A., Walker J.D. (1973) *J Biol Ed*, 7, 37-42.

[96] Diamond R.H., Benton A.H. (1970) *J Biol Ed*, 4, 111-114.

[97] Marinos N.G., Lucas A.M. (1971) *J Biol Ed*, 5, 109-113.

[98] Brewer I.M. (1974) *J Biol Ed*, 8, 101-112.

[99] Roach D.K., Hammond R. (1976) *Studies in Higher Ed*, 1, 179-196.

[100] O'Connell S. *et al*. (1976) *A rationally designed laboratory mini-course*. I.E.T. Report, University of Surrey, England.

[101] Bridge W., Elton L.R.B. (eds.) (1977) *Individual Study in Undergraduate Science*, Heinemann Educational Books, London.

[102] Keller F.S., Sherman J.G. (eds.) (1974) *P.S.I.: The Keller Plan Handbook*, Benjamin, U.S.A.

[103] Peterson D.L. (1977) *J Chem Ed*, 54, 362-364.

[104] Palma R.J. (1975) *J Chem Ed*, 52, 116-117.

[105] Splittgerber A.G. *et al*. (1971) *J Chem Ed*, 48, 330-332.

[106] King J.G. (1966) *Am J Phys*, 34, 1058-1062.

[107] Soules J.A., Bennet R.B. (1968) *Am J Phys*, 36, 1068-1072.

[108] Finegold L. (1972) *Am J Phys*, 40, 1383-1388.

[109] Finegold L., Hartley C.L. (1972) *Am J Phys*, 40, 28-32.

[110] Graetzer H.G. (1972) *Am J Phys*, 40, 270-276.

[111] Ivany J.W.G., Parlett M.R. (1968) *Am J Phys*, 36, 1072-1080.

[112] Sokolov V., Pavlov V., Grishina L. (1969) *J Biol Ed*, 3, 23-35.

[113] Smyth J.C. (1974) *J Biol Ed*, 8, 285-293.

[114] Kormondy E.J. *et al*. (1974) *Am Biol Teach*, 36, 217-220.

[115] Cochran J.C. *et al*. (1972) *J Chem Ed*, 49, 630-633.

[116] Brown T.L. (1972) *J Chem Ed*, 49, 633-635.

[117] Michael J.V. *et al*. (1972) *J Chem Ed*, 49, 636-638.

[118] Wartell M.A. (1973) *J Chem Ed,* 50, 361-362.

[119] Pearson W.A., Finholt A.E. (1975) *J Chem Ed*, 52, 236-237.

[120] Chisholm M.G. (1975) *J Chem Ed*, 52, 739-741.

[121] Bobbitt J.M. *et al*. (1974) *J Chem Ed*, 51, 58-60.

[122] Klatt L.N., Sheafer J.C. (1974) *J Chem Ed*, 51, 239-242.

[123] Bramstedt W.R. *et al*. (1973) *J Chem Ed*, 50, 252-255.

[124] Brown D.B., Friedman L.B. (1973) *J Chem Ed*, 50, 214-215.

[125] Buono J.A., Fasching J.L. (1973) *J Chem Ed*, 50, 616-617.

[126] Nujent M.J. (1972) *J Chem Ed*, 49, 491-492.

[127] Aldridge W.A., Feldker P. (1969) *Phys Teach*, 7, 321-326.

[128] Tubbs M.R. (1968)*Physics Education*, 3, 189-192.

[129] Black P.J., Whitworth R.W. (1974) in [18].

[130] Smithers A.G., Hambler D.J. (1969) *J Biol Ed*, 3, 209-220.

[131] Goodlad S. (ed.) (1975) *Project Methods in Higher Education*, Society for Research into Higher Education, London.

[132] Gull H. (1933) *Projects in the Education of young Children,* McDougall, London.

[133] Dronsfield A.T. (1975) *Education in Chemistry*, 12, 112 and 114.

[134] Clausen D.F. (1974) *J Chem Ed*, 51, 120-121.

[135] Harper J.L. (1972) *J Biol Ed*, 6, 318-321.

[136] Thomson N. (1977) *The Assessment of Student Performance in Honours Degrees in Physics,* Report to the Nuffield Foundation, London.

[137] *A Question of Degree* (1975) Group for Research and Innovation in Higher Education, The Nuffield Foundation, London.

[138] Anderson W.F. *et al.* (1974) *Am J Phys*, 42, 944-947.

[139] Breslin L. (1974) *Am J Phys*, 42, 948-951.

[140] Cohen S.A., MacVicar M.L.A. (1976) *Am J Phys*, 44, 199-203.

[141] Downie T.C. (1974) *Education in Chemistry*, 11, 42-43.

[142] Parsons M.L., Bentley G.E. (1975) *J Chem Ed*, 52, 396.

[143] Scalzi F.V., Kovacic P. (1973) *J Chem Ed*, 50, 205.

[144] Waddington D.J. (1974) *Education in Chemistry*, 11, 41.

[145] Courts B. (1974) *Education in Chemistry*, 11, 47-49.

[146] Black P.J. *et al.* (1968) *Physics Education*, 3, 289-293.

[147] **Barr G.C., Macqueen D.** (1971) *J Biol Ed,* 5, 80-82.

[148] Joner P.E. (1974) *J Biol Ed*, 9, 80-82.

[149] Gerber B.R., Dreskin S.C. (1971) *J Chem Ed*, 48, 464.

[150] Bliss J., Ogborn J. (1977) *Students' Reactions to Undergraduate Science*, Heinemann, London.

[151] Urickeck M.J. (1972) *J Chem Ed*, 49, 259-262.

[152] Brooks D.W. *et al.* (1972) *J Chem Ed*, 49, 622-623.

[153] Mellon E.K., Dence J.B. (1971) *J Chem Ed*, 48, 674-675.

[154] Thomas M (1977) M.Ed Dissertation of Chelsea College, London.

[155] **Parlett M., Miller C.M.L.** (1974) *Up to the Mark*. Society for Research into Higher Education, London.

[156] Friedman C.P. *et al.* (1975) *Am J Phys*, 44, 204-211.

[157] Zinberg D.S. (1976) *Social Studies of Science*, 6, 215.

[158] *The Programme at Two* (1976) U.N.C.A.L. University of East Anglia, England.

[159] **King J., Parlett M** (1971) *Concentrated Study*. Society for Research into Higher Education, London.

Project Work in University Science

W.H. Dowdeswell and N.D.C. Harris

1. Introduction

As an educational device, the project may well be one of the least cost effective yet devised. Its requirements of such precious commodities as time, manpower, space and equipment, far exceed those of other methods for the teaching and learning of science. Yet it is a strange paradox that in spite of these manifest drawbacks, it is a mode of learning which finds widespread acceptance among the tertiary educational establishments of Europe, and to a lesser extent in the United States. Not surprisingly, the majority of published accounts of project work and its uses emanate from these two sources. [1,2]

In the following pages we shall attempt to explore briefly the background to this paradoxical situation, to assess the validity of the claims put forward in support of project work and to weigh up some of the advantages and disadvantages inherent in this approach. But proceeding further, it is necessary to attempt to answer the basic question — what is a project?

2. Defining a Project

Attempting to define a project is rather like trying to define "life"; there is no single description that covers all aspects even within the somewhat restricted compass of university science. Like "life", projects manifest themselves in many different ways which, if viewed more closely, nonetheless reveal a number of features in common[3]. Thus, project work always involves students working singly or in small groups of two or three at the most. This means that the numerical ratio of students to staff is usually one to one or nearly so, a situation which inevitably influences the role of the supervising tutor. Thus, instead of being authoritarian and dogmatic as is the tendency in lectures, in projects it becomes mainly advisory and stimulatory.

Again, a project usually involves investigation and the solution of a problem. This may be of a theoretical kind such as the designing of a computer programme, or demand laboratory or constructional work. The work is usually allotted a finite length of time, ranging from a mini-project lasting a week or so[4] to a more extensive project occupying a year or more[5]. The end-product is generally clearly defined and may take the form of a report or a physical model, or both.

Most projects call for certain behavioural attributes in students which can be grouped together as higher educational activities — creativity, enterprise, persistence and dedication. Such objectives belong largely to the affective domain [6, 7, 8] and although highly desirable, are difficult to assess. Indeed, it can be stated as a generalisation that the conflicting requirements of learning and assessment pose one of the major problems inherent in the organisation of project work[9]. A further intellectual activity associated with projects is decision-making. Whereas in other forms of teaching and learning the sequence of activities and their eventual outcome are mainly under the control of the teacher, projects are essentially student orientated. The student is required to make decisions and to live with their consequences.

One of the aims of project work in science (p. 205) at the tertiary level is to enable students to gain some insight and experience in the techniques of research. However, only on rare occasions will it be possible to enable a class of students to embark upon a range of project topics all of which are truly original. More often than not, a subject will have been researched many times before but this does not necessarily invalidate it as an area for a satisfactory project. As the American educationalist Dewey once remarked[10], "a fact discovered by a person for himself—although it is well known to a large number of people — is still a new discovery to him". Herein lies the essence of project work; it is not the topics themselves which matter but rather the context in which they are investigated. Many of the tutors who supervise students on project work will themselves be able researchers; by no means all of them will possess a knowledge of teaching methods as well. The project provides, as it were, an interface where these two sets of attributes can most fruitfully meet. An influential writer during the early years of this century who drew attention to this fact was the distinguished chemist, H. E. Armstrong, who propounded the then revolutionary view that students "should find things out for themselves", which was frequently interpreted by antagonists as suggesting that pupils were expected to make new discoveries[11]. In fact, Armstrong was expounding his heuristic method of teaching in much the same sense as Dewey, quoted earlier. Today we realise that the original heuristic approach tended to overstress student responsibility and to underestimate the role of the teacher. Its modern derivative, sometimes referred to as neo-heurism[12], is best described as the process of guided enquiry, in which the tutor plays the important but supplementary roles of adviser and catalyst. Ideally, the teacher exerts an influence on the student without his realising it! However, the ideal situation is seldom attained, since students require assistance in greatly varying degree. For some a light advisory hand will suffice; for others the teaching techniques employed will resemble more closely those habitually used in classwork (p. 215).

3. Aims of Project Work

As Kelly has pointed out[13], the stating of educational aims and objectives can be approached from a number of different viewpoints. Firstly, there are those aims which apply specifically to the student[14] and the changes in him or her that projects are intended to facilitate (*student aims*). Second, there are aims related to project work itself and its modes of conduct (*project aims*). These will be complementary to student aims but not necessarily identical with them since they are seen from a teaching standpoint. Lastly, we must not overlook the fact that project work is but part of a wider curricular spectrum and that some of its aims (*implicatory aims*) will have a relevance for kindred areas of teaching and learning.

When attempting earlier (p. 203) to define what is meant or implied by a project, we pointed out that no definition can be of universal application on account of the diversity of purposes to which this kind of approach is applied. Nonetheless, we believe that an attempt to state broad aims in terms of the three categories defined above can serve a useful purpose.

Student Aims
The student should,
i) adopt an active approach to the attainment of knowledge and experience through recognising and solving a problem in as real a context as possible,
ii) assume greater responsibility for his own learning,
iii) acquire a greater depth of knowledge in a limited area based on his own interests and study,
iv) bring together existing skills and techniques of various kinds while also developing new ones.

In addition, the student may be required to,
v) work in collaboration with other students, thus acquiring the necessary experience in communication, co-operation and compromise,
vi) work in an interdisciplinary context.

But why are these student aims peculiar to the project method of learning? The reason is that active learning methods predominate in preference to passive means of assimilation. The student assumes increased responsibility because of the need to explore his subject in depth. Motivation is generated through a problem being as real as possible; thus, the need to design an agricultural implement to meet a particular requirement is infinitely preferable to a set of theoretical calculations based on second-hand information. In order to solve a real problem the student will have to bring together experiences and skills of various kinds such as experimentation, apparatus design and knowledge derived from the literature. Some of these experiences and skills may need to be developed specifically to solve the problem. Report writing and communication in seminars require additional skills such as those of presentation. On occasions projects may involve groups of students working together which will require the development of interaction skills in facing a common challenge. It may also be necessary to use knowledge from a variety of other disciplines[15], not only mathematics and statistics, which are familiar tools of all scientists, but also from neighbouring disciplines such as economics and sociology.

Project Aims

The project should encourage the student attitudes included under Student Aims and,

i) provide an atmosphere in which the student can feel the maximum of involvement,

ii) generate an atmosphere of reality and/or research,

iii) have a reasonable chance of success,

iv) generate a close relationship between student and supervising tutor,

v) provide an atmosphere of minimum constraints,

vi) discourage passive assimilation of knowledge,

vii) discourage the uncritical use of evidence,

viii) encourage students to think outside their immediate area of enquiry.

Project Aims supplement Student Aims in attempting to ensure success in learning. Such learning needs to be as realistic as possible in order to generate maximum student motivation[15,16]. The degree of success achieved will depend upon the experience of the student, the nature of the topic, the time and facilities available, and the knowledge of the supervisor. Just as a research or design team work together on a common venture, so in project work a relationship conducive to learning must be built up between students, if it is a group project, also between each individual student and his supervisor. Once such relationships have been achieved, one of the main constraints to a successful outcome will have been overcome.

Implicatory Aims

i) As a teaching method, project work must be sufficiently adaptable to satisfy the needs of a wide range of different situations.

ii) It must fit in with and be complementary to other methods of teaching.

iii) Its nature must be such as to constitute an integral part of the whole curriculum.

iv) Its demands must not be so exacting as to exceed the availability of time, manpower and resources available.

v) The process and its end products must be assessable. Moreover, the process of assessment must be acceptable to students and staff, and not involve an excessive expenditure of time and manpower.

In the preceding summary we have purposely refrained from being too specific when defining the intentions of project work, for these will inevitably vaɪy somewhat from one subject to another.[17]. However, for the efficient management of projects by university staff and a clear understanding by students of what is required of them and how their work will be assessed, it will generally be necessary to provide for each project a more precise description of what is expected[18]. This is best done by drawing up a set of objectives which will constitute not only a guide for supervising tutors and students, but also a framework on which assessment will eventually be based.

4. Selecting a Topic

Our ability to learn is largely determined by two factors— intelligence and motivation. In the past we may well have misjudged somewhat the optimal balance between the two for successful learning, overestimating the significance of the first and underestimating the second. From educational psychology there is much evidence that we learn best what we want to learn, and as we have seen in the previous section, the maintenance of motivation in a student is a prime function of a project supervisor. Equally, motivation and preference for a particular member of staff play an important part in the preliminary stages of a project involving the selection of a topic and deciding on the line of investigation to be followed.

In order to ensure maximum personal involvement students should, ideally, have a free hand in the selection of a topic. In practice, this arrangement never obtains for a variety of reasons. What we find is a spectrum of situations ranging from light handed and minimum guidance by a tutor at one extreme, to the presentation of a *fait accompli* at the other, in the form of a list of predetermined topics from which the student is permitted to select one out of several alternatives.

When deciding on the suitability of a topic for a project, the following considerations should be borne in mind:

i) what is the likelihood of achieving a successful outcome in the time available?

ii) has the student the necessary competence in the area of knowledge involved?

iii) is the project suited to the student's personality and temperament?

iv) is the knowledge of the supervisor appropriate for such supervision?

iv) are the necessary resources available such as books, research papers, space, equipment and technical help?

vi) can the associated problems of management be overcome, such as the need to look after animals over week-ends or to obtain readings from experiments at unusual hours?

The fewer the likely constraints, the easier it will be to give students a relatively free hand in the choice of topics to investigate. The biological sciences have always been noted for project work, perhaps because the subject presents such an enormous range of possibilities. On the other hand, subjects associated with an elaborate technology such as engineering and physics face a difficult situation, with resources inevitably restricted both in quantity and quality, leading to a far more limited range of alternatives. But even under the most ideal conditions students will still need some degree of guidance in choosing project topics. What we are emphasising here is that such guidance should be given with circumspection and not as a stated dogma. There are obvious advantages in tutors steering students towards their own areas of research and interests, and success in this can usually be achieved in the end provided the approach is made in the right way.

5. Management of Projects

From the previous account it will be seen that project work, when properly carried out, can be more exacting than any other form of teaching. Besides making considerable demands on the student, it also requires effective management by the teaching staff.

Managerial responsibilities occur in three main fields of activity — the learning process, personal relations between tutors and students, and the provision and utilisation of resources.

Management of learning

Bearing in mind the heterogeneous nature of project work, it is not surprising to find that models proposed by different authors to cover the sequence of phases vary greatly in complexity. Taking two divergent examples, that of Bligh[6] represents a relatively simple sequence, while Adderley et al[1] propose a more complex chain of events. For comparative purposes, the two can be summarised as follows:

(Bligh)	(Adderley et al)
i) Selection of problem/theme /issue to investigate.	i) Perception of problem.
ii) Selection of procedure for solving problem.	ii) Definition of problem and design of brief.
iii) Data collection.	iii) Definition of context of problem.
iv) Plan organisation and presentation.	iv) Selection and retrieval of data.
	v) Conceptions of solution.
	vi) Testing and evaluation (at each stage)
	vii) Selection of solution and development.
	viii) Handling of feedback.
	ix) Use of appropriate communication technique.
	x) Evaluation of process of realisation.

In the previous pages we have emphasised that no project will be successful without a clear-cut plan of action which must be sufficiently flexible to allow for appropriate modification as the investigation proceeds. Any such scheme must be fully understood and agreed between tutor and student, including the procedure for assessment (p. 216).

As Black has pointed out[18], the concept of project work is now so familiar to many teachers that they tend to assume that students are automatically aware of what is intended. All too often this is far from the truth, and much of the value of projects can be lost if students only realise belatedly the distinction between this approach and their other routine laboratory activities. This serves to underline the point made elsewhere (p. 205) that it is desirable not only to establish broad aims for project work in general but also to draw up more precise objectives for each investigation. For instance, a student will need to know from the outset the nature of the end product and to whom it is to be addressed (e.g. the supervisor, university department or outside professional world). It is also desirable that students should be encouraged to write down their interpretation of the objectives laid down by the supervisor. This can have the dual benefit of avoiding misunderstandings later on, and ironing out any obscurities of meaning. Teachers who have never attempted to draw up educational objectives covering a particular curriculum are commonly under the mistaken impression that this is an easy matter. Nothing could be further from the truth. Factors such as content, presentation, assessment and feed-back interact in a complex manner so that, in practice, it is sometimes only possible to agree on the objectives of a course after the course is over!

Another important aspect of project management concerns the student's use of his time. Our natural tendency is to procrastinate and in a situation where the optimal use of time is crucial, students should be required to submit a schedule of their activities covering the whole project period. This can take the form of a work-plan which is submitted to the supervisor and approved by him. Such a scheme may sound pedantic and irksome, but its advantages far outweigh its defects. Not only does it provide an orderly basis for periodic "stocktaking" (p. 215) but it also helps to avoid recriminations should a supervisor maintain that a student has been too ambitious, or a student claim that the tutor did not advise him in time that he was taking too long over a particular phase of his investigation.[18]

Documentation associated with the management of projects varies greatly from one situation to another. Some departments require weekly progress reports to be recorded in log books which are scrutinised and signed by supervisors every four weeks. Again, students may be required at regular intervals to give seminars on their projects attended by other students and staff; they may even have to prepare at least one interim report during the allotted time.

Another scheme[18] requires the student to think out the various components of his programme and to set them down in the form of a network through which he can determine the critical path. Once the network is agreed with his supervisor, the student is then expected to devise a system of monitoring his own progress in the form of a Programmed Evaluation and Review Techniques chart. In order to introduce an element of realism into the time scale, the project is sub-divided into a sequence of activities and the student is required to compute an estimated time allowance in weeks for each activity under the headings: optimistic — likely — pessimistic — expected error (Standard Deviation). The sequence of events is thus as follows. After completing the network and chart, the student calculates the standard deviation for the critical path together with its time. Finally, from this he deduces a t-factor and the probability of completion in the time available.

Such elaborations may serve a valuable purpose on occasions, but before introducing them as an integral part of a scheme, it should be borne in mind that anything which tends to increase the load on the student is likely to have a comparable or even greater effect on that of the supervisory staff.

Management of personal relations

Most of the methods used for teaching science in universities are essentially impersonal, although the smaller the student groupings, the more will discussion play a part and the more personal will the role of the tutor become. This increase in the personal element can have both advantages and disadvantages. On the positive side it can lead to a relationship between staff and students involving a degree of friendship, trust and mutual respect which could hardly be achieved in any other way. It is difficult to specify precise rules of conduct for achieving such relationships but, for the tutor, two of the most important considerations will be to avoid unwarranted preconceptions where students are concerned, and to let relationships develop gradually rather than trying to force the pace[20]. At worst, collaboration in a project can lead to a head-on clash of personalities between tutor and student. Such occurrences are regrettable and with the exercise of a little forethought and restraint on both sides, they can frequently be avoided. The fact is that, as Jenkins has stressed[21], in project work the roles of both tutor and student change. Moreover, the situation is fluid, the one having to adjust to the other as the association develops with increasing experience and continued personal interaction.

Inevitably, supervisors will themselves assume varying degrees of involvement, even to the extent of directing the project for the student, which largely defeats the whole purpose of project work. On the other hand, it must be realised that not all students take to projects equally readily. Some (not necessarily the most successful in other spheres of learning) accept the approach at once and need little guidance beyond periodic encouragement. Others (usually the majority) need some help in coping with unforeseen problems and maintaining motivation. Others again (fortunately a minority) have considerable difficulties and may never come to terms with their project. Handling such students requires great patience and often a disproportionate expenditure of time. Problems can arise through inadequate background knowledge, lack of imagination in overcoming obstacles and poor motivation, to mention only a few reasons. Difficulties are often exacerbated when one of these problem areas reinforces another.

Working on a project can demand such a variety of activities, many of which will be unfamiliar to students, that it is important for the tutor to set aside regular times for taking stock. Such tutorials can serve many different purposes besides a review of progress—to provide encouragement and stimulate motivation, to overcome difficulties, to provoke discussion, and to help students to learn from their own mistakes. In this context, if is important not to rule out students' ideas just because they may not necessarily lead at once to success. One of the principal difficulties in supervising project work is that the tutor may find himself acting in four capacities at the same time—as planner, consultant, controller (teacher roles), and assessor. In order to avoid conflict between the roles of teacher and assessor it is essential that both tutors and students should be fully conversant with the methods of assessment to be used and their significance in the wider context of the course as a whole.

As we have already seen (p. 203), a feature common to all projects is that they demand and seek to develop in students, attributes which can be grouped together as higher educational activities[22]. Personal qualities such as self-confidence, enterprise, clear thinking and the ability to work with others are requisites for success in most professions. In project work they find expression not only in an ability to work with a tutor, other members of the teaching staff and fellow students, but also to co-operate with and learn from technicians. Moreover, there will be occasions when experts outside a student's department need to be consulted, also possibly other students based elsewhere. One of the principal justifications for projects is that, no matter in what subject context they occur, they can help to equip students in more than just a narrow academic sense. By helping them to exploit and develop their own strengths while becoming aware of their limitations, they are the better equipped to face the challenge of professional life later on.

The desirability of enabling students to develop fully their own strengths has encouraged at least two European Universities to develop courses based largely on projects[23]. At Roskelde University Centre in Denmark the two year basic course is developed entirely round project work and a problem centred approach, with no fixed syllabus. The design of buildings and the faculty structure are so arranged as to enable students to work in small groups on projects. Similarly, courses at Bremen University, West Germany are based on project learning. Both institutions have encountered problems in some disciplines; thus it is reported that physicists at Bremen now wish to include a taught basic core course. This is the more typical approach in universities where there is an element of government control.

In the USSR each student in Plant-establishments for Higher Technical Education is required to undertake an individual project[24]. As is typical of projects in engineering, the student is required to present both a written synopsis and to distribute, or present verbally, his report to other students in seminars under the supervision of the teacher. This style of project is carried out with the acceptance of and assistance from the Plant. It is interesting to contrast such a scheme with those at Roskelde and Bremen which tend to orient their projects towards environmental or socio-political areas.

Management of resources

Of all the factors determining the success of project work, the availability of resources can exert the most powerful influence. Indeed, it would be most unwise to embark on this form of teaching without prior planning for resource allocation. This is particularly true in subjects such as physics where expensive electronic apparatus may be required, and in engineering where rigs may have to be constructed. For the purpose of discussion we can group resources under three headings — physical resources, time and finance.

Physical resources include a wide range of items such as technical equipment, laboratory space and library facilities whose relative importance will vary greatly from one subject area to another. Their availability may ultimately determine whether particular topics should be studied by individuals or by groups of students, or indeed, whether they can be studied at all.

When attempting to define a project (p. 203) we pointed out that such work always occupies a finite period of time representing a specific portion of a course. We also stressed at the outset how time-consuming project work can be. The load can become particularly heavy for supervisory staff if they are to carry out their duties conscientiously. In planning, an appropriate allowance must therefore be made in their teaching programme. Similarly, for a major project students will be expected to expend up to fifty hours or more, so that not only must their time-table be planned accordingly, but the requisite working space and other physical resources must be continuously available, free of interruption and interference.

Mention has already been made (p. 203) of the low cost-effectiveness of project work, although it must be admitted that objective evidence is hard to obtain. The true picture is complicated by the fact that a substantial portion of the total cost is hidden. This includes the monopolisation of bench space, the cost of consumables such as chemicals, and requirements for living materials which have either to be grown on the premises or procured. Obviously, a design project in architecture or engineering where the end product is a model and associated drawings will be cheaper than say a physics project employing specialised apparatus, which may not be readily usable again. Final year projects in physics at Bristol University[25] have been estimated to cost £25 per project in expendable equipment. A total of £300 per year for the whole class was spent on commercial items for project work, the equipment being destined eventually to become laboratory stock. Occasionally, a special capital allowance was necessary (e.g. for the purchase of oscilloscopes). At Bristol, the cost of equipment for physics projects has been found to be similar to that of running normal laboratory courses; but where particularly sophisticated apparatus is required, the reason for its use, and eventual value of the project need very careful consideration.

A further hidden cost is in the use of support staff (e.g. technicians). Taking Bristol as an example, 80 final year students have been estimated to use about 1000 hours of workshop time in the building of apparatus for projects, most of this work being carried out under the guidance of a skilled technician. Again, if reports are to be presented as an end-product, are these to be handwritten or typed? If the latter, who should pay for the typing? At Bath University students are usually expected to pay for their own typing and in the School of Architecture they also pay for the materials used in any photographic work carried out on their behalf.

The principles of recouping the cost of projects, at least in part, can be extended to the charge of a bench fee which includes the purchase of expendable items, students being refunded any portion of the fee remaining unused at the end of the project. Some university departments regulate expenditure by fixing an upper limit for each student, thereby influencing materially the kinds of projects that can be attempted.

6. Assessment of projects

There are two basic reasons for assessment: to provide feedback to students keeping them informed of their progress, and to discriminate between the performance of different students in making awards such as degrees.

The provision of feedback to students is a requirement for all teaching methods but may sometimes be omitted in project work, its presence or omission depending upon the purposes of the learning. Often, feedback between students and their supervisors is of an informal or even involuntary kind, but sometimes[6] this is deliberately withdrawn by a tutor in order to encourage students to work on their own. On occasions when discussions take place and projects are being assessed for degree purposes, some record or diary of these discussions needs to be maintained[26]. Not only will this provide useful information about the amount of help that has been given but it will also indicate how much of the developmental thinking has been contributed by the student and how much by the supervisor. As in all forms of assessment, there is a danger that the grades or marks awarded may be a measure of the efforts of the supervisor rather than those of the student.

Discriminative assessment can assume a number of different forms which can be summarised as,

i)   contracts
ii) assessment related to objectives
iii) ranking
iv) romantic
v)   performance

Different methods can be used in combination and all of them can be adapted for the awarding of grades, or marks. The characteristics of the various procedures can be summarised briefly as follows.

Contracts

This type of assessment was developed in the United States and depends upon a written agreement being reached between student and supervisor regarding the nature of the project, its mode of conduct and the end-product required.[18] In a sense it can be regarded as a contract in which the mode of assessment is closely related to the nature of the learning experiences. A possible routine for this method might be as follows:

i)   Before the session likely topics are submitted by students or tutors and a panel of supervisors reviews them. The proposals will include information on previous or related work, likely demands on resources, and students' task objectives such as the review of existing work, apparatus, methods of analysis, and the likelihood of original results being obtained.

ii)   Supervisors and students meet in a 'market place' situation where the available topics are discussed and selected.

iii)   Students are given a hand-out explaining the general purposes of project work and indicating how the project will be assessed.

iv)   A contract of expectation is drawn up between each supervisor and student. This will include task objectives and their relative importance, a brief statement of possible outcomes, and a list of special needs such as computer access, materials and workshop facilities.

v)   The assessment procedure begins immediately: the student is required to submit a work plan and maintain a log-book or diary. Part of the supervisor's form for assessment used in the School of Engineering at Bath University[18] and based on a six-point scale, is included at Appendix A.

vi)   Students are required to present a verbal paper on their work after an appropriate period of time, say two terms if the project is due to last a year. This is assessed and counts towards the final grading.

vii) Students are provided with instructions in the form of a hand-out on how to present a final report.

viii) The draft manuscript of the final report is handed out to the supervisor who criticises and assesses it.

ix)   The final report is submitted and assessed.

x)   Assessments are moderated (see p. 225).

    This method can be very effective if carefully applied, but its success depends upon a clear understanding between supervisors and students of the objectives of project work and the expected outcomes[18, 26, 27, 28].

Assessment related to objectives

    For this method the objectives of the project work need to be clearly specified; these may include cognitive, affective and psychomotor aspects[6]. A possible routine for such a method could be as follows:

i)   Define clearly the objectives of the project work (see p. 205).

ii) Decide on the weighting of the marks to be allotted to each objective.

iii) Provide the students and supervisors with either complete or simplified versions of (i) and (ii).

iv) Students carry out the projects under the supervision of their tutors.

v) A questionnaire is designed (see Appendix B) requiring answers by supervisors on a yes/no basis. The questions relate to the students' attainment of the objectives enumerated in (i) above.

vi) The questionnaire is distributed to all assessors/supervisors for completion.

vii) Marks are allocated in accordance with the weightings in (ii).

viii) Assessments are moderated (see p. 225).

This method tends to produce a distribution of marks with a concentration on the high side; it also leads to a somewhat stereotyped approach. The questions included in Appendix B have obvious limitations and the method leaves little room for subjective interpretarion [26, 29].

Ranking

The previous methods, because of their clear-cut specification and comprehensiveness, tend to produce project marks at the higher end of the spectrum. If a more uniform distribution is required covering the whole mark range available, the contract and objective methods have undoubted limitations. One way of obtaining a wide range of marks is to design deliberately an assessment procedure to give such a distribution. This is the principle underlying Ranking. A possible routine for this method might be:

i) Each assessor quickly assesses the projects and their reports and places them in three groups: the top ten per cent of students, the bottom ten per cent, and a middle group comprising the rest.

ii) A moderation procedure is then carried out (see p. 225).

iii) The number of students in the top and bottom groups are then adjusted on the basis of the moderation.

iv) The remaining projects and their reports are now sub-divided into three further groups, for example, 20 per cent, 40 per cent and 30 per cent, or in some other agreed proportions.

v)   A further moderation is carried out.

vi) Further sub-divisions can be used if finer differences are required.

vii) The groups are now allocated their final marks.

This method has the advantage of producing a range of marks approaching a normal distribution. It is basically a competitive method in that it discriminates as widely as possible between the performances of different students. However, it allows no comparisons from year to year and gives little useful information or guidance to students when embarking on their projects.

Romantic

This method depends upon an entirely subjective marking system, each assessor using different criteria, or none at all! Clearly, any system which is open to such a wide range of interpretation can cause great difficulties, not least in discriminating between the relative contributions of supervisors and students. The method is also open to criticism on the grounds that different assessors are likely to have greatly differing standards[1]. On the other hand, the advantage claimed for it is that the assessor is not tied to a rigorous quantitative framework and he is therefore able to use his "feel" for the effectiveness of the student's work. An added source of error is that the expectations of the supervisor/assessor will change as the student progresses. One procedure that is claimed to overcome this difficulty is to let the assessor have only the student's final report. Assessment then becomes a measure of the student's ability to communicate what he has done. Although communication may be an important aspect of project work, nevertheless there are other areas of the curriculum under which this can be tested. If this is the only method of assessment employed, it calls into question the need to use a project for the purpose.

Performance

The basis of this method is the selection of a number of specific areas or operational divisions for assessment (see Appendix C). Some possible areas could be:

exposition	—	mathematical accuracy, clarity, literary presentation,
literature	—	evidence of reading basic and unusual sources, understanding of sources,
originality	—	examples cited and constructed, new treatments of standardised results, simple generalisations, original design of or use of equipment,
scope	—	conceptual difficulty, technical difficulty, relationship with previous investigations/studies, relevance of material included, coverage of topic.

Alternatively, a list could be constructed based on behavioural characteristics such as personal qualities, resourcefulness, creative thinking, perseverance, initiative and ability to work in a team.

It will be clear from this type of catalogue that any such assessment model is inevitably limited in its scope. Certain features appear under more than one heading. For example, "evidence of reading", "examples cited", "relationship with previous investigations/studies", can give an unintentional bias to mark schemes. The concept of "originality" is also fraught with difficulties in interpretation. Usually, tutors will agree that original work is patently obvious and confined to the rare few; but it is the bulk of students about whom more detailed information is required. Perhaps some sort of profile of abilities is required so that the really diligent, hard-working, well-read student can be discriminated more clearly from the innovative, rather lazy genius?

In order to operate the Performance method of assessment, two prerequisites are necessary—the clarification of the areas to be assessed and the weighting of marks to be applied to each[4]. A possible routine could be as follows:

i) Supervisors and assessors list possible areas for assessment.

ii) An agreed list of operational divisions and mark weightings is drawn up (see Appendix C).

iii) The method of assessing each operational division is agreed.

iv) Assessors use the methods and weightings to assess the students' projects.

v) Assessments are moderated (see p. 225).

Comparison of the five methods of assessment

In the previous pages we have attempted to describe some of the characteristics of project work and means by which it can be assessed. The fact that it is used so widely as a method of teaching science in higher education presupposes certain expectations in relation to assessment. These in turn raise a number of questions. Thus it is assumed that the purpose of projects is to develop and test students' abilities outside the normal range covered by examinations, practical work and course work. It follows that we would not expect marks gained for projects to correlate closely with those obtained from other examinations, thus indicating that we are measuring other student attributes. However, such marks, when added to the total accumulated from other sources, will tend to cause a regression to the middle of the overall scale, thus reducing discrimination for classification purposes. Comparable problems arise if projects are assessed in a rank order when it comes to adding their contribution to other marks. Again, could project work be allotted a fixed percentage of a student's possible score? If so, on what basis should that percentage be determined?

To varying extents, these are questions common to all methods of project assessment. Perhaps we may appreciate their implications more clearly by itemising the five methods of assessment in subjective terms.

Method	Advantages	Disadvantages
Contracts	Student knows the objectives.	Marks tend to bunch at the top of the scale.
	Supervisor and student can communicate easily.	
	Changes in expectation are recorded.	
	Appears to motivate most students.	
	Assessment is closely related to learning experience.	

Objectives	Students and supervisors are able to determine what is required. Both are working together towards a common goal: the objectives.	Relationship between student performance and marks is rather artificial.
	Motivates some students but not all.	Communication between supervisor and student can be limited to "beating the system".
	Different assessors have similar standards.	Little room for subjective interpretation.
	Easy to compare one year with the next.	Marks tend to bunch at the top of the scale.
	Assessment is related to learning.	
Ranking	A clear distribution of marks can be obtained.	There is no relationship between different student performances other than on a competitive basis.
	Motivates those students who can adapt to this rather unstructured method of learning.	There is no clear expectation for supervisor or student.
	Similarities between different assessors' grades.	The value of communication between supervisor and student is limited unless the supervisor knows the relative performance of other competitors.
		No motivation for poorer students.
Romantic	The supervisor has a completely free hand.	There is no basis for standards or comparability.
	Motivation level is high for a small proportion of students.	Communication tends to be directed towards getting a good project result (so that the supervisor appears in a favourable light?)
		Tendency for other assessors to examine the supervisor's contribution rather than that of the student.
		Changes in expectation continually occur

Performance	Easy to relate assessment to specific areas such as exposition, literature consulted, originality and scope.	The distribution of marks is unpredictable.
	Marks are allocated for a specific product or process.	Deflects students' attention from basic objectives to the end processes and products.
	Allows some subjective interpretation.	Unlikely to give any evidence of the effectiveness of projects in developing such characteristics as personal traits.
		Tendency to assess the same items more than once.

Assessment of group projects

As we pointed out earlier (p. 203), in project work there is a tendency for tutors to require students to work individually rather than in groups. One of the principal reasons for this is that grouping tends to create problems in assessment.[1, 9] In fact, students will seldom if ever work entirely on their own since they will need to communicate frequently with their supervisor. Moreover, there is bound to be, in varying degree, interchange between the students themselves. On grounds of economy in staff and facilities, there is much to be said for the group project. It also has the added advantage over the individual investigation that it helps to develop in students the readiness and ability to co-operate with others. University departments where habitual use is made of group projects make light of the problems of discriminative assessment, for instance by requiring that a detailed schedule of work be submitted for each group and a statement signed by the participants of the part played by each member.

Mixing methods of assessment

From the previous account it will be seen that each method of assessment has its strengths and weaknesses. Most systems in operation are a mixture of more than one method, for there seems little doubt that a scheme which helps students and supervisors to communicate more effectively, but which leaves a margin for subjective impressions within specified areas, provides a useful compromise. Some departments emphasise fairness to students by instituting a viva voce examination on the project similar to that for higher degrees, and allowing a possible adjustment of the total marks as a result. In others only the reports are marked. However, it is difficult to prescribe an ideal mix to cover all circumstances, for as we have already seen, project work varies greatly in its manifestations, while the preferences of departments and individuals play a powerful part in deciding what in projects should be assessed and how.

7. Moderation procedures

Project assessment usually requires more than one assessor and in a large department, may involve a considerable number. As a prelude to obtaining the final marks, the standards of marking by the different assessors must be equated and appropriate adjustments made for variations where necessary. This is the process of moderation which usually involves only departmental tutors but, in universities, may involve one or more External Examiners.

In carrying out moderation, two basic procedures are possible—continuous and end point moderation.

Continuous moderation

This system requires the use of two assessors, one usually being the supervisor and the other independent. Each assessor works with two or more different supervisors and vice versa. The procedure can operate either with the second assessor being brought in at certain fixed phases of the assessment, as in the contracts assessment method, or only at the end. In either event, where a specific mark scheme is in operation, both assessors must use the same system. Each project is assessed by the assessors individually and their data compared. Where small discrepancies occur the mean can be taken; where large differences exist the assessors must discuss them in detail. If they are unable to resolve their differences the Head of Department or External Examiner can act as arbitrator.

A problem often occurs when five point scales are used. This is best illustrated by taking an example based on a project assessment scheme using five grades and four criteria. The sample is 65 students so 260 grades are to be allocated to the four criteria by pairs of assessors using continuous moderation. The resulting distribution is shown below in Table 1.

Grade	Criterion	1	2	3	4	Total
A (Distinction)		1	4	4	2	11
B (Good)		25	32	24	24	105
C (Pass)		29	25	26	23	103
D (Border)		9	4	11	13	37
C (Fail)		1	0	0	3	4
Total		65	65	65	65	260

Table 1. Distribution of grades allocated to 65 students

From the table the following points emerge,
i)   only four students were judged to be failures on any criterion
ii)   the heaviest weighting was given to Criterion 2 which shows the least distribution.
iii) most assessors used a two or three point scale
iv)   105 ratings were given as B (good) out of 260 possible ones.

It is clear that the assessors tended to play safe just above the middle of the range, giving a heavily skewed distribution of grades. The final project grades will have even less distribution because students gaining A grades on one criterion may finish with a B grade overall, similarly students with only one E may end with a C grade. As can be seen nearly all students will end up with Grades B or C. The problem is common for this kind of moderation procedure which tends to provide a low level of discrimination.

End point moderation

Each assessor marks his allotted number of projects and an appropriate number of moderators is provided, say one per 30 students. The moderator quickly reads and/or views the projects, sorting them into three categories:
i)   the best   (about 3)
ii)   the worst   (about 3)
iii) the middle   (about 24)

Where several moderators are involved, they must compare their samples of the best and worst in order to determine standards.

The procedure is now repeated for the middle group, splitting these into say 6, 12, 6 students. Again, if there is more than one moderator, samples must be compared.

The moderator assigns no marks to the reports or projects, the basic assumption of this method being that the supervisor is in the better position to rank students in his own area of expertise, but the moderator is the better able to compare one supervisor's students with another's.

Two alternatives are now possible—the moderator can assume a ranking role and produce a distribution covering the whole mark range, or he can proceed according to the scheme outlined below. Table 2 represents a typical situation requiring the moderation of six student projects.

The assessor fills in columns 1 and 2, and the moderator completes column 5. The moderator now has frequencies for all grades—3 for grade 2, and 1 each for grades 3, 4, 5. These grades are now distributed in column 3 in the order that the assessor ranked the students. Where the grades only disagree by one, the assessor's grade is used. When the discrepancy is greater then one one of the following alternatives is possible:

Student (1)	Assessor's Score (/34) (2)	Assessor's Moderated Grades (3)	Frequency (4)	Moderator's Grades (5)
e	30	2		2
d	29	2	3	3
a	28	2		2
f	26	3	1	2
c	25	4	1	5
b	25	5	1	4

Table 2. Moderation of six student projects

i)   to check the student's report along with the supervisor's:
ii) to check the detailed assignment of grades/marks;
iii) to discuss the work with the student and/or supervisor.

In the event of option (iii) being adopted, it is desirable to prepare specific questions in advance rather than allow a general discussion to take place. If none of these alternatives succeeds in resolving the problem, it can be referred to the arbitration of the

External Examiner. No matter what methods are selected, it is important that adequate records be kept of all moderation procedures, including discussions with students and supervisors.

8. Relationship between Project Marks and Examination Marks

It has been suggested in the previous sections on assessment that the marks awarded for projects may be higher than those awarded for examinations. In Figure 1 a distribution has been plotted (using 5 per cent intervals) showing the difference in marks between

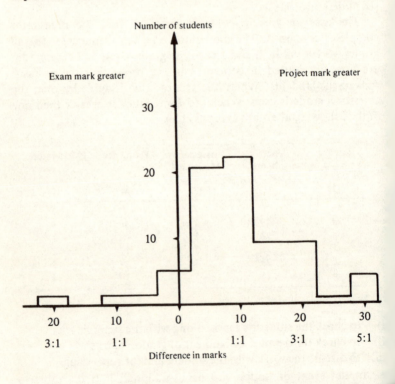

Ratio of marks (examination : project) to give a 5% gain/loss in total from the project.

Fig. 1. Comparison of examination and project marks for Engineering students (N = 76).

projects and examinations in an Engineering Department. The sample represents 76 students; 68 have a higher mark on the project, 3 have a higher score in examinations (shown as a negative difference) and 5 have the same marks. Some of the differences are quite large with 4 students having a mark 30 per cent greater on the project than on the examination.

However these differences are only part of the picture, the key to the relationship being the weighting given to the project when compared with the examination. Table 3 below shows the effects on the final mark using various weightings:

It can be seen that even with a 5:1 ratio student A has gained little benefit from his project relative to student D. At a ratio of 7:1, which was used in the Engineering Department concerned, the effort put in by staff and students seems of doubtful value for classification purposes when candidates A and E ultimately have the same mark. The system is heavily biased in favour of the 3 candidates (Figure 1) with higher marks in the examination.

Student	Examination mark (a)	Project mark (b)	1:1	2:1	3:1	4:1	5:1	6:1	7:1
					Final mark. (Ratio a:b)				
A	50	80	65	60	58	56	55	54	54
B	50	70	60	57	55	54	53	53	52
C	50	60	55	53	52	52	52	51	51
D	50	20	35	40	43	44	45	46	46
E	54	50	52	53	53	53	53	53	54

Table 3. The effects of different weightings (all marks are shown as percentages)

For a gain of 5 per cent in the final mark relative to the project mark, a ratio of 3:1 would require a 20 per cent greater mark on the project, but for a ratio of 7:1 the student would need a mark on the project which is 40 per cent greater. With a 7:1 ratio it can be seen that the chances of a change in classification of degree attributable to project work are very small. The ratios shown in Figure 1 are at the mark differences which will provide a gain or loss of 5 per cent on total marks attributable to the project mark.

A similar effect is found for a Pharmacy Department, the results being reproduced in Figure 2. In this sample of 53 students, 37 have higher marks in the project than in the examination. The differences are similar to the previous example but with a smaller

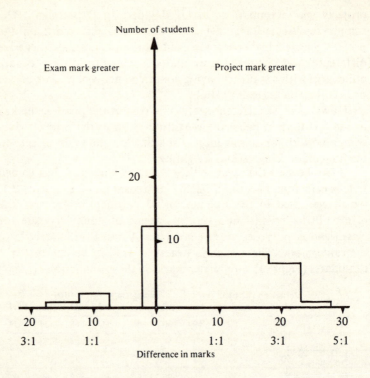

Ratio of marks (examination : project) to give a 5% gain/loss in total from the project.

Fig. 2. Comparison of examination and project marks for Pharmacy students (N = 53).

range of variation, nevertheless there are students with a difference greater than 20 per cent. The ratio is used in this instance for examinations: projects is 17:3, and only two students show a gain of over 2.5 per cent on the total which is attributable to the project. Once again the system is heavily biased in favour of the three candidates who had a higher examination mark than project mark. Even with a small change in weighting, two of those three students would probably have been awarded a lower degree.

On many university courses students spend a large proportion of their time in their final year on project work. Yet ratios for the marks given for examinations and projects are typified by the following:—

Engineering 7:1; Chemical Engineering 7:1; Physics 6:1; Pharmacy 6:1; Architecture 1:2.

Apparently, Architects are the only academics in this group who have any real confidence in the role of the project in contributing to the overall assessment of students.

A more statistical approach to the problem of weighting is to consider the correlations between the examination marks and the project marks. Using a product moment correlation the figure for the Engineering Department quoted was 0.35 and for the Pharmacy Department 0.15. This means that for the Engineers only about 40 per cent of those who were in the top quartile for examinations would have been in the top quartile for projects, and similarly for the bottom quartile: for the Pharmacists the percentage would have been about 30 (i.e. there are nearly equal chances of students being found in each quartile).

Another measure of weighting that can be used[30] is to calculate a ratio for the proportion of time spent by the student on a project to the proportion of marks given for the project. Ratios as high as 2:1 or higher are found using this basis of computation, which only emphasizes the extent to which the project can be deliberately devalued as an assessment procedure. Perhaps the real question is: do you trust the project mark as an indicator of student ability in preference to the conventional formal examination?

9. Some Unanswered Questions

In the preceding pages we have posed, at least by implication, a fundamental question concerning the use of project work. Should projects be regarded primarily as a contribution to student assessment or as a means of teaching and learning, or as a mixture of both? As we have seen in Sections 6-7, there are many ways of assessing projects and moderating them. But all too often the credit accorded to students for project work bears little relation to the time and energy expended on it and to marks gained in other ways. The essence of any good assessment scheme is that it should be seen to be just by both students and staff alike, be closely related to course objectives, provide appropriate incentives and be sufficiently sensitive to discern differences in attainment between one student and another. Judged by these criteria, project assessment has certainly made headway but it still has some distance to go, for instance in the introduction of more realistic methods of mark weighting and moderation. As we have repeatedly emphasized, the setting up and management of student project work is not easy, and there may well be a case for special instruction, not only of students before they begin their projects, but also for supervisory staff as well.

On the intellectual side it is clear that projects should not be looked upon primarily as a road to the acquisition of specialized factual knowledge, but rather as a means of generating certain attitudes, and of acquiring and practising new skills. But many of the elements of a project can be taught and assessed just as readily by other means; for example, simulation can be used in problems of design by means of computer programmes. Moreover, it is a common experience among those who supervise undergraduate projects that some students adapt to them far more readily than others, while a few find great difficulty in coming to terms with them at all. Should we be exploring possible alternative methods of catering for such students for whom the need to undertake project work may well be doing a disservice? Perhaps such difficulties could be overcome to some extent through a more widespread use of group projects. Requiring students to work as a team can undoubtedly help to promote a "real life" situation and a better understanding of what collaboration with others really involves, but it brings with it corresponding difficulties where the need for assessment arises.

It may well be that the most important justification for the lavish expenditure of resources on projects derives from the area of personal relations and understanding that can develop between tutors and students, and between the students themselves. Much of the research that has been carried out so far on the effectiveness of projects has been of a comparative nature with other methods of learning. In particular, comparisons have been used on the retention of individual facts or areas of knowledge. When the aims of projects were outlined earlier (p. 205) the acquisition of factual knowledge played a relatively insignificant part. The curious paradox that such research has tended to be devoted to areas that are relatively atypical perhaps explains why, as yet, we have only an incomplete idea of what this unique method of teaching and learning really achieves.

ACKNOWLEDGEMENTS

We would like to thank the following for critical comments and suggestions: Mr. D.W. Clemson, Mr. J.I. Harris, Dr. W.H. Humphreys, Mr. P.J. McMahon and Dr. P.H. Redfern. We are also grateful to Miss Sheila Hones for conducting a literature search and to Mrs. I. Irving and Mrs. J. Steer for preparing the typescript.

REFERENCES

1. ADDERLEY, K, *et al* (1975) *Project Methods in Higher Education,* London, Society for Research into Higher Education.

2. STEVENSON, J.A. (1921) *The Project Method of Teaching,* New York, MacMillan.

3. DOWDESWELL, W.H. (1970) "Are Projects Worthwhile?" Educational Technology Bulletin *4* 1-3 (University of Bath).

4. NUFFIELD FOUNDATION, (1973) "Mini Projects in Metallurgy". *Newsletter, 1,* 14. Group for Research and Innovation in Higher Education.

5. NUFFIELD FOUNDATION, (1974) "Project Assessment in Physics and Mechanical Engineering". *Newsletter, 4,* 37. Group for Research and Innovation in Higher Education.

6. BLIGH, D.A. (1975) *Teaching Students,* Exeter, Exeter University Teaching Service.

7. HEWTON, E. (1975) "Project Work in Universities", *Physics Education, 10,* 20-24.

8. KRATHWOHL, D.R. *et al* (1964) *Taxonomy of Educational Objectives, 2,* London, Longmans.

9. HARDING, A.G. (1973) "The Project: Its Place as a Learning Situation", *British Journal of Educational Technology, 4,* 216-32.

10. DEWEY, J. (1916) *Democracy and Education. An Introduction to the Philosophy of Education,* New York, MacMillan.

11. BROCK, W.H. (Ed) (1973) *H.E. Armstrong and the Teaching of Science, 1880-1930.* Cambridge, Cambridge University Press.

12. NUFFIELD FOUNDATION, (1974) "Heurism". *Newsletter 5,* 14. Group for Research and Innovation in Higher Education.

13. KELLY, P.J. (1975) "Nuffield A-Level Biological Science Project", in SCHOOLS COUNCIL *Evaluation in Curriculum Development: Twelve Case Studies.* London, MacMilland (pp 91-109).

14. HARDING, A.G. (1973) "The Objectives and Structures of Undergraduate Projects". *British Journal of Educational Technology, 4,* 94-105.

15. MORGAN, A.S. (1976) "Learning through Projects". *Studies in Higher Education, 1,* 63-68.

16. TRIBUS, M. (1971) "Education for Innovation". *Engineering Education, 61 (5),* 421-423.

17. HARRIS, N.D.C. (Ed) (1975) Editorial (including summary of project aims in seven disciplines at Bath University), *Educational Services Bulletin, 13,* 29-37. University of Bath.

18. BLACK, J. (1975) "Allocation and Assessment of Project Work in the Final Year of the Engineering Degree Course in the University of Bath". *Assessment in Higher Education, 1,* 35-53.

19. MIDDENDORF, W.H. (1971) "Pacing Engineering Design Projects". *Engineering Education, 61* (6), 532-3.

20. LANCASTER, O.E. *et al* (1974) *Effective Teaching and Learning,* New York, Gordon and Breach. (p. 157).

21. JENKINS, D.E.P. (1972) "Group Projects in Engineering", in UNIVERSITY TEACHING METHODS UNIT *Varieties of Group Discussion in University Teaching,* London, University of London Institute of Education.

22. BLOOM, B.S. (1956) *Taxonomy of Educational Objectives, 1.* London, Longmans.

23. CORNWALL, M.G. (1975) "Authority v Experience in Higher Education", *Universities Quarterly, 29* (3), 272-298.

24. TCHETVERIKOV, V.N. (1976) "New Forms of Higher Education in the USSR" in ZEILER, H. (Ed) *New Forms of Higher Education in Europe Bucharest, CEPES.*

25. MANSELL, T. (1973) "Project Work in the Final Year of the Physics Course in the Department of Physics at Bristol University". NUFFIELD FOUNDATION, *Studies in Laboratory Innovation.* Group for Research and Innovation in Higher Education.

26. BLACK, P.J. (1972). "Group Discussion in the Planning and Reporting of Projects" in UNIVERSITY TEACHING METHODS UNIT: *Varieties of Group Discussion in University Teaching.* London, University of London Institute of Education.

27. DEERE, M.T. (1974) "The Assessment of Project Work" in MACINTOSH, H.G. (Ed) *Techniques and Problems of Assessment,* London, Arnold (pp 102-145).

28. TRICKER, B.J.K. & DOWDESWELL, W.H. (1970) *Projects in Biological Science* London, Penguin (Nuffield Advanced Science Series).

29. BRUNER, J. (1976) "Beyond the Information Given" in ENTWISTLE, N. and HOUNSELL, D. (Ed) *How Students Learn,* Lancaster, Institute for Research and Development in Post-Compulsory Education, Lancaster University.

30. HARDING, A.G. (1971) *The Objectives and Assessment of Undergraduate Projects,* Unpublished M.A. Thesis, University of Exeter.

Appendix A   ASSESSMENT BASED ON A CONTRACT

UNIVERSITY OF BATH	FINAL YEAR PROJECT	PROJECT MEMO
SCHOOL OF ENGINEERING	GRADING ASSESSMENT PROFILE	NO.

STUDENT'S NAME:

PROJECT TITLE:

NO.

Supervisors should enter their grading of the student's performance under these headings:
they should indicate where they are inapplicable, and add any special aspects in section 4.
The items are not weighted, so there is no requirement to convert the gradings into marks.

O = Outstanding   E = Excellent   G = Good   S = Satisfactory   P = Poor
I = Inadequate

1. CARRYING-OUT	O	E	G	S	P	I	COMMENTS
1.1 _Approach_							
Exploration & enquiry							
Literature & background search							
Setting objectives							
Preparation of programme							
1.2 _Implementation_							
Decisions on test facilities & instrumentation							
Design of rigs and apparatus							
Building & commissioning rigs							
Setting-up calibration							
1.3 _Experiments_							
Logical planning							
Accuracy & relevance of measurements							
Overcoming difficulties							
Modifications during progress							
1.4 _Computing_							
Modelling							
Programming							
Analysis							
Presentation							

	O	E	G	S	P	I	COMMENTS
1.5 *Evaluation*							
Study of previous theories							
Prediction based on theory							
Analysis of experimental results							
Relation between theory & results							
1.6 *Log-book*							
Maintained as instructed							
Standard of entries							
2. *MANUSCRIPT DRAFT REPORT*							
Structure of report							
Clarity of argument							
Balance of sections							
Validity of results							
Justification of conclusions							
Details; figures; titles; reference							
Achievement of objectives							
3. *FINAL REPORT*							
Response to criticism of draft							
Lay-out of report							
Standard of execution							
Style							
4. *SPECIAL ASPECTS*							

5.   *SUPERVISOR'S COMMENTS ON STUDENT'S PERFORMANCE & ATTITUDES*

e.g. Response to advice and criticism, initiative, determination to succeed, dependence on instruction, powers of innovation, enthusiasm, perseverance

MARKS ALLOCATION

Carrying-out	(50%)	%
Log-book	(5%)	%
Draft report	(30%)	%
Final report	(15%)	%

Appendix B   ASSESSMENT RELATED TO OBJECTIVES

This form will require answers of YES or NO to the questions listed below for each of the chosen experiments and project. Spaces will be included for reference to specific points in the journal and report, and other comments.

1.   Has the candidate elicited any valid hypothesis from any set of observations ?

2.   Has the candidate shown mathematical ability in the formulation or moderation of hypothesis ?

3.   Has the candidate shown initiative in deciding the experimental procedures to be adopted ?

4.   Has the candidate shown initiative in devising or assembling experimental apparatus ?

5.   Has the candidate shown any understanding of the relative importance of the various experimental errors incurred in the course of this work ?

6.   Has the candidate discussed alternative approaches or solutions ?

7.   Did the candidate independently formulate the problem in a manner appropriate for its solution ?

8.   Does the candidate both show any recognition of any implicit assumptions (e.g. recognition of the limitations of physical laws) and assess their importance ?

9.   Has the candidate made a valid critique of his work ?

10.   Has the candidate been skilful or resourceful or thorough in the application of established design, craft or assembly procedures, or in the methodical (or statistical) handling of results ?

11.   Did the candidate make a significant contribution to the work plan ?

12.   Has the candidate used the work plan with intelligence ?

13.   Has the candidate made use of and indicated relevant and independent sources of information available to him?(e.g. has he consulted books to which he was not directed ?)

14.   Is the final report both clear and complete ?

Appendix C   **ASSESSMENT BASED ON PERFORMANCE**

Project Assessment Form

Name of tutor
completing the form

Number of students

		Operational Divisions								
		(I)	(II)	(III)	(IV)	(V)	(VI)	(VII)	(VIII)	
No.	Candidate's name	Statement of problem	Selection of topic for investigation	Investigation of background knowledge	Planning of procedure	Recording	Inference from practical work	Relating inferences to background knowledge: suggestions for further investigation	Bibliography and acknowledgements	TOTAL GRADE SCORE

Appendix D   **ASSESSMENT BASED ON MULTIPLE CHOICE QUESTIONS**

Criteria with respect to the project

PLANNING   Grade

In planning the project the candidate:
recognised relevant factors, discussed their importance
sensibly, drew up detailed specification in practical terms
and mapped out a reasoned plan of campaign   3

as above but lacked one feature   2

made some attempt to analyse the problem in
practical terms   1

made little attempt to analyse the problem   0

EXECUTION

In executing the plan the candidate:
gave thorough consideration to realistic alternatives at
every stage, and made a reasoned selection of the
optimum solution in each case   3

gave consideration to realistic alternative solutions with
inadequate reasons for selection   2

gave some attention to the consideration of alternative
solutions   1

paid little attention to this aspect of the work   0

DESIGN ACTIVITY

In relation to the design for all or part of the project with
respect to procedure or artefact the candidate produced:
a markedly significant and original contribution to   3
an original contribution   2

a new device by applying a standard design technique   1

little or no design activity during his work on the project   0

USE OF RESOURCES

In relation to the resources and time available the candidate:
used them well throughout the project   3

used them reasonably well for much of the project   2

failed to make reasonable use of them over significant periods
of the project   1

made little use of them throughout the project   0

CRITICAL REVIEW

In comparing the final product or outcome with the original
specifications the candidate has produced:
a thorough and objective discussion in which consideration has
been given to all major aspects of the work including suggestions
for further development and a critical appraisal of the conduct
of the project with a clear indication of the lessons learnt   3

a reasonable depth of discussion which, however, lacks either
objectivity or coverage   2

some significant comparison   1

a discussion of little significance   0

PERSONAL CONTRIBUTION

In planning, executing and appraising the project the candidate:
exercised initiative throughout   3

lacked initiative and judgement at times   2

made little personal contribution   1

relied entirely on external help   0

A Challenge for Interdisciplinary Science

V.M. Showalter

1. A Challenge for Interdisciplinary Science

One hundred years ago the problems of educating a fledgling scientist or a novice physician or a person aspiring to some other endeavor requiring a university education, were relatively easy especially in terms of science. For the neophyte scientist, all that was required was to teach him the contents of six textbooks and apprentice him to a real scientist. The aspiring physician studied three or four of those same textbooks and was then apprenticed to a practising physician. The education citizen-to-be studied the same texts as the physicians but tended to forget what he learned.

Since then, things have changed. The amount of scientific knowledge has expanded at an ever increasing rate and it has become necessary to make some compromises with what had been regarded as a "complete" education in science relative to the aspirations of the individual. To educate the scientist, the compromise was to direct the person into specialized sub-divisions of science. The overall effect was to cause individuals to learn more and more about less and less as the specializations became ever more narrow. If this trend is projected a few more decades, it would seem that the freshly graduated scientist would soon know everything about nothing.

At the other extreme, the trend for liberally educated non-scientist graduates seems to have been to learn less and less about more and more. In this case, the ultimate end may be to know nothing about everything, which is equally undesirable.

For physicians and other professions that use science in general, the trend seems to be to learn the same things as a hundred years ago with a few topics, such as DNA and nuclear fission, thrown in to give the appearance of modernity.

One of the consequences of these trends is that many scientists have come to view their work as completely separate from the concerns of non-scientists, the professionals, *and* scientists in other fields of specialization. To most people in the 1960's, this situation was natural because everyone "knew" that Newtons and Humbolts could not occur because of the sheer mass of existing scientific knowledge.

A further complication in the general problem is that most universities and colleges now admit a much more diverse student body. The diversity of students is reflected in broader ranges of abilities, aspirations, favoured learning styles, previous experience, etc.

The present situation clearly calls for serious reconsideration of the classic question, "What knowledge is of most worth?" Probably the most promising approach to providing significantly new answers to this question are those that involve interdisciplinary thought.

For those science educators interested primarily in preparing scientists, the push to interdisciplinary thinking has been accelerated by several emerging realities of the career scientist's life. First of all, an increasingly significant amount of contemporary research is being conducted by teams of scientists representing diverse fields of specialization and dealing with problems that are not easily identified with any pure specialization. Secondly, it seems that any new scientist can look forward to changing his field of speciality at least once in his career as new areas of research open and old ones close in terms of available support money. Thus, there is a need to educate scientists with a speciality but also with sufficient cognitive and affective links to other disciplines to enable the kind of flexibility demanded by the future.

For those science educators primarily interested in the science education of non-scientists, exposure to introductory courses in two or three of the specialized sciences does not seem particularly appropriate in view of the very large number of sciences many of which are more directly relevant to the citizen than those that had been taught traditionally. Philosophy of science courses might provide a desirable level of generality to serve the educated citizen but these courses too had developed their own peculiar levels of specialization and abstraction that eliminate much of the nitty-gritty of science from the courses.

Although the problems of overspecialization and solutions in interdisciplinary approaches seem intuitively right, science educators have found it difficult to establish clearly defined goals and objectives for the new approaches. The problem is even more acute for the scientist-to-be because most suggestions for interdisciplinary approaches seem to be accompanied by lowered levels of "quality" and "rigour" even though these concepts are rather difficult to define in operational terms.

The concept of "scientific literacy" has been invoked frequently in the past decade as the primary goal of an educational programme in science to meet the needs of non-science majors. Since specialization in science is, in itself, no guarantee of scientific literacy, some educators have suggested that the concept also has usefulness for guiding development of programmes for science majors assuming that adequate rigour can be maintained.

For many years the concept of scientific literacy was inadequately described in terms of just what is constituted. One of the few efforts to synthesize a comprehensive yet functionally concise statement of scientific literacy components was made by the Centre for Unified Science Education and was based largely on consensus derived from a diverse collection of articles and books extant in 1974. The statement exists as a "working document" and contains seven dimensions of scientific literacy. Each dimension is explicated by ten to thirty "factors" which represent the core of each dimension. The dimensions are:

I. *The scientifically literate person understands the nature of scientific knowledge.*

II. *The scientifically literate person accurately applies*

appropriate science concepts, principles, laws, and theories in interacting with his universe.

III.   *The scientifically literate person uses processes of science in solving problems, making decisions, and furthering his own understanding of the universe.*

IV.   *The scientifically literate person interacts with the various aspects of his universe in a way that is consistent with the values that underlie science.*

V.   *The scientifically literate person understands and appreciates the joint enterprise of science and technology and the inter-relationships of these with each other and with other aspects of society.*

VI.   *The scientifically literate person has developed a richer, more satisfying, and more exciting view of the universe as a result of his science education and continues to extend his education throughout his life.*

VII. *The scientifically literate person has developed numerous manipulative skills associated with science and technology.*

There is not much literature beyond the scientific literacy document that can be used to provide a guiding framework for the development of interdisciplinary science in the great variety of tertiary institutions around the world. And yet, there is a general feeling that interdisciplinary approaches to science curriculum should be useful in most if not all situations. The lack of a proper theory to work with or from, is a common shortcoming of education in general. Maybe this void can be filled on a local needs basis until something like a universal theory is developed if that is possible.

A local theory to be used in guiding interdisciplinary curriculum development could consist of a series of statements or guidelines outlining the goals, beliefs, constraints, premises, and principles on which the local group can agree. The next step would be to forge ahead and try developing some interdisciplinary courses. Following some type of evaluation, the working guidelines would be substantiated and/or modified and the loop repeated.

The purpose of this paper is to provide a kind of vicarious experience base for the reader that will be useful in pursuing interdisciplinary science further whether the reader is starting at ground zero or has already been involved in an interdisciplinary effort.

Part 2 is intended to identify and define operationally the elements of interdisciplinary science that are useful in thinking about educational programmes. Part 3 contains descriptions of six generalized exemplars of interdisciplinary courses or programs. Part 4 identifies eight crucial questions that need to be answered locally in connection with any interdisciplinary effort along with some selected comments relative to each question. The key questions have been derived from a large number of reports and articles on case histories of actual interdisciplinary efforts.

There is a tendency for any thoughtful person immersed in a given specialized science discipline to argue that his or her discipline is somehow *the* one that brings all the others together in a sensible way. These arguments are always cogent and well reasoned. However, productive interdisciplinary thought requires that we try to set aside these biases in the quest for educational goals shared by all who work in the name of science. The challenge of interdisciplinary thought for all science educators is to find common goals and pervasive ideas and use them to develop improved courses, programmes, and other learning experiences in science so that the contribution of science and its value in the world of tomorrow can be maximized.

2. Terminology for Interdisciplinary Science Teaching

One of the frustrating realities of working with education innovations is that the terminology involved is inconsistent from one locale to another. Some linguists insist that creative thought depends on terminology that is relatively imprecise. For many scientist-educators, such looseness is contrary to their usual way of thinking and so most try to start their thinking about interdisciplinary courses and programmes with working definitions of key terms.

In spite of several noteworthy attempts to standardize terminology used in thinking and communicating about interdisciplinary courses and programmes, there are no universally accepted definitions. The problem is that different people use the same term to mean differing things and also use different terms to mean the same thing.

The next few pages of this paper are devoted to establishing some working definitions that will be used in the remainder of the paper. These working definitions are not set forth in the usual dictionary style because the discussion will also serve to set the stage for subsequent sections and therefore includes definitions for basic elements of the university teacher-learning situation as well as for terms needed to differentiate various aspects of inter-disciplinarity.

"Student" is taken to mean a person enrolled in a degree programme in a post-secondary institution of higher learning. Ordinarily this person will be 18-25 years old and will be pursuing a baccalaureate or higher degree. He or she may be designated either as a "Major" or "non-major" in a science or science related field.

"Teacher" is a person with responsibility to direct and catalyze the learning of one or more students. The teacher may lecture but ordinarily invokes additional methods and may even act as a co-learner with students from time to time. An implicit responsibility of the teacher is to establish, usually in collaboration with one or more colleagues, goals or objectives expected of students, and to evaluate individual's achievement of these.

"Programme" refers to the combination of learning experiences that are prescribed for the student prior to receiving a certain degree or certification. Ordinarily, the components of a programme are courses but may be specified as competencies to be met by working with a given teacher or group of teachers in a less formal organizational structure.

A "course" is an administrative structure of convenience which ordinarily brings a group of students together at regular intervals and which is presided over by one or more teachers. Typically, the course sessions involve 30-60 hours of direct interaction between the teacher(s) and involved students and may be spread over as little as two weeks or as many as 18 weeks. Some "courses" may be sequential and extend over a period of a year or more. Courses may be either required or optional (elective) for specific degree programmes.

A "unit" is a subdivision of a course and may consist of a topic or chapter or be organized around some other conceptual theme that is consistent with the course. The unit is a convenient entity and may be changed as the course evolves. For some teachers, the course itself is a sufficiently small organizing entity, however, the unit concept seems especially useful when a course is designed by a group. An "activity" is a coherent bit of learning activity that is conducted or experienced within a unit. It may consist of a single lecture or film, or a laboratory exercise, or any one of a variety of possibilities. Two different teachers may teach the same course but use different units and/or activities.

The "purpose" of a programme, course, or unit describes what its designers (i.e. teachers) aspire to accomplish by conducting it. Thus one purpose of the course might be "to show some of the interconnections among the various sciences." A purpose for a unit might be "to explore some of the ways chemistry can be used in improving the environment." It should be noted that these are in teacher terms and specify little if anything about what the students are expected to learn.

"Objectives" are statements describing what students are to learn. They are usually written for and are most useful at the level of courses and/or units. Objectives are written in student terms and may be classed as "general" or "performance." Many heated arguments have taken place on the question of which type of objective is more useful or whether either is of any value. Arguments for performance objectives are usually based on the belief that they provide a concrete basis for evaluation although it must be admitted that there is a tendency for these to proliferate for a given course until there may be a thousand separate objectives each of which is trivial when considered by itself. Arguments for general objectives are usually based on the desirability of a teacher and student having five or six well defined and important but open-ended directions toward which progress should be made. A relatively recent middle position and one that capitalizes on the strengths of both extremes has been established by Gronlund in which each unit or course has several major general objectives in student terms *and* for each of these objectives two or three related performance indicators are specified.

A "realm" is one "way of knowing" as conceived by Philip Phenix and serves to place science in perspective to other of mankind's ways of knowing. Phenix' categories are based on the nature of knowledge and accepted procedures of generating new knowledge. In addition to science ("empirics"), Phenix denotes symbolics, aesthetics, synoptics, ethics, and synnoetics. Although, as with any categorization system, the dividing lines among realms are not always perfectly clear cut, the problem of designing and developing interdisciplinary programmes and courses may be more complicated if boundaries between the realms are crossed. Each realm is characterized by its own epistemology and mixing of these in a single course may be very difficult to resolve especially in the minds of students.

A "discipline" is defined as a subdivision of a realm that is associated with people who label themselves as practitioners of the activities that characterize the discipline. Within the realm of science, a discipline is established by a research tradition which includes such things as one or more journals, university departments, and people who persist in using a professional label derived from the name of the discipline. Thus, the existence of the *Journal of Geology,* many departments of geology, and people who proudly label themselves geologists are taken as conclusive evidence that there is a discipline of geology. The conceptual structure of geology is then taken as the language, procedures, models, research goals, concepts, theories, etc., that geologists use in generating new knowledge and that have been used in generating existing knowledge.

It should be noted that this operational approach to defining a science discipline does not preclude the formation of other disciplines within an older discipine (eg. petrogeology) or of combinations of two or more disciplines to form a separate discipline (eg. geophysics).

"Interdisciplinary" science education, in this paper, is used as an umbrella term to include any one or all of the different ways science disciplines can be used in concert with each other and with disciplines from realms other than science to serve the purposes of educational programmes and courses. Most of the specific interdisciplinary approaches referred to in this paper have their origin and emphasis in science or technical concerns.

In a "co-ordinated" approach, interdisciplinary relationships are acknowledged and promoted between and among separate courses. Thus, a physiology course may acknowledge what students have studied previously or are presently studying in a chemistry course. In fact, teachers of the two courses may have collaborated in planning the two courses. It is possible to have an entire programme result from this approach. Teachers retain their traditional disciplinary identity in teaching the courses resulting from this approach and students are expected to reflect the right professional identity at the appropriate time.

In a "multidisciplinary" approach, several disciplines are brought together in a course and in each of its component units, although a special effort is made to maintain the identity of each discipline as it is used in the course. Often this approach results in a course with several teachers, one for each of the disciplines represented. The students themselves usually retain the identity of their major field in multidisciplinary courses.

In an "integrated" approach the resulting course contains elements from several disciplines but each unit within the course maintains an identity with a certain discipline. On the other hand, the teacher projects no identity with a particular discipline and the students are expected to do the same.

In a "unified" approach, all disciplinary identifications as such are minimized within a unit in favour of certain ideas that characterize all or most of the disciplines within a realm. Thus, each unit within a course may, on a given day, have the external appearance of being associated with a given discipline but in the context of several sessions will be seen as utilizing disciplinary materials or activities as useful vehicles for attaining objectives derived from the whole realm of science.

3. Generalized Exemplars of Interdisciplinary Science Courses and/or Programs

Each of the exemplars in this section has been derived from several existing courses and/or programs. The decision to use generalized exemplars rather than specific examples was based on several reasons. First of all, there are so many well conceived and effective interdisciplinary efforts that to select a few as illustrative examples would be to do an injustice to many. Further reasons for avoiding actual cases are to avoid nationalistic biases and thus give the exemplars greater universal interest among those contemplating interdisciplinary efforts of their own.

The fact that most interdisciplinary courses and programs are in a more or less continuous state of evolutionary change makes any description obsolete almost before it can be written. This state of flux associated with most interdisciplinary efforts seems to be one of the most important factors in the vitality of the effort as all persons involved get caught up in the business of doing something for rational reasons as opposed to institutional reasons. The latter often seems irrational to many progressive teachers and students.

Each of the exemplars was selected to illustrate one aspect of the diversity in interdisciplinary approaches. In reading the exemplar descriptions it must be remembered that the specific course structure and teaching methodology for a given target group will vary from one real life situation to another and that which is given in the exemplar should be viewed as only one workable structure. Certainly this brief collection of six exemplars does not exhaust all possible combinations of target groups, interdisciplinary structures, staffing arrangements, and teaching methodologies.

Alpha University

Natural Science I and II were instituted as a two term sequence of integrated science two years ago. These integrated courses were intended as an option for the first year student who would ordinarily take separate introductory courses in biology, chemistry, and physics. By eliminating repetition and reordering elements of the older courses, it was expected that both student and faculty time would be conserved and that a satisfactory basis would be established for second level courses in the specialized disciplines.

Both science majors and non-majors may select Natural Science with approval of the teaching staff. The teaching staff's approval of individuals desiring to enter the course is required because the staff felt that doing so would help assure the success of the course sequence in its formative years. Since the courses are a departure from tradition, they could be subject to criticism for any shortcoming whatever the real cause, and such criticism could be magnified to the detriment of the courses.

The present teaching staff numbers three, one from each of the departments of physics, biology, and chemistry. These three have done most of the development work on the course and feel they risk criticism from some colleagues in their own departments for taking on this particular assignment. However, the administration of Alpha University has been very supportive of the effort while at the same time emphasizing that the teaching team will need to produce some substantive evaluation data within a few years to support continuation of the courses.

A modest grant from the national government subsidised the first two years of course development and revision. The amount of the grant was equivalent to two staff persons' annual salaries, and was used to buy both staff time and some materials.

The sequence of units in Natural Science I and Natural Science II is: 1—Ecosystems, 2—Macroscopic Aspects of Natural Systems (mechanics, kinetics), 3—Microscopic Aspects of Natural Systems (particles, atomic structure), 4—Aggregate States of Natural Systems (solid, liquid, gas), 5—Elements (bonding, transformations), 6—Molecular Structures (Macromolecules), 7—Cellular Ultrastructure, 8—Chemical Dynamics, 9—Cellular Processes, 10—Organisms (structure, function), 11—Regulatory Processes within Organism, 12—Genetics, 13—Organic Evolution, 14—Origin of Life.

Enrollment in the course numbers around eighty. Lecture sessions are conducted for one hour in a well equipped lecture hall four times per week. Four separate recitation groups meet for one hour each week. Each teacher has responsibility for at least one recitation group. Each teacher lectures in his field and the other two usually attend. A total of 20 two-hour laboratory sessions is conducted during the two courses. Six laboratory sessions are conducted in each of the physics, biology, and chemistry facilities which are shared with students from the traditional introductory courses. Each member of the teaching team supervises the laboratory sessions in his or her area of specialization. Although each teacher has expressed an interest in having some first hand experience in the laboratories of the other areas, this has not yet been possible. Two laboratory sessions are conducted with an interactive digital computer in the mathematics department.

The teachers evaluate students on standards they feel are comparable to those used with students in the regular introductory courses. Grades in the integrated courses are running slightly above those in the regular courses.

The cost of conducting the integrated course sequence is presently about the same as for the regular courses. However, the teachers feel that the integrated course would be much better if they had an expanded budget especially for films to illustrate the interdisciplinary links among biology, chemistry, and physics. The cost to students is about the same as in regular courses since they use the same three textbooks that are used in the regular courses.

Evaluation of the integrated course has been mainly informal, although a few formal questionnaires have been distributed at the end of the course. About 90% of the students report strong satisfaction with the integrated course although it is difficult to make comparisons since no similar data has been obtained from students in the regular courses. The teachers of the integrated course would like to formally evaluate the course in terms of success of the students in later subsequent science discipline courses. However, they feel that lack of both time and money has prevented this. On an informal basis, it appears that students from the Natural Science sequence do as well in advanced science courses as do those from the traditional introductory courses.

About 75% of the students that choose the integrated course are pre-med majors and have been alerted to the course by their major advisers. The integrated teachers feel that the advisers vary in their understanding and enthusiasm for the course. There is hope that extra efforts to further inform the advisers about the course and its results with students will improve this situation.

Additional future plans include getting additional colleagues involved in teaching the integrated course and in expanding student enrolment. The integrated course teachers would like to develop improved laboratory work and to articulate it more closely to the lectures. There may be an opportunity to expand the interdisciplinary effort to include other departments at Alpha University but the present integrated course teachers are not certain as to who should take the initiative to include the others.

Beta College

Unified Science 1, Unified Science 2, and Unified Science 3 were developed as a three term sequence in direct response to what were perceived as the unique needs of prospective primary school grades 1-6 teachers enrolled in the Beta College degree program. Each term is one-half of the academic year or about 18 weeks in length. The full sequence has been in operation only one year.

Historically, prospective elementary teachers enrolled in the same introductory science courses as did science majors because it was thought that doing so gave academic respectability to the education degree. Even though the old plan enabled the individual to choose two or three courses from five or six available, the courses emphasized the abstract aspects of science and omitted "hands-on" inquiry aspects of science. Primary school teachers with the old science background have found it difficult to make the transition to "new" activity centred programmes that they are required to teach in the schools in spite of the fact they experienced methods courses that aimed to prepare them for inquiry teaching. Teachers tend to teach science as they have been taught science rather than as they are expected to teach science.

A four person team representing four Beta College departments, biology, chemistry, earth science, and physics was established to prepare an appropriate sequence of courses for prospective primary teachers in which the medium would be a large part of the "message" and which would be individualized to some extent. A further and important part of the charge to the team was that the resulting courses should be academically respectable. The development team accepted the task with its many challenges after first getting Beta College administration to agree that the team would also be the teachers of the course and that a specific classroom, laboratory, and office complex would be devoted exclusively to the Science 1, Science 2, and Science 3 courses.

The team's first task was writing purposes for the sequence of courses and which would be used as a guide to designing and eventually evaluating the courses. They decided on a list of twelve which included: a—to help the student learn the processes of scientific inquiry; b—to help the student learn some of the major concepts that are important in science; c—to help the student see that science is a part of the everyday work; d—to help the student gain confidence in his or her ability to "discover" things by doing scientific inquiry; etc.

The course sequence now consists of a mixture of short and long units. The long units each last about three weeks (nine one-hour sessions) and are organized around selected processes and concepts of science. Each unit has objectives stated in Gronlund style. Each of these units is taught to the whole class using a mix of lecture, laboratory, audio-visual, etc., methods which are facilitated by the ready availability of a combination classroom-laboratory. The short units last about one week and are organised around certain natural phenomena.

In both kinds of units, materials from various sciences came together as appropriate to the course purposes, the unit objectives, and the knowledge level of the students. Some of the unit activities were adapted from existing primary science materials and upgraded to college level. Each of the units is fairly independent of the others although the team has tried to impose some order in terms of increasing levels of difficulty.

The organizing themes for the long units include processes such as classsifying, interpreting data, controlling variables, etc., and concepts such as models, populations, systems, etc. The shorter units include themes such as soil, birds, pendulums, magnets, rocks, trees, etc.

The long and short units differ also in the way they are taught. The long units are required and taught in a conventional class group setting although the teaching-methods minimize but do not abolish lecture and strongly emphasize manipulative and audio-visual activities. The short units are individualized in that each student chooses from about 30 available units and then works through that unit by himself or herself or with one or two other students on a co-operative basis. A student may undertake as many optional short units as he or she can find time to do. The student's course grade depends on how many options are completed, on end of unit tests, and on end of course test.

Each course in the sequence contains four of the long units leaving enough time for at least six of the short units. Some students are able to complete as many as ten or twelve short units since they are able to work in the science area at odd hours when it is not occupied by regular classes. The teachers monitor the work on short units co-operatively and at least one is always "on duty" during the day and two evenings each week.

Students enroll in the unified science course sequence during the second year and first term of the third year in the four-year teacher preparation programme. A course in methods of teaching science is given in the second term of the third year and is planned to articulate with the three science courses. Ordinarily there are two sections of each course in the sequence and each section contains about thirty students. Assignment to one section constitutes one-third or one-half of a teacher's full "load" depending on how much time is assigned to monitoring the science area during non-class time. There is no single text for the course although each unit is accompanied by a bibliography of articles and books which are readily available on a loan basis.

Future plans for developing Beta College's unified science sequence include redesigning several of the long units and preparing additional short units. The teachers feel that development work on the units should occur every year in order to maintain the vitality of the courses. To do so will require time and therefore some budget allocation from the administration which will need to be convinced that such continuous expenditure is justified. The cost of conducting the courses and maintaining the facility is about 30% more than for conventional courses at Beta College.

Evaluation of the course sequence has been based on end of unit tests, an end of sequence questionnaire, and the teachers' subjective opinions. All are very positive (especially the students' enthusiasm for the courses) although the teachers admit they really do not have any "hard" baseline data from the "old" style courses for comparison. As yet, it has not been possible to determine whether people going through this new sequence actually make better primary teachers. The person who teaches the educational methods course that follows the sequence would like to do a formal research study as a follow-up because he feels that the students have developed a better understanding of the nature of science, and will be better teachers and are far more interested in science than previously. However, he feels the study would be too much for him to undertake along with current responsibilities.

Gamma University

Science for Citizens is a one term unified science course for non-science majors designed and developed by faculty from the university's psychology, physics, chemistry, and civil engineering departments. The idea for the course arose in an informal discussion that occurred in the Faculty Club and was based on the premise that although most students learned some science they never had an opportunity to learn how or what science could be applied directly to human affairs. The group agreed that science thought could be applied as effectively by people in careers other than that of professional scientist.

The Science for Citizens course is elective for upper level undergraduates and is conducted as a seminar with only twelve to fifteen students per teacher. The class meets five times per week for one hour for twelve weeks. The course is divided into four or five units each of which is organized around a theme that corresponds to a persistent problem that exists at the interface of science, society and technology. The number of units is indefinite because it varies from one term to the next depending on who teaches it and, to some extent, on student interest. Although one teacher meets with the group through the whole term, the other faculty members occasionally meet with the group as do people from other departments who make guest appearances to present information or concerns from their field of expertise as it applies to the particular unit problem theme.

The number of class sections has varied from none to six per term depending on student enrolment and faculty availability. In the six years the course has been taught, student requests for it have risen steadily. The teachers of the course believe that this trend represents a profound and positive evaluation of the course and therefore have not pursued any other evaluative procedures other than that needed to evaluate student achievement for grading purposes.

The problem themes have been selected and outlined by the four originators of the course and include: The Game of Science (how science operates in the real world), Whose Rights Are Right? (human rights regarding birth and death), Where Is Mother Hubbard? (food supply and distribution), Lord Mr. Ford What

Have You Done? (technological impact and the future of the automobile). A Clockwork Orange (behaviour modification). The Affluent Effluent (how should the price of pollution be reckoned?), Garbage In, Garbage Out (limitations of computer capability innate and controlled), Alternatives to Growth (limits to technological and biological growth), and Nothing from Nowhere (alternative energy sources and usage). Reading materials for each theme have been assembled by the staff. Two of the units rely heavily on unit materials from the Science in a Social Context (SISCON) Project. The original decision to give the units "catchy" titles may be reversed since most students prefer to refer to the units by simple single word descriptions such as "energy", "food", etc.

The materials for each unit are updated regularly and stored in file cabinets in the psychology department office which is the departmental office closest to the classroom used for the course. The file cabinets also contain materials that are not readily available in the university library and are accessible to students under the supervision of the psychology department's secretary.

The course is conducted solely by lecture, reading, and discussion methods. There has been some serious discussion among the teachers as to whether or not some laboratory or practical activities should be included sometime in the near future. The main arguments for doing so are that this would give the students a first-hand feeling for the value, limitations and difficulties of obtaining useful empirical data as related to the unit problem themes. Also, to do so would qualify the course as counting toward Gamma University's requirement that all students take a minimum of three science courses as part of a liberal education standard. At present, the Science for Citizen's course does not count toward this requirement.

Arguments against the inclusion of practical laboratory work are based on both the increased cost that this would incur and real doubts that data collected by students would be sufficiently "good" to replace the vicarious data presently used in class discussions. Also, there are some doubts that the present group of teachers could handle the increased number of students. The latter is already becoming somewhat of a problem and next year it will be necessary to add an "outsider" to the team because of the anticipated increase in the number of class sections.

Three of the present group of teachers are looking forward to the addition of "new blood", but one is fearful that the present team spirit and accord may be threatened. The additional person will come from either the botany or zoology department, neither of which has faculty members that have expressed an interest in the type of interdisciplinary science taught in "Science and the Citizen". Some have expressed the feeling that the course is not "science" even though the present teachers can show how "good" science comes into each unit and can claim that many students seem to learn certain principles, concepts, and laws for the first time even though they have been exposed to them in one of the standard science courses. The original four teachers have recently decided to embark on some type of "public relations" effort, to convince those in other science departments that "Science and the Citizen" or something like it is not only legitimate science teaching but also important in terms of the university's declared purpose.

University of Delta

The University of Delta is a medium size multi-purpose institution and has been in existence only since 1970. When the university was formed, its founders were mandated to incorporate innovative curriculum and teaching/learning procedures. Among these innovations have been several interdisciplinary efforts, one of which is the multidisciplinary Third Year Project. Participation in a Third Year Project is required of all students at the University of Delta, regardless of their planned curriculum or major field.

Each student is assigned to a project group that includes an adviser-teacher and a total of 8-12 students. The project group is allocated two full terms (nine months) to initiate, conduct, and report on a project that involves a real problem situation that persists in the local community and that has strong implications for science and technology. It is assumed that each student will spend about one-third of his or her time in activities associated with the project.

About forty (40) project groups are active at any given time. Their work is co-ordinated by the Third Year Project Director who also has the responsibility for assigning individuals to groups, allocating working space for the groups, and providing appropriate materials and services for the groups. His method for doing this is to obtain a list of three or four promising project topics or themes from each faculty member that will be a project group adviser and then to assign individual students so that each resulting group has a mix of backgrounds and specialities among its members. This procedure results in considerable diversity among the group members, but each is from a major discipline area that has direct relevance for all of the potential topics that each adviser has submitted. In many cases, advisers post their list of potential topics and students may express personal preferences to the Project Director prior to his making group assignments.

At the first meeting of the group, the project adviser introduces the list of potential project topics and describes each in view of the project goals and objectives. When the Third Year Project was first conducted, the students in each group were allowed to identify their own project, but this was very time consuming and denied the values of the adviser having given some thought to the matter previously.

Project themes have not always been the same from one year to the next and many of the faculty feel that they can be effective with a given theme only once every five or six years. Examples of project themes that have been used in recent years are: Community Food and Food Service Regulations, Public Transit System, Crime, Solid Waste Disposal, Proposed Motorway to Connect Airport Directly to Central City, Proposed Dam on the Delta River, Traffic Regulation System, Drinking Water, and Consumer Protection Laws and Regulations.

Although there is considerable flexibility in organizing the individual projects, several of the advisers feel that one of the most effective is to simulate the approach of a government sponsored commission to investigate the current status of the theme, to devise feasible recommendations for future action, and to report both. Student and teacher enthusiasm for the project are enhanced if they are able to identify a specific community or national agency to whom their final report can actually be submitted. This gives a feeling of real value as opposed to that of an intellectual exercise for the whole project.

In the past two years, increasing numbers of projects have been reported by way of a public forum in the local community or by means of a video-tape presentation. These are usually limited to 20 or 30 minutes and are in addition to some type of written report.

Activities within the project after topic selection generally involve: identification of project goals in terms of the product or products that will result; determining the specific tasks that need to be done; establishing a schedule of deadlines for the task; organizing project people to best accomplish the tasks and to fulfill individual interests; conducting the tasks. Each student in the group plus the adviser is a contributing member of the team effort. Each member carries the identity of his major discipline or academic interest and his or her contributions are recognized as coming from that discipline. However, there is frequent interdisciplinary collaboration as well as co-operation. For example, an economics student may well work with a chemistry student in analyzing the water quality in a local reservoir during a Drinking Water project. In the same project, a bacteriology student may work with a sociology student and an engineering student to forecast the community's water needs for the next 100 years. Thus, disciplinary identities are constant although roles shift frequently. Skills and conceptual knowledge are developed incidentally as needed either by individual study or special topic lectures.

Each project group has an office in which the whole group can meet at one time and where project materials can be stored. The ''office'' may be only part of a room with a desk, a filing cabinet, a bookshelf, and some chairs, but it is dedicated solely to the project. Often students with teacher encouragement, identify the area with a distinctive insignia which seems to contribute significantly to the *esprit de corps* of the group and which is an important factor in the success of the project.

There has been some talk about working up direction manuals for conducting a project since many faculty members believe that the quality of the projects has been erratic in the past. Others believe that to do so would be a waste of effort since there are so many unpredictable variables that can cause differing levels of satisfaction with a project and the manuals would stifle efforts to try new projects and the excitement of risking failure that goes with doing something new. They also believe that the manual would cause certain themes to become institutionalized the avoidance of which was the reason for the university being innovative in the first place. There may be a compromise in assembling a book of guidelines which would be less prescriptive than a manual, contain suggestions for projects, and be revised frequently.

Most of the teachers who advise projects do so as one-half of their assigned "load" as the other half may be either research or other teaching. Most feel that advising a project is an exciting and rewarding, although sometimes frustrating experience. It is very difficult to be a teacher in a course in which not all students can be expected to learn exactly the same things. Some objectives can be stated for all students such as, "To learn ways and means by which concepts, knowledge, and procedures from ones own discipline can be applied in understanding and treating community problems". Other common objectives can be specified in terms of attitudes and communication skills. It is almost impossible to specify many cognitive objectives that have to do with technical concepts, such as thermodynamics, bond resonance, cloning, etc., in advance although it is entirely possible that everyone in the project group might learn some of these things.

One promising approach to incorporating some cognitive objectives into each student's project experience is for the teacher to confer with each student about one month after the project has started and the project's main tasks and individual responsibilities have been identified. In this conference, the student and teacher may have a basis for specifying a few things that the student can reasonably be expected to learn as a minimum during the remainder of the project.

Evaluation of the multidisciplinary Third Year Project is very difficult. A survey shows that 85% of the students feel that they learned more than they would have in the same amount of time spent in conventional courses. About 8% of the students feel they would have learned more in conventional courses and the remaining 7% either did not have an opinion or thought it did not make any difference.

Epsilon University

The course "Systems Science" was introduced as an open elective for upper level undergraduates by two of Epsilon University's engineering faculty. These two, who have been colleagues and friends for many years, became interested in general systems theory five years ago.

Their interest in and enthusiasm for general systems theory led them to the conclusion that the combination of concepts embodied in systems thinking provided the nearest thing to a single, general framework for *all* science. As such, it should be of lasting interest and value for all people working in the realm of science. Systems theory would enable practitioners of any science discipline to communicate with each other and a systems approach to problem solving could facilitate research by interdisciplinary teams.

The two faculty members tried to convince the curriculum committees of the various science and engineering faculties to require a single uncomplicated course in general systems theory. Their proposals have been rejected although they have been encouraged to offer the course as an elective. The two faculty members feel that the rejections have been caused mainly by the fact that most faculty in the science departments are not knowledgeable about general systems theory and that these other faculty are fearful lest a new required course in systems theory might cause some of their "own" courses to lose "required" status The two systems oriented teachers are endeavoring to overcome this resistance by conducting an informal campaign to educate various science faculty in systems theory. The campaign has very low visibility and consists of distributing short articles dealing with systems theory at an introductory level, engaging individuals in systems based conversations at lunch, and publicizing systems related lectures by visiting off-campus people.

Epsilon University requires that all students regardless of specialization complete at least two introductory science courses as part of the student's general education program. The "Systems Science" course has been proposed to the university-wide curriculum council for approval as meeting part of the general education requirement. The reasoning behind the proposal is that if any educated person were forced to know some science, it should be that which has the broadest utility. The proposal was rejected because "Systems Science" has no practical laboratory activity in it and, therefore, in the view of that committee is really a philosophy course and not a science course.

Thus "Systems Science" remains a rather obscure low-enrollment elective course in spite of very enthusiastic evaluations by students who have completed the course.

Ordinarily only one or two "Systems Science" classes of 15-20 students are conducted during each 12-week term at Epsilon University. Classes meet for one-hour, twice per week. The first half of the course is directed to developing basic systems concepts including: boundary, hierarchy, subsystem, input-output, parameter, feedback, etc. These basic ideas are developed using a rich assortment of examples taken from many disciplines including the behavioral and social sciences as well as the "natural" sciences. The teacher of each class tries to avoid emphasis on examples taken from the students' fields of specialization as the last half of the course is occupied by each student presenting applications of systems theory in his or her own field of emphasis. Each presentation and group discussion of it lasts about one hour. If the class is unusually large, extra sessions are scheduled so that each student may have a full opportunity to participate. Student interest has been sufficiently high that there have been no serious objections to the extra sessions.

Some students choose to report on a systems view of an avocation such as winemaking or photography rather than some part of their major discipline in the university. The teachers encourage the students to attend meetings of the local chapter of the Society for General Systems Research.

The cost of conducting the "Systems Science" course is demonstrably low. However, other objective evaluations of the course and its impact on students have not been done and are not anticipated in the near future due to the preoccupation of the two teachers with obtaining institutional recognition for the course.

A collection of up-to-date readings on general systems theory has been assembled by the two teachers. Although one teacher has the sole responsibility for a class, the other is a frequent visitor. These visits often result in some argumentive discussion between the two teachers which seems to promote the same kind of action among students and between individual students and the teacher. These spirited discussions are evaluated very highly by students and teachers when the overall course is considered in retrospect.

There are formal objectives for the course and both teachers feel that individual student's achievement of these can be assessed accurately by analyzing the student's participation in class plus responses to a one question end-of-course examination. That question is based on a two-hour evening visit to some unexpected site such as a local restaurant, a local horse racetrack, the local zoo, etc. The one question is always the same, but the site never is. The question asks the student to describe the place visited in systems terms and to identify the least effective subsystem.

The "Systems Science" course is somewhat unique in that it is both "unified" and "multidisciplinary" as the unified teacher brings many sciences together in the big idea of "systems" and the learners retain their identity with a specific discipline. In the last few terms, increasing proportions of the classes have been composed of students who are majors in the school of business administration and in the environmental planning programme of Epsilon University.

Zeta University

Zeta University is an old well-established institution that has a tradition of academic excellence, a mature faculty, and a strongly entrenched departmental organization. A few years ago the university's top administrative positions were reorganized and filled with new people from the "outside". With the reorganization came a mandate from the Governing Board to produce some graduates in traditional discipline areas with a "marketable" background that would appeal to environmentally oriented employers such as certain governmental agencies and industries.

The new administration has responded to the mandate while at the same time retaining the strength of the university's traditional discipline oriented courses by establishing a programme in Environmental Management. In this programme, a student essentially completes a four-year degree in a conventional science area such as chemistry, zoology, botany, etc. However, in addition to the usual courses, the student participates in three additional types of activities: Co-ordinating Seminars, Field Experience, and Special Courses.

During the Student's second, third, and fourth year in the programme, he or she participates in an ongoing co-ordinating seminar comprised of one teacher and 8-10 students, all of whom are in the same year of the programme.

The seminar meets once a week for two hours throughout the whole academic year. The seminars involve rather informal discussions in which current topics being treated in the students' ongoing courses are related to environmental problems or applications. Thus, a typical discussion might be initiated by the question, "What implications does your current course work on aromatic hydrocarbons have for water pollution?"

The key questions for discussion are usually established by the teacher a week or two prior to discussion, although with third and fourth year groups, many questions are suggested by students. This method of operation requires a teacher with a broad background and, more importantly, a secure individual who is not afraid to show his or her ignorance in some areas but is willing to be a continuing learner. The teacher needs to be aware of what is happening in the student's various courses and be sufficiently knowledgeable and creative to establish meaningful discussion questions. Often teachers of the Co-ordinating Seminar will "sit in" on lectures in certain courses. At first this caused some feeling of uneasiness by both the lecturer and the seminar teacher but that has diminished in time. In fact, some lecturers feel that the visitors have had the effect of improving their lectures.

Each Co-ordinating Seminar teacher works with a given student group for only one year although there has been some discussion of a teacher continuing with a given group for two or even three years.

An early concern that students majoring in the same discipline as that of the seminar teacher's departmental affiliation would have an unfair advantage over students from other areas has not materialized.

Teachers of the seminars are assigned as needed by chairmen of the various departments co-operating in the programme. Those assigned tend to be among the younger members of their respective departments and report that the experience is very rewarding to them personally. However, the seminar teachers unanimously express a concern that their work with the seminars may not weigh very heavily toward future promotion within their own department.

The Field Experience aspect of the programme involves a practical internship during summers following the second and third years of course work. Each student spends four to six weeks working in an industry or government agency as a field or laboratory assistant or in some equivalent professional apprenticeship role. The students are paid a nominal amount which usually is just sufficient to cover living expenses.

Most students report that this phase of the programme is very valuable in linking their formal studies to the real world. A few report that the experience is a waste of time. The industries and agencies report that most of the students are enthusiastic, responsible, and reasonably competent in their assigned tasks.

The third aspect of the Environmental Management programme is a group of special courses that are conducted in response to timely environmental concerns. Each course is offered no more than once in a given three-year cycle. One of these courses is "Environmental Advocacy and The Law." When it is offered, students in all three years of the programme are required to enroll. Other special courses have been, "Temporary Organizations for Community Action" and "Oil Spill Prevention and Treatment." Since these courses are based on current concerns, it is anticipated that some may be dropped after being offered only once as other concerns displace them in priority of public interest.

There has been no formal evaluation of the programme in empirical terms nor is any planned since nearly everyone agrees that the programme is successful. From the administrator's point of view, the main criteria for success are: (1) graduates have found jobs rather readily and (2) the programme does not add significantly to the university's already overburdened budget. From the teacher's point of view, the main criteria for programme success are:
(1) employers report satisfaction with graduates' capabilities, (2) students seem enthusiastic, and (3) the programme attracts a large number of students without apparently detracting from conventional courses.

There has been some speculation in Zeta University that the Environmental Management Programme might lead to the establishment of an independent department. However, this would require one or two equally unlikely events. Either the university's budget would be augmented or several existing departments would decide to merge and form one.

4. Planning for future Interdisciplinary Courses and Programmes

There seems to be an aura of intellectual excitement around present day interdisciplinary science courses and programmes that will undoubtedly be sufficiently contagious to cause other colleges and universities to become involved in similar and extended efforts. As one looks to the future however, there are many questions that must be considered in the light of past experience by others. A few of the more important questions that have been answered by all the designers and developers of successful courses in the past follow in no particular order of importance. As with all lists, answers to the questions presented here should be regarded as necessary but not sufficient for future course and program development.

4.1 What purpose will be served by developing an inter- disciplinary science course or programme?

To design, develop, and enroll students in an interdisciplinary course or programme purely for the purpose of doing something interdisciplinary will probably be an unsatisfactory experience for both students and teachers. There are many legitimate purposes to be served by interdisciplinary courses and programmes. Those illustrated in the generalized exemplars are only a few. The best purposes are probably those that are student oriented although some institution oriented purposes, such as cutting costs, are certainly legitimate. It can be argued that serving institutional purposes also serves students indirectly. Nevertheless, if a group is setting out to design a course or programme the task is easier and more stimulating if the primary purposes involve student gains.

The history of educational innovation has many instances of faddism in which innovations became widespread because they were fashionable. In many of these cases, the innovation was abandoned more rapidly than it was adopted because the adopters really had insufficient student oriented purposes to take the time and trouble to ascertain whether the innovation would better serve these purposes than traditional instructional patterns.

A case in point of such an innovation that was adopted rapidly in the United States and generally dropped just as rapidly by most institutions is programmed instruction even though some prestigous educators had claimed publicly that everything can and should be taught in this way. The reactions against programmed instruction were so great that some institutions are unable to use it for those situations in which it is superior to other instructional methods.

Interdisciplinary courses and programmes are not educational cure-alls. They should be practiced only when there has been a critical examination of proposed courses in relationship to the purposes to be served.

4.2 Can an interdisciplinary course or programme be "exported" successfully to another institution?

A high proportion of successful interdisciplinary courses and programmes are organized around problem themes that are of local interest. Many teachers in these courses and programmes report that the unique local character of these problems provide the relevance ingredient that many students feel is seriously lacking in conventional courses. They also report that both teachers and students seem to function at higher levels when they know they are working on something that is unique to them. This is the "Hawthorne 'effect" that has been known to social psychologists and educators since the 1920's.

On the basis of the foregoing, it would seem that one institution's effort to replicate another institution's course or programme is bound to achieve substantially less success although the quantitative extent of the Hawthorne Effect has never been established clearly.

Good teachers have never tried to replicate someone else's course even when they have used a single textbook in a very conventional course. On the other hand, poor teachers have often been accused by students of merely "reading the book" during lectures.

Another indicator of the difficulty (impossibility?) of adopting someone else's course can be found in the few interdisciplinary science courses that have been discontinued. In most every case, discontinuation of a course followed the departure of a key organizer and teacher of the course. This does not mean that departure of the leader in an interdisciplinary course development necessarily signals the death of the course provided that other teachers understand and feel the same way about the course's purpose, methods, and spirit.

There are ways to benefit from other people's experiences and products associated with interdisciplinary course development without trying to duplicate the courses. The usual channels of communication (publications, conferences, etc.) can be used to determine what others have done and produced and how the products can be adapted in a local effort once a purpose has been determined.

4.3 What organizing themes can be used for inter-disciplinary courses?

Often the specific purpose of a course makes theme selection almost automatic. Thus, if a course is intended to show how various disciplines can work together to understand environmental problems, a very natural theme for part or all of the course depending on anticipated depth of treatment would be a specific environmental problem such as, "air pollution." The problem type of theme is currently popular because in many countries science is being required to justify its existence in terms of social utility and because such problems form an increasingly frequent arena for interaction among practicing scientists.

A second type of theme is that of an intellectual topic such as *"Metaphor in Science and Society."* Again, this type of theme could be applied to a whole course or some part of it. Occasionally, this type of theme arouses less intellectual excitement among students and teachers since it seems to be less of a departure from tradition and, in fact can often be found as a title of, or chapter heading in, a textbook associated with some discipline.

Another theme type that has not yet been fully exploited is that of a natural phenomenon such as rain, trees, plastics (assuming that man-made things are "natural"), etc. In spite of traditional "proprietary rights" to certain phenomena by some disciplines, many phenomena can only be understood in a holistic way by utilizing several disciplines each of which contributes to overall understanding by adding its own unique aspects which ordinarily are consistent with each other.

A fourth type of theme is the basic concept that is more or less universal through the science disciplines. Thus, "equilibrium", "energy", "system", etc. are used in many if not all sciences. For non-science majors, this type of theme seems to be especially valuable as it serves to focus on one of a relatively small number of powerful concepts that are more or less unique to science.

4.4 What organizational structure should be used within an interdisciplinary course?

If a course of six weeks duration or longer is based on a single theme, there seems to be a human tendency to perceive the day to day activities as separate entities. There seems to be growing evidence that a given theme is only functional as an organizing theme for three to five weeks. Thus, if institutional constraints dictate that course length be ten weeks or eighteen weeks or something in between, it would be wise to construct the course around several units each of which has its own organizing theme and is more or less related to the other themes. However, a growing number of educational theorists doubt that the exact sequencing of units in a course is as critical as was generally believed a few years ago.

In this connection, it is interesting to note that several collections of published instructional units (or modules) of relative short length have appeared in recent years that, in effect, advocate use of the units in any combination or sequence that makes sense locally. Specific reference is made to interdisciplinary units developed by the Science in a Social Context (SISCON) Project in the UK and the disciplinary units developed by the BSCS Collegiate Minicourse Project in the USA. An increased number of available units such as these might well enable institutions to minimize the task of designing their own interdisciplinary courses by using an eclectic approach in selecting units along with an admixture of as many local units as time and resources permitted.

A set of generalized guidelines for an ecletic approach to interdisciplinary unit design has been developed by the Federation for Unified Science Education (FUSE) in the USA and other models will probably be formulated in the future. The FUSE model is intended primarily for non-science majors.

4.5 What teaching and learning methodology should be used in interdisciplinary courses?

Some interdisciplinary courses seem to have been initiated as a reaction to dissatisfaction with traditional lecture methods as much as to establish a departure from traditional content structures. This does not mean that traditional methods of teaching and learning should be discarded completely. It does mean that the best method of teaching and learning in interdisciplinary (and other) courses is a mix of methods.

An eclectic effort to match teaching and learning methodology with the nature of that which is to be learned is consistent with the spirit of interdisciplinary thinking. Thus, lecturing is a very appropriate method when the lecturers unique point of view or association with a specific topic is important. On the other hand, if that to be learned is an exposition of a well established theory, reading may be a more appropriate method since, for most university students, it is more efficient of time and permits immediate review.

Programmed instruction as mentioned earlier was hailed as the panacea of teaching/learning problems for all age levels in the early 1960's. As the realization that programmed instruction had its serious shortcomings occurred, several other things happened. Traditional teachers who had refused to incorporate programmed instruction withdrew even further into their steady self-satisfying routine of pure lecture. Those who had committed themselves totally to the bandwagon of programmed instruction abandoned that vehicle of learning completely. Cynics and perpetual critics of education had more ammunition for their attacks on the "establishment".

And yet programmed instruction is a very efficient methodology of teaching/learning undisputable aspects of a discipline such as the terminology of special subdivisions of the discipline or of certain precisely defined constructs such as "vector".

There are many teaching/learning methodologies from which to choose the most appropriate for a given situation. Among some of the less widely used are: role play simulation, computer simulation, gaming, data bank analysis, and film production. Each of these puts the learner in a more active role than that of passive receiver of a lecture. And yet each of these methodologies has its limitations and each can be misused by a well meaning but unskilled teacher who sees the method as an end in itself.

The best interdisciplinary courses of the future will be those that incorporate a variety of learning methodologies appropriate to the purposes and objectives of the course and conducted by teachers who are skilled in and knowledgeable about these methodologies.

4.6 Who should teach an interdisciplinary course?

It is almost a foregone conclusion that the best teacher (or teachers) of an interdisciplinary course will be a person (or persons) who has shared in the design and development of the course. If this policy is followed, there is reasonable assurance that the course will be taught in the same spirit and level of enthusiasm with which it was conceived.

Many interdisciplinary courses have been initiated and taught by a team of teachers representing several disciplines. This approach has usually been motivated by a psychological need on the part of the teachers to avoid personal confrontation with subject matter out of their field of speciality. After all, the ideal model of a university teacher has traditionally been that of an expert, possessing "complete" knowledge of his discipline.

Nevertheless, one of the purposes of many interdisciplinary courses often relates to enabling students to perceive the basic unity of science or to project the notion that in solving real world problems, the student should be able to access relevant knowledge and procedures regardless of disciplinary origin. Therefore, the more courageous teachers felt they should project a model consistent with the purposes of the course and undertook the total teaching responsibility for the course. In being so presumptuous to break from tradition, these teachers did not pretend universal expertise. They had to learn how to say, "I don't know." More important, they had to learn how to be co-learners with the students.

The trend of staffing for interdisciplinary courses seems to be toward that of a single teacher for each section of a course with an interdisciplinary cadre of other teachers and experts available for help either as guest lecturers or as consultants to the teachers.

4.7 What evaluation procedures should be conducted in connection with an interdisciplinary course?

Evaluation problems associated with an interdisciplinary course are of two kinds. One is the problem of evaluating individual student's achievement. The other is that of evaluating the course itself which usually requires procedures different from and in addition to evaluation of individuals.

In dealing with evaluation of individuals, interdisciplinary courses cause some unique problems in that the courses are often so individualized that not all students are expected to learn exactly the same things. For example, a multidisciplinary course on "Systems" might have as a principal objective that each student would learn how systems thinking can be applied in his or her own discipline. Thus, a single examination question could have a variety of "right" answers and may invoke completely different concepts from systems thought.

The problem of evaluating individual achievement will be minimized if a set of objectives for students can be clearly set at the beginning of the course. Such a set of objectives can be phrased in terms that specify what is to be learned and, if appropriate, qualified for application to special cases. Another way to handle the problem would be to specify fifteen (for example) course objectives and give students the option of being examined on any ten at the end of the course. Ordinarily, these objectives would be in terms of what is to be learned not what is to be done in the course.

To write a paper analyzing the local water pollution problem is not a proper learning objective. It comes closer to being an objective if criteria to be met by the paper are specified. Writing a paper is in itself a physical task and says nothing about what is to be learned. On the other hand, to learn the various parameters involved in water pollution may be a desirable objective and writing a paper may be *one* way to demonstrate that the learning has occurred. There may also be other ways to show the same learning besides writing an examination and could include an interview by a teacher or preparation of a tape recorded report in place of a paper.

Some interdisciplinary courses have included affective or attitudinal and psychomotor or skill objectives along with the more usual cognitive or knowledge objectives and these require evaluation techniques different from the usual written examination.

Evaluating a course requires data on how well the course has achieved its purposes. Traditionally this has been done more or less intuitively by the teacher or department staff. Today there seems to be a trend toward obtaining more objective data. Some have gone so far as to seek job performance data after graduation although the effects of a single course at that late stage may be indistinguishable from those effects caused by a multitude of other factors.

Obtaining data on the degree to which course purposes have been achieved is simplified if the course purposes have been written with eventual evaluation in mind. One of the simplest techniques for obtaining data to evaluate the course is a questionnaire to students and teachers and which is responded to anonymously.

In planning the course evaluation phase of any interdisciplinary effort it must be remembered that it will be expensive in terms of teacher time and the results may be such that a valid comparison to previous courses may not be possible. For a comparison to be made both courses would require the same purposes which is rather unlikely.

Nevertheless, course evaluation is extremely valuable in terms of guiding the evolutionary development of the course in subsequent years and should have high priority in planning and allocation of time and resources. Often it is wise to involve the assistance of an "outsider" who is able to discern the outcome variables from a less biased point of view than the teacher or teachers directly involved in conducting the course.

4.8 What side effects can be anticipated as a consequence of establishing an interdisciplinary course?

Possible answers to this important question will vary widely from place to place. About the only thing certain is that there *will* be side effects. Some of the possible side effects may well be serendipities but generally those that are cause for the greatest concern while a course or programme is in its formative stages are those which are undesirable. In some institutions a large voluntary enrolment in a new interdisciplinary course might cause a drastic decline in the enrolment of an established course and consequently cause serious "rumblings" within the institution.

If potentially undesirable side effects can be identified *before* they actually occur, something can usually be done to minimize the resultant "rumblings" or to avoid them entirely. In the example cited above, the teacher of the course with potential declining enrolment might be made a part of the interdisciplinary development team or if he or she is not interested, it may be possible to arrange new challenges in other directions so that the loss of enrolment and maybe even of the old course itself will not be so traumatic. In some colleges and universities it is as difficult to discontinue a given course as it is to abolish a commission or agency of the national government, and practically never happens. Many large state supported universities in the United States have been criticized for never offering a course for the last *or* first time.

Two interesting and worthwhile techniques exist that can help in anticipating side effects. These are role-play simulation and modified Delphi techniques. In the former, specific individuals who might be concerned with possible side effects of a new course are identified and a profile is written which summarizes each one's biases, interests, professional commitments, etc. A group is then assembled and each is asked to play one of the roles (not oneself!) in a hypothetical situation. The situation could be as formal as a faculty meeting or as informal as a conversation in a local bar. A scene should be set and could be as simple as "one month after the new course has been underway" or as complex as "Professor Newton of the Physiology Faculty has asked The University Senate to investigate a new biophysical chemistry course."

It is important that each of the role-players stay in character and make a conscious effort to eliminate his own personal biases, interests, etc. The role play is concluded either by time limit or by the group reaching some kind of consensus (or impasse!). Then, the players drop their roles and the group debriefs on whatever crucial happened during the role play. Actually debriefing is the most important part of the exercise as it is during this phase that potential undesirable side effects (and other problems) are identified.

In a modified Delphi technique, a description of the proposed interdisciplinary course is circulated to all those people who could conceivably be affected by the course. Each is asked to respond in writing by identifying the six (for example) most important side effects of the course that each envisions. The responses are tabulated on a single list with number or percent of people who had each item on their list. The summary tabulation is circulated to the same people as previously and each is asked to either rank the items in order of decreasing importance or to select the six (for example) most important side effects as they now perceive them. After the responses are received, a second tabulation is made and the process repeated until a clear consensus has developed.

There are methods of forecasting future side effects of a new interdisciplinary course which often work as well as these two. However, these two provide an element of objectivity and ordinarily result in a more clear cut consensus than do other methods. It should be noted that if serious undesirable side effects are identified and cannot be resolved, that the plan for a new course might justifiably be scrapped or at least radically modified. Although it is very unlikely that all undesirable side effects can be removed even if they are identified, the potential benefits from the projected interdisciplinary effort may outweigh the undesirable side effects no matter how numerous or serious the latter may seem to be. It is generally accepted that "tradeoffs" accompany any innovation and may be risked with some level of confidence especially when they have been considered carefully before the innovation is implemented.

The future of interdisciplinary science is bright, promising, and exciting for students and teachers alike. Imagination, a good perspective of science as a human endeavour, and realization that college and university courses exist for students will help interdisciplinary approaches to realize their full potential.

ACKNOWLEDGEMENTS

The people listed below were instrumental in providing material describing interdisciplinary science from their region of the world. Sincere appreciation is due to them for their invaluable help.

IAN BLOCH, IPN, Kiel
DENNIS CHISMAN, The British Council, London

CECIL CRELLIN, UNESCO, Jakarta
ROBERT HOWE, ERIC, Columbus
MYRIAM KRASILCHIK, Cidade Universitaria, Sao Paulo
VICTOR MONTVILOV, UNESCO, Paris
TED SANDERCOCK, Sturt CAE, Bedford Park
BARBARA THOMSON, FUSE, Columbus

REFERENCES

Bremen Conference on Project Orientation in Higher Education—Working Papers March 23-26, 1976, University of Bremen. 1976

DALE, L.G., "Integrated Science in Tertiary Education" in *New Trends in Integrated Science Teaching—Volume II*, P.E. Richmond (editor), UNESCO, Paris. 1973.

GRONLUND, N.E., *Stating Behavioral Objectives for Classroom Instruction*, Macmillan, New York, 1970.

Integration, Co-ordination or Separation of Sciences at University Level International Council of Scientific Unions (ICSU) Paris, 1974.

Interdisciplinarity—Problems of Teaching and Research in Universities Centre for Educational Research and Innovation (CERI), Organization for Economic Co-operation and Development, Paris, 1972.

PHENIX, P. H. *Realms of Meaning*, McGraw Hill, New York, 1964.

Proceedings Project Directors Meeting, Materials and Instructional Development Section, Division of Higher Education, National Science Foundation, February 10-12, 1974, ERIC Information Analysis Center, Columbus, Ohio 1974.

Science and Mathematics Curricular Developments Internationally, 1956-1974, J. D. Lockard (editor), Science Teaching Center, University of Maryland, College Park, Maryland, 1975.

SHOWALTER, V. M. "Scientific Literacy" in *What Is Unified Science Education?* Federation for Unified Science Education (FUSE), Columbus, Ohio, 1976.

Broadening Courses

W.F. Williams and J. Lipscombe

1. Introduction

The English education system is renowned (or infamous?) for its specialisation. The seeds are sown in schools where it has long been the case that pupils have to decide at an early age (often 13 or 14) whether to opt for a science based range of subjects or an arts based one. Once this basic decision has been made the number of subjects in that range is quickly whittled down, usually to three by age sixteen, so that in depth studies can be made of a small number of subjects to fit the academically able students for university entrance. University science degrees were (and often still are) very specialised and oriented mainly towards preparing students to take their places in academic life. At the end of their first degrees they should be able to move forward, equipped with sufficiently detailed knowledge of that subject and its methodology to carry out research in that subject. In addition there has always been a variety of 'general' science degrees, aimed at the 'second class citizens'; the would-be scientists who fail to make the high standards required either for university entrance to single honours or at various stages along the way. It is this image, that of the failed specialist, which tends to overshadow all attempts to broaden science courses. The general belief then is that first rate students read for single honours degrees whilst second rate ones have to settle for an easier option; a broad course which covers a variety of subjects in less depth and which is, as a consequence, less intellectually demanding.

In our view this represents a misunderstanding of the philosophy and aim behind many 'broad' science degrees. It also underestimates both the depth of understanding required by such courses and their value. In this article we set out to destroy the myth of this inferiority of broad science courses and to show the valuable and important role which they play. To do this we shall look first at what is meant by 'broad' courses and investigate why there is a significant movement in British Universities and Polytechnics towards them. Having established, we hope, our case, we then turn to some of the problems which people have encountered in devising appropriate and effective courses and look at how different institutions have tackled the problems. We do not suggest that devising successful broad courses is easy. It has to be done with great care to ensure that high standards are set and maintained and the education thus provided is appropriate and meaningful as well as intellectually stimulating and demanding.

In stressing the problems, however, it is not our wish to discourage institutions from introducing broader courses. The rewards are high for those who succeed. These will come from the satisfaction of attracting students back into science courses at a time when, in spite of the growing importance of science and technology in society, young people seem to be increasingly rejecting science education.

2. What do we mean by broadening?

Quite simply broadening is taken to mean in this article the extension of a science degree course to include elements not normally considered appropriate to a traditional single honours degree. Single honours degrees are usually designed to allow students to make an in depth study of the subject matter and research techniques and methods of a specific discipline in isolation. In such courses no attempt is usually made to relate the discipline to other disciplines or to put it into a wider context, either historically, or as a contemporary study. What other subjects *are* taught alongside the main subject for part of the three years are usually chosen because they provide related knowledge or techniques important for a full understanding of the main subject. Hence maths is often studied alongside physics or chemistry to facilitate understanding of the science. It is more convenient to teach the necessary maths as a separate subject rather than attempt to integrate the maths into the science teaching. Broad courses in various ways go beyond this minimum involvement with essential supportive studies. They deliberately set out to extend the students' horizons. Such an imprecise definition leaves many questions unanswered and covers a multiplicity of possible course constructions; by the time you reach the end of this article we hope you will have a much clearer idea of what broadening really means both conceptually and practically.

One small point of clarification is necessary here. There is obviously bound to be some overlap between 'broad' courses and 'interdisciplinary' courses. The latter topic is covered in detail in a separate article in this series, but you should note that some of our examples, although by no means all of them, can be considered to be interdisciplinary.

There are innumerable ways of setting up broad science degree courses. The Nuffield Foundation Group for Research and Innovation in Higher Education has analysed the whole range of course types (see their 3rd and 4th Newsletters, published in October 1973 and April 1974 respectively) and it will be useful here, as a means of setting the scene, to consider very briefly their analysis.

They have identified a number of categories of broad science degrees. Their categorisation is based on the assumption that broad courses have sprung out of the specialist degrees which typify the British University system. They have divided these specialist degrees into two main basic types: (i) Professional and (ii) Single honours. Such degrees as engineering, medicine, law and social administration are classed as 'professional'. Professional education of this sort serves two purposes: to transmit the essential core of knowledge; and to inculcate professional norms of behaviour. Single honours degree courses—physics, biology, chemistry etc.—are centred on a single discipline and in addition to transmitting knowledge about that discipline try to develop a distinctive style of thinking and approach which may be transferrable to problems outside that particular discipline.

In the view of the Nuffield Group these two basic types, the professional degree and the single honours degree, have each given rise to different patterns of broadening courses. For example, some professional degrees have been adapted to include some social science or a study of a related current social issue as a means of putting the professional knowledge into the social context within which the professional must operate. Another frequent ploy is to have a common core course e.g. basic engineering, upon which specialist expertise can be built, to prepare professionals for later re-training or changes in specialism.

The main forms of broadening, however, for professional studies, are seen as the move towards the inclusion of general/liberal/complimentary studies components and the growth in courses emphasising the social responsibility of professionals. The first of these can be illustrated by the way in which CNAA requirements for degrees to meet their general educational object- ives are often met by the inclusion of general/liberal/compli- mentary studies components which cover anything from beer brewing to the sociology of science. Such courses as 'Community Medicine' and 'Engineering and Environment' are used as examples of the second type, a concern with social responsibility.

Turning to single honours schemes, the pattern of broadening courses which emerges is one of joint honours (which the Nuffield Group see as a dilution of single honours rather than a 'true' broadening type); general degree schemes involving three or more subjects; systems of major and minor subjects; unit/module systems where students build up their own combination of subject matter from a variety of possibilities; systems, which have a common general scheme for all students, which attempt to give an over-view of the map of knowledge to which the student can relate his particular discipline; and finally systems which provide some broad interest subjects which are studied to supplement the discipline and which are available to students from a variety of departments and faculties.

This analysis seems to be based entirely on examining what happens as broadening is built onto traditional courses. One area which seems to be omitted is the science studies type of course, which is designed to be broad from the outset and is not a broadened science course. This type of course is discussed further in Sections 5 and 8.

All these patterns are of interest to anyone contemplating the possibility of initiating a broad science course. In Section 8 we look in greater detail at some actual courses so that you can consider specific examples of what has already been tried. Before we do this, however, it seems appropriate to spend some time looking at the rationale behind them. Why do we want broad courses and what problems have been experienced in devising them? The next two sections are concerned with these two aspects.

3. Why Broaden?

There is nothing new about the idea of providing a general or broad science education at university level. Throughout this century there have been numerous attempts to do this. One example is the London B.Sc. General which has appeared in several forms over the years. These attempts represent the deep-seated belief among a significant minority of university scientists that there is some special virtue in a broad course in science which transcends the particular subjects and there will be advantages both to the individual and to science which accrue from this. This belief continues to be held and there are an increasing number of attempts being made to provide such courses. It has been strengthened in recent years by a number of factors which seem to be becoming increasingly important.

The first of these factors is the trend for specialist scientists to take up generalist or non-science based employment. For example a considerable number of single discipline sciences graduates take up positions as general management trainees every year. Similarly many others embark on professional post-graduate training which bears little or no relationship to the subject of their first degree: a physicist becomes an accountant; a chemist a personnel officer. This is partly because of the rapid expansion in tertiary education in recent years which has resulted in a big increase in the numbers of science graduates without an equivalent increase in job opportunities in particular specialisms. Another factor, however, is the reluctance of many graduates to pursue careers in science. There are a variety of reasons for this, but one of some importance is the effect of early specialisation at schools. Many students see single discipline science honours courses as the only possibility open to them at university and pursue this in the hope that the degree they so obtain will prove to be the key to open a variety of doors. (See the Swann Report* for more detailed discussion of this aspect). Such people change direction out of choice and not because of the lack of opportunities for them to practise their specialism. Surely it would make more sense to recognise this fact and design some science based degrees which gave a broader education more appropriate to the type of jobs that are sought by so many science graduates?

The second factor is the increasing concern which is being felt about the social impact of science and technology. Until relatively recently advances in science and technology were seen as almost invariably benefiting mankind. Medical science was overcoming disease and pain, mass production technologies encouraged economic growth and provided consumer goods at prices the majority could afford, labour saving devices brought more leisure and less drudgery. Health, welfare and happiness for all were thought to be the products of science and technology. Today, however, there is increasing concern that all is not well. Health, wealth and happiness may be attained by some, but vast problems lie in the wake of technological progress. Such diverse difficulties as depletion of resources, energy shortfall, food shortages, population explosion, dereliction, the increasing gulf between rich and poor nations, social breakdown—the list is endless, are increasingly being blamed on short-sightedness and ignorance about the full implications of the application of science and technology. With this goes the demand for a greater awareness amongst scientists and technologists of the complex inter-relationships between science, technology and society, and a more socially responsible approach to their work. Science graduates should not just be super-technicians, they should be educated in the fullest sense of the word so that they understand how their subject relates to other subjects and to society.

Thirdly there is the basic problem of matching supply and demand. Statistics show that science and engineering courses have

* *The Flow into Employment of Scientists, Engineers and Technologists.* (The Swann Report) Cmnd. 3760: 1968. London: H.M.S.O.

failed to attract as many students as they might have expected in the post-Robbins era of expansion. The overall proportion of applicants to universities and polytechnics for places in science and engineering courses has steadily declined, as the figures UCCA reports show. There are thousands of unfilled placed on science and engineering courses. Although we are continually told that the country in general and industry in particular needs more scientists and engineers, prospective students have voted with their feet, opting for courses which they feel offer more relevance or satisfaction. Of course the reasons for this are complex and we must not overlook the shortage of maths and science teachers in schools which undoubtedly contributes to a reduction in the number of suitable students who could apply for university or polytechnic admission to such courses. Nevertheless a significant number of potentially suitable students opt out of science and technology and we cannot escape the conclusion that this is largely caused by disillusionment with what science education and a career in science have to offer. And yet science, by which we mean to include technology, is the most social of man's activities in this day and age, the activity which has the greatest impact on our daily lives. At the same time it is the greatest and most powerful of our cultural activities in western civilisation, the activity which most influences our modes of thought and our outlook and approach to art, music, literature, religion, drama and philosophy. The interest and excitement of science and its great relevance to the world in which we live ought to be reflected in the courses available to students in universities and polytechnics. If this *were* the case students would once again be attracted to science and engineering courses in increasing numbers.

A further look at UCCA statistics will show that some science courses, if not single honours ones, are increasingly popular with students. For example the number of applicants for combined science degrees, increased from 1000 in 1963 to 6000 in 1975. Many 'broad' degrees are over-subscribed whilst traditional science and engineering courses remain half empty or have to lower entrance standards significantly to fill their places.

Another aspect of meeting demand concerns the growing number of students with mixed arts and science 'A' levels. The traditional split is breaking down in schools and institutions of higher education must recognise this and provide courses which are appropriate for such candidates. Many of the 'broad' science courses which are being developed are suitable for people with this mixed background. Such students do not wish to be pigeon-holed *either* into a particular discipline—physicist, geologist, mathematician—*or* a specific faculty—scientist, engineer, social scientist. Their interests range across subjects and faculties. There is no natural law which prohibits abilities and interests developing in individuals which cut across traditional departmental/faculty boundaries. Hence a student may want to pursue mathematics and music or be especially interested in applying mathematical methods in the social sciences. Conventional specialist degrees do not allow such combinations. Broad courses can cater for this and may well lead to new research into hitherto unexplored areas. Unthought of relationships might well become apparent as students develop familiarity with areas not previously studied in concert. New doors are being opened, doors which have remained closed because the expertise and understanding required to discover this knowledge was not developed by specialist degrees. This knowledge is not less valid because it is not traditionally recognised as an academic discipline. Consider for example the development of ecology. This was once a small branch of biology but is now a fast-growing discipline in its own right, a discipline which many consider to be the basis for an integrated understanding of the whole living world. This arose through broadening biology to consider the relationship between species and their environment. Biochemistry is another example of a subject, now a specialist discipline in its own right, which grew out of exploring the interface between biology and chemistry.

The overall picture seems to be one of not moving with the times. University courses which were probably very successful when their main purpose was to train a scientific elite going on either to research in academia or industry or to teach the next generation of prospective scientists do not seem to be adequate for today's needs. Not only do they fail to prepare scientists to play their full role in society, they are also rejected by the very people they hope to attract. This is happening at a time when science and technology are having an increasing effect on everyone's life and there is a need for everyone to understand science, its application and implications.

4. The Problem

The range and variety of broad courses which have been introduced over the years is one indication of the difficulties which are faced in devising successful courses of this nature. The first attempts were mainly in the area of 'general' science courses and, on the whole, these were not very successful. By examining these we can draw out lessons and guide-lines which are useful when considering other alternatives.

The usual pattern of such courses, in England at least, is for students to study three subjects in parallel. The subjects would normally be closely related, for example maths, physics and chemistry, and would be studied in less depth than was required for single or joint honours candidates. Breadth, not depth is the characteristic of such courses. The syllabus is selected in a fairly arbitrary manner, perhaps the easier sections of single discipline degrees, often with no overall structure or apparent linkage within or between the three subjects. Entry standards are lower than those of single honours courses, low priority and importance is given to the course by staff. Students are abandoned between three stools, have no department with which they can identify or associate and have low status. All this leads to low stimulus and motivation for students and, naturally, poor results follow. Course standards then tend to be lowered giving another twist to the downward spiralling standards. Staff and students alike become disillusioned and attempts are made to rethink and reorganise, whereupon the same pattern repeats itself. Consequently general degrees have a poor reputation and so only those students thought not to be sufficiently academically able to cope with the rigours of specialist degrees are encouraged to apply, a further factor contributing to the downward spiral.

Such pitfalls must be avoided if other broad degrees are to have more success. We can specify a number of criteria which should be met if broad science degrees are going to fulfil the needs outlined in Section 3.

The first of these is that a broad degree must be as challenging and exciting *in its own way* as specialist degrees are in theirs. In a specialist degree the intellectual challenge and excitement come from pursuing a discipline in depth: the student begins to appreciate and understand what distinguishes his subject from others, how different aspects of the discipline relate to each other, the structure of the intellectual framework on which the detailed knowledge rests, the methods by which 'knowledge' in that field is established and so on. The challenge from a broad course can be similar to this. For example in combined honours courses this opportunity to study a discipline in depth remains an important aspect. In this case two disciplines would be covered and compensation for a somewhat restricted range of topics in one subject comes from covering two specialisms in some depth with the added advantage of understanding something of the relationship between two subjects and/or appreciating differences in approach, subject matter, methods and philosophy.

It is often argued, with much conviction, that integration and cross linkages are at least as challenging as in-depth analyses within the bounds of a particular discipline. When it comes to applying knowledge most problems and their solutions do not recognise what are after all man-made artificial boundaries between disciplines. The effects of technological innovation are not limited to technical ones. Hence, for example, the solution to the population explosion might be seen as devising more effective methods of contraception, but the chemist who sees 'effectiveness' as purely a question of technical efficiency is only seeing one part of a very complex problem. He may devise a highly effective and reliable method of controlling fertility but it will only do this if women have access to regular supplies, are not prevented by cultural pressures from using it, are able to understand how to use it and so on. The chemist who understands the cultural and social implications of his work is more likely to develop truly effective methods for a particular culture. It is this sort of challenge, to understand how one discipline relates to others and how it interacts with society, that is being built into many broad courses and which *must* be captured by such courses if they are to succeed.

Our second criterion is one of quality. Any degree course must produce able graduates. This immediately begs the question: able for what? Our answer to this must be: able to play a full and valuable role in the complex world in which we live. This includes playing their part as citizens and human beings as well as doing their job in industry, commerce, education, administration and so on. Most attempts at broadening would consider this to be an important aim. For example such components as general studies or liberal studies introduced into otherwise specialised courses are often justified as trying to produce the humane, professional graduate, one who is truly educated.

In most people's eyes, however, the question of ability is more importantly related to ability as a 'chemist' or 'doctor' or 'engineer'. This brings us once more to the need for such specialists to understand how their subject relates to the world in which they practise their discipline. Remembering, too, that many science and engineering graduates move into non-technical positions, either immediately or late on in their working lives, ability must relate to competence in considering and taking into account in decision-making all the related aspects of complex problems. A broad education which is science based should prepare graduates for such positions, particularly where decisions have technological aspects. This is increasingly the case as science and technology impinge further and further into every aspect of society.

The third criterion is closely related to ability. It is the need for graduates to be questioning and critical in their approach. In our view it is as possible to encourage this attitude through a broad approach as it is through a single subject approach. It is necessary, however, to achieve this to avoid the trap of superficiality. Before students can develop the ability and confidence to criticise in a constructive manner they must appreciate the need to make a thorough examination of a problem. Otherwise criticism can only be based on partial understanding and is consequently not very valuable. Such an appreciation can come in broad courses by constructing the course around specific themes e.g. systems, materials, mathematical studies, biological studies. A case study approach is useful here too in encouraging a detailed examination of a specific problem from a number of aspects.

5. Some Practical Considerations

In Section 2 we outlined a variety of alternative types of broadening courses. Apart from the differences in detail touched upon there we can identify two distinctly different approaches.

The first approach is that of continuing to produce specialist scientists who will have the knowledge and expertise necessary to become practising scientists but who will also have a fuller understanding of how their subject relates to other disciplines or to society. The normal starting point in such situations would be an existing single honours degree. On to this broadening elements would be superimposed. Hence for example chemistry students might have to take a course in History and Philosophy of Science or the Environmental Implications of the Chemical Industry. This could be done either through a system of major and minor subjects or through subsidiary subjects or through a modular scheme. Whatever system is chosen it does mean giving up some time previously devoted to the main subject; students could not be expected to devote time to such broadening elements on top of the typically crowded timetable of lectures and practical classes.

Combined honours degrees would also fall into this category. Their normal starting point is two single honours degree courses which are amended and juxtaposed to give a coherent combined degree. One of these principal subjects could be History and Philosophy of Science or a similar 'broadening' subject. Alternatively a student following a combined degree in, say, Physics and Mathematics could add broadening subsidiary elements in the same way as the specialist student. At the end of such a degree students could normally expect to follow a career in one of these two subjects if they so wished.

This type of approach will be the one most commonly adopted by science departments. Their main objective will remain that of producing 'chemists' or 'physicists' or 'biologists'. What is changing is the concern of what education is appropriate for such specialists.

The second distinct approach is that of designing a broad science degree course from the ground up. Here the aim is no longer to produce specialists with a broader based education, but to produce generalists with a science-based education. This approach which for convenience we will call 'integrated science' is not only more difficult in execution it is more contentious in concept. Essentially it is an attempt to produce a graduate with the outlook, methodology and approach of the scientist, with a good knowledge of the concepts and achievements of science, with an understanding of the interaction between science and the society on which it is based, but *without* the extensive technical skills both theoretical and experimental of present day specialist science graduates. In short the aim is to produce the science generalist who can take his/her place in an advanced technological society confident that he/she understands the nature of that society and the role that science and technology take in it. Such a graduate will not normally be competent to do a bench-based research or development job, but will be particularly well equipped for the large variety of jobs in industry, government, administration which requires an understanding of science and technology.

Conventional departments are unlikely to have the interests or skills to be able to devise and conduct this second type of course. It may well require the setting up of a new department or unit, for example the School of Science and Society at Bradford University, or the Technology Policy Unit at Aston. Such a department can attract staff with a wide range of disciplines and experience who can pool their expertise. Setting up such a department has the additional advantage or providing a base for the students. An alternative approach is to set up a course team of lecturers drawn from a variety of disciplines, who, while retaining their departmental allegiances also have a commitment to 'the course'.

Before embarking on a broadening exercise you should be quite clear what your objectives are and then select which of the above approaches seems most appropriate. If it is to be successful much planning and preparation will have to go into the new course, once the idea has been accepted and course plans can go ahead.

Some of the considerations which should be taken into account are:

What teaching expertise is available?
What teaching methods are appropriate? (see Section 6).
Will co-operation be available from other departments when required?
What new books and teaching aids are required?

How much time is to be devoted to broadening elements?

or   What weighting should be given to different aspects of a broad degree?

What form will assessment take? (see Section 7).

Failure to prepare adequately is bound to result in poor courses with critical student response. This will perpetuate the second rate image which still persists from some general degrees and put even more obstacles in the way of other people trying to make similar innovations.

We now turn to a more detailed look at some of the options available.

(i) Combined Honours Schemes

These have been introduced in an attempt to escape from the unsuccessful general degree approach. The structure of the combined degree differs from place to place, but, generally speaking it is designed to avoid the shortcomings of its predecessors. The student concentrates on two subjects in the final year(and sometimes in the penultimate year). The subject matter in each discipline is carefully selected and treated in depth, high standards are set throughout and every attempt is made to provide the student with an adequate stimulus even at the risk of over-working him. Usually a quasi-department is set up to provide both an academic and a physical home for the student within the university and, increasingly, a head of department under various titles is appointed to act as 'defender of the faith'. The scheme operating at Leeds University which is now in its 15th year and has 560 students is discussed more fully in Section 8 as a specific example.

(ii) Modular Schemes

These usually refer to schemes which offer a large number of self-contained relatively short units which can be put together on a 'cafeteria' principle to earn sufficient 'credits' to obtain a degree. An individual programme can be either narrow or broad, depending on the choice made and 'the rules of the game'. Some schemes have a system of prerequisites whereby satisfactory completion of specific modules is necessary before certain other ones can be embarked upon. Probably the best known example of this type is the Open University system. Where this system operates in conventional institutions a number of difficulties not faced by the Open University have to be overcome. These include either great strains on time-tabling *or* time-table limitations on student choice *or* much duplication/multiplicity of classes. Its over-riding attraction is the great facility it affords for programmes of studies to be tailored to suit the individual student.

(iii) General/Liberal/Complimentary Studies

This approach to broadening began some years ago with the introduction of a small non-vocational and usually non-specific component into an otherwise highly specialised science programme of studies. Such components are drawn from a great range of subject matter. Some might be regarded as being professionally useful, for example communication and business studies, but sometimes they are quite unconnected with the principal subject of study, as in the case, for example, of music and art appreciation, religious studies and politics; classes are intended to add a thin veneer of 'liberal education' to otherwise technical studies. They are seldom taken seriously either by students or by the staff giving them or by the staff of the parent department. This is not surprising. The time allocated is small, the pressure applied is effectively nil, the student's attainment is not usually assessed—all indicators of lack of esteem. Many recent attempts to use this existing infra-structure to provide opportunities for some consideration of the social aspects of sciences have been hampered by the low status accorded by both staff and students to 'general' studies. This is particularly the case in polytechnics where staff engaged in teaching social aspects of science and technology have found it very difficult to escape this image and establish academic acceptance and respectability.

(iv) Integrated Science

The biggest danger with such courses is that students will find it difficult to identify the integrating concepts. Having abandoned specific disciplines which normally provide the skeleton on which to build the detailed knowledge, course designers will find it necessary to provide an adequate alternative. Otherwise there is a danger that the course will jump from one topic to another without opportunity either for in-depth study or for students to relate the parts to an overall picture. 'Grasshopper' minds may result which fail to make the inter-connections and the integration which are so important if such a course is to succeed. Students may become jacks-of-all-trades. The alternative which seems to be effective is to construct the course around one or more linking themes. One course which does this is the Integrated Science Studies degree at Aston University. Here the linking themes are materials, systems and 'science, technology and society'.

6. Teaching Methods

Course structure and content are only one aspect of designing a successful course. Another very important consideration is the teaching methods to be used. Different methods are appropriate in different circumstances with such factors as the level and type of student, the subject matter, overall teaching objectives being important. Traditionally science degrees have been taught by a mixture of "chalk and talk" and laboratory exercises. It is quite clear that such a pattern will not always, or even normally, be appropriate in many of the broad courses we have been discussing. Without knowing precisely the scheme in question it is impossible to give detailed advice on what is appropriate. Many of the other articles in this series deal in some detail with other methods which could well be appropriate in broad science courses. Hence Group Methods, Adapting Instructional Method to Class Size, and Laboratory Work in Undergraduate Teaching should each offer invaluable advice relevant to particular circumstances.

Teachers would wish to obtain satisfactory results from innovation in education must consider methods as much as structure and content. The Siscon Project (Science in a Social Context) provides us with one example where this was recognised from the start. Siscon has been largely concerned with producing teaching/learning materials in the area of the social aspects of science. The materials are designed to encourage active student participation, something which the project members felt was crucial to the successful teaching of social aspects of science. Students must see themselves as involved—reading, writing, discussing—if the objectives are to be reached. Further details of Siscon are given in Section 8.

7. Assessment

Examinations

Most of the examination assessment of broad degree courses is no different from the examination/assessment of single subject science courses. Much has been said about this elsewhere; it is not our intention to repeat it here. There are one or two points which are especially relevant and are therefore worth emphasising and there are a few considerations which are peculiar to broad degree schemes.

Firstly, when some injection—small or large—of liberal or general studies is used as the broadening element in an otherwise conventional course it is important that a) it is assessed and b) the assessment contributes significantly to the overall assessment or classification of the degree scheme. If the rest of the degree scheme is assessed and the liberal studies component is not, the differentiation will be seen by some students—probably by most—as a clear indication that liberal studies is relatively unimportant and they will treat it accordingly. Secondly the components of a broad course will differ more in their subject matter than those of more conventional courses and require a correspondingly wide range of examining techniques: the conventional unseen 3-hour paper, open-book papers, pre-set papers, essays, dissertations, projects— all have their place and should be used as most appropriate.

The project both as a mode of assessment and as a teaching/learning method has a special application in broad degrees. An inter-disciplinary project can be very valuable in helping the student to relate and to integrate the different elements in his studies. Supervision and assessment present problems for which there are several possible solutions. In our opinion joint supervision—one supervisor from each specialism involved—and separate assessment—each specialism assessing the worth of the project in that particular discipline—work best. This approach is not without its difficulties and requires close collaboration between the supervisors but it presents less problems than any of the alternatives.

Finally there is the problem of conflation. Were it acceptable to produce a profile assessment, showing the student's level of attainment in each element of a broad course, final assessment would pose no especial difficulty. But that is not the case; the longstanding tradition of aggregating performance into one final class dies hard and broad degrees must conform. That being so the problem is one of how best to conflate the student's performances in the various elements of his course—a problem not limited to broad degrees but perhaps requiring more explicit consideration in such courses. The questions that have to be answered are:

(1) Are *marks* or *classes* to be awarded for each component? If marks are used how comparable are the mark values and mark spread in the different subjects? If classes are used are *they* awarded on a comparable basis in the two or more subjects?

(2) What weights are given to the different components and why?

(3) In a multi-component scheme are early components and late components to be weighted equally or weighted differently?

(4) In a multi-component scheme must the student attain a certain level (pass) in all components? If not what is the maximum number of 'fails' allowed and what is the minimum acceptable mark?

(5) Is the Finals Board of Examiners to be a large one on which all subjects involved in the broad scheme are represented? In which case will all take a part in decisions about every candidate though most of the examiners present will neither have taught nor examined a particular candidate? Or, a small one comprising only representatives of subjects concerned with a particular group of candidates plus perhaps the external examiner(s) or assessor(s) and a chairman? In which case complex schemes with many components require several—sometimes many—such Boards; much time may be required and there is difficulty in maintaining parity of treatment.

(6) If a dispute arises who has the authority to decide?

(7) Perfect foresight being a rare thing, what provision should be made for modifying the arrangements in the light of experience?

These are difficult questions not always recognised explicitly nor given much thought when formulating proposals for a broad course. But nonetheless some answer to most if not all of them is implicit in the arrangements which are proposed.

There is no ideal set of model answers to these questions; every scheme has its special features requiring its own answers and different examining arrangements (if the implications have been well thought out beforehand and there is some flexibility included) can be made to work satisfactorily. We can best illustrate the resolution of these questions by summarising the procedures in two schemes and referring the readers to others.

Combined Studies, Leeds

Here the final classification is done by numerous small boards, one for each combination, each having one examiner from each department concerned, the Director of Combined Studies in Science (as Chairman) and an External Assessor. The guidelines issued to all departments, which will be seen to be fairly simple and to allow considerable flexibility, are as follows:

(a)   Papers will be marked in the individual departments in accordance with the normal practice, the departmental external examiner(s) being involved in the usual way.

(b)   Your departmental examiners' meeting should arrive at a classification (Fail, Pass, III, II(ii), II(i), (I) taking into account all matters which you consider relevant (i.e. which you would consider in the classification for your own single-subject degree). In those cases where you consider a candidate to be very much on the Fail/Pass borderline, and where you are prepared for the result in the other principal subject to be the deciding factor, a result of 'Fail/Pass' should be returned.

(c)   You should bring to these meetings *all relevant information about the candidates*. It is most important that you should be able to say whether a particular candidate is regarded as being at the lower end, the middle, or the upper end of the class to which he/she has been graded.

(d)   The classification for each candidate will be made by the appropriate meeting on the following basis:

   (i)   A failure in either principal subject will result in failure in the final examination for the degree. Those returned as Fail/Pass will be resolved by discussion in the light of the performance in the other subject.

   (ii)   The class awarded will be the 'average' of the two classes in the individual subjects; normally, the class awarded will not be higher than that class next above the lower of the two classes for the separate subjects.

   (iii) Such other evidence as the committee may agree to accept (e.g. the candidate's programme and performance in ancillary courses) may be taken into consideration in resolving difficult cases.

NELP Science Course

By contrast the B.Sc. Science Degree at North East London Polytechnic is a complex multi-modular scheme built around core studies. The Board of Examiners is huge, consisting of some 40 internal and 10 external examiners meeting under the Chairmanship of the Dean of Science. The main annual meeting is preceded by several subject board meetings and sometimes also by a meeting of the external examiners. There is also an Appeals Committee. The rules are too extensive to be summarised briefly and although much care went into their preparation the Board still finds it necessary to adapt them in the light of experience. The examination procedures are fully documented (in a book not much smaller than this) and these are subject also to the rules laid down by the CNAA. Those readers wanting more detailed information should write to Mr. Paul Dye who is in charge of the scheme.

Two other examples of significantly different type are provided by the Modular Degree Scheme at the City of London Polytechnic and the Combined Science scheme at the University of Liverpool. Enquiries should be addressed to Mr. Michael Brandon-Bravo at the City of London Polytechnic and the Director of Combined Studies in Science at Liverpool University.

It is, of course, the borderline and generally unsatisfactory students who raise the problems and to whom much of the procedures are addressed. We should emphasise that, diligent and conscientious as examiners in these and other schemes most often are, there are no ideal solutions. There will inevitably be shortcomings in any system which attempts to fit a large number of students of very varied and assorted talents and attainments into five or six categories.

8. Some Examples

Finally we turn to some specific examples of what has been tried. The examples have been chosen to illustrate a wide range of approaches, and their degree of success varies considerably. They are *not* models put forward as 'ideal' types for you to follow but they do show how the different approaches have tried to overcome some of the problems discussed in the earlier sections.

(i) Combined Studies in Science, Leeds University

66 combined science degrees in science are offered, involving 17 science subjects, 8 applied science subjects, 4 arts subjects and 3 subjects from social sciences. The student graduates in two principal subjects and also studies another subject until his penultimate year. Usually the other subject for one student will be a main subject for another; it is therefore easy to change from one combination to another as shown in Figure 1 which illustrates a three-year degree scheme.

		Year 1	Year 2	Year 3	
	(	Physics 1A	Physics 2A	Physics 3A	)
	(	Maths 1A	Maths 2A	Maths 3A	)
Courses	(	Computational	Computational	*or*	
studied	(	Science 1A	Science 2A	Physics 3A	)
				Computational	)
				Science 3A	)
				or	
				Maths 3A	)
				Computational	)
Fig. 1.				Science 3A	)

In addition to the normal three-year scheme of study for each combination there is a four-year scheme for those entrants who, for any reason, are deemed to require the longer course. For example entrants to the Geography/Geology course with an Arts bias in their Sixth Form work need the additional time to cope with a scientific course content.

The standard of students admitted to combined science degrees is fairly high, judged by A level achievement. For example admissions in October 1976 had average grades of BCC. The final degree is awarded on the two principal subjects only. Each department examines the student independently using its own method of examination and assessment and deciding on a classification in consultation with its own external examiner. The final combined honours classification is arrived at by representatives of the two departments, the Director of Combined Studies and an external assessor. The Combined Studies scheme in its present form started in 1962. High standards have been set and maintained and the results to date have been good. (See Table 1).

Table 1. The figures given below refer only to Science in Leeds University. The first row summarises the classification proportions over many years, the second row covers the period 1965-76 and the third row covers the period up to 1964. In this last category the ratios in many institutions have been much worse.

Type of Degree	% in Class in final degree				
	I	II.1	II.2	III	Ordinary/Pass
Single Subject Honours	10	26	35	18	11
Combined Honours (943 Graduates)	9	26	32	15	18
General Honours	13	16	25	25	21

The whole scheme is administered by the Director of Combined Studies, (who is a member of Senate with a status roughly equivalent to that of a Professor and Head of Department), aided by an Assistant Director and several part-time tutors who are members of subscribing departments. Both Director and Assistant Director are permanent full-time academic appointments. It is their responsibility to deal with all aspects of combined studies in science: enquiries, admissions, introducing new combinations, liaison with departments, examinations etc. But most important of all it is their job to know all combined science students, to help them over their difficulties and to deal with and forestall the problems of the combined degree student outlined earlier in this article. Until 1966 Combined Studies occupied temporary accommodation but now has a custom built Combined Studies Centre comprising offices, a common room, a students' study, tutorial rooms—in short a physical nucleus which combined science degree students can identify as their base within the University.

An Example: Physics within combined studies

The Combined Studies scheme at Leeds is extensive and complex and its operation can, perhaps, be demonstrated by following the 'fate' of one subject, physics.

There are seven combined degrees of the normal type in which physics is one principal subject and the other is one of: chemistry, computational science, earth sciences, history of science, philosophy, statistics or mathematics. In all but the last mathematics is the essential third subject and all are flexible in the manner illustrated in Figure 1. There is also another combination: Physics and Electronic Engineering which, for Leeds, is atypical. In this scheme all the courses have been carefully tailored to fit together and the mathematics is a selection of topics designed to meet the needs of the Physics and Electronics courses. It is hoped that it will produce a graduate with a marriage of the outlook of the scientist and the approach of the engineer and satisfy a very pressing and growing need in the graduate market. Applications to all physics combined degrees have declined from about 20% of all applicants (500 out of 2,500 in 1970) to 12.6% in 1976 (266 out of 2,112) although it has to be borne in mind that many new non-physics combinations have recently been introduced. Over the last five years the intake has been between 20 and 30 students each year, compared with about 60 students per year entering the single subject physics course. The two groups of students, combined physics and single subject physics, attended many physics lectures together and use the same laboratories and equipment; the combined students spend less time in practical classes. The Physics Department makes every effort, both in academic and social matters, to differentiate as little as possible between the two groups of students and this policy has paid off handsomely both for the students and the department. The mathematics courses studied by the two groups are different. The combined students (with the exception of the Physics/Electronics group) follow a course in which there is mathematics from pure, applied and applicable branches—a considerably abbreviated form of a straight mathematics degree. The mathematics is not essentially subsidiary to the physics; the flexibility of the schemes, as mentioned before, is dependent on this. The single subject physics student (plus the Physics/Electronics group) follow a course in mathematics for physics, essentially a course in applicable mathematics.

Within the physics combined degrees the distribution is not even. There is strong preference for Physics/Mathematics and Physics/Electronic Engineering as might be expected. Both these options are important in their different ways. The former is an admirable introduction to theoretical physics, better than most undergraduate courses labelled theoretical physics. The latter is a better preparation for many fields of work in the electronics industry and in electronics research than either the physics degree or the electronic engineering degree. It is hoped that the interest in these combinations will continue and that the intake will increase. At the weak end of the spectrum are Computational Science/Physics, Physics/Statistics and Physics/History of Science or Philosophy (the last two are linked because they share a common year). Although there have been some transfers into these schemes from other degrees the numbers of graduates have so far been very small. Each of these degrees are seen as both interesting and important—increasingly important in years to come. The development of complex large-scale physics with its emphasis on computing, with on-line experiments, the ever greater need for statistical treatment (both in design and analysis) convinces Leeds of the desirability of the first two combinations. Many physicists derive great interest from reading about the history of science and its philosophy, interest which is transferred to studies in physics itself. Combined degrees including these subjects, as well as having intrinsic academic value, could prove to be a sound training for physics teachers. For these reasons therefore the small numbers in these four combinations is seen as a weakness in the present situation.

(ii) B.Sc. Science: North East London Polytechnic

This is a three year full-time course, first offered in the 1974/5 session, essentially modular in construction but incorporating a common core. The core occupies about 15% of the student's time and is intended "to develop the intellectual skills and background necessary for a critical understanding of the complex nature of science and its place in society, together with the ability to use that understanding to guide (the student's) future work in science". As well as this major objective the core also attempts to give all students basic mathematical and information retrieval skills. The more substantial part of the core is concerned principally with consideration of the scientific approach, using both methodological and historical treatments, and with the subject of 'science in society'. The teaching/learning methods are appropriately varied and include interdisciplinary seminars on topics of interest to a range of subject groups. The core studies all lead up to the students, working in small groups, preparing case studies on social aspects of science, describing the problems and discussing the possible solutions. In addition to the core each student must complete three modules each year, a total of nine in all. There are sixty-seven modules from which to choose (eleven offered in the first year, the remainder in second and third years) drawn from a wide range of subject area: Biology, Biochemistry, Physiology, Psychology, Chemistry, Physics, Mathematics, Computing, Statistics. The modules are arranged to allow both for a continued, developing study in depth and for divergence from a given starting point. Almost all the second and third year modules are based on a first year module and a few also have a second year prerequisite. Students are provided with a very clear chart showing possible sequences of modules and are helped in making their choices by course tutors, year tutors, guidance tutors, and by the director of the scheme who has the status of a head of department. Although it is by no means the largest or the most complex modular system in existence it is nonetheless complex enough, complex without being confusing. The core system holds it together; the modules are sufficiently numerous to provide adequate choice, sufficiently interdependent to give the student's studies sufficient cohesion, not so numerous as to make those studies too fragmented. The core helps the student to understand the purpose, methods, limitations and direction of science; the modules give a sound basis in the techniques and subject matter of some part of science. The procedures and methods of assessment have been constructed with care and are mentioned elsewhere in this book.

Indeed the whole scheme clearly shows the thought and care which went into its preparation; a team of academics and educational technologists was brought together specially for this purpose and worked on the proposals for two years. Then followed a period of discussion with the Council for National Academic Awards and some consequent modification. Even so, the limited experience to date has suggested some variations in the content and scope of modules, in tutoring procedures, in examining procedures and regulations. The closely-knit and committed team of lecturers, tutors and administrators responsible for the conduct of this course are still learning.

The 'economics' of this scheme is interesting—the economics of all schemes are interesting (and important); we introduce it here only because it is a particularly straightforward case, easy to explain. The college admits about 100 students each year. If we treat the core as equivalent to a module each student must attend 3 modules + core, i.e. 4 modules—equivalent in each year of the course. So in the first year where 11 modules + core are offered the average number of students per module is about 33, assuming all modules are populated, as in practice they are. Very healthy. In the second and third years allowing for some wastage by transfer, failure etc., a similar calculation gives a figure for the 56 modules + core of about 12 students/module, again assuming all modules are populated. This is not so comfortable a figure. A few modules not 'running' will improve the situation but not by much. If the average over the three years is calculated we find students/module works out at about 16. All of which means either (a) that a scheme like this cannot work sensibly without an intake of 100 students/year or more *or* (b) it is unwise on an intake of 100 to offer more modules or (c) it would be more economical to offer some second and third year modules on alternate years. Remember, these calculations assume four module-equivalents being studied at any one time. A scheme which differed in any essential respect: size of intake, number of modules being studied simultaneously, number of modules offered in each year or semester, will require a different but similar calculation.

(iii) The Honours School of Liberal Studies in Science at the University of Manchester

That rather cumbersome heading is the official description of an important approach to broadening science education offered by Manchester since 1966 and commonly known by the more convenient title of 'Science Greats' or, recently, 'Science in Society'. The governance of the course is in the hands of the Liberal Studies in Science Department, the members of which, all qualified scientists, teach the social aspects of science and technology; the remaining half of the teaching is provided by members of the economics and various science and technology departments. The whole comes under the general supervision of a Board of Studies. The three year degree programme, which contains various options as we shall explain, is essentially a science-based course designed to develop in the student *both* the traditional science skills *and* what has been called scientific literacy: the study of science from economic, sociological, political, historical and philosophical points of view. *All* students study the Science in Society component for approximately half their time throughout all three years. Coupled with that they may study one of three opinions: Physical Science (Physics/Engineering) *or* Physical science (Chemistry) *or* Life Science. In addition, during the first two years, they attend a subsidiary course. The arrangement of the scheme of study is most easily understood from the chart on the next page. Educationally, one of the prime virtues of the course is that the students learn a balanced set of skills. The concepts, theories, laboratory skills and theoretical skills of traditional science education are married with an understanding of how science affects, and is affected by, society, of scientific methods and of what makes science 'scientific'. This latter area of study develops both written and verbal skills and encourages serious consideration of the problems—internal *and* external—of science. In all parts of the course the teaching and examining methods used are those most appropriate to the material studied.

We could go on at length about this course. Much as been said and written about it, both because it has been successful and because of its seminal role in encouraging other institutions to explore ways of broadening science teaching. Perhaps, however, our purpose can best be served by quoting one small section from

COURSE STRUCTURE

Course	Science in Society	and Physical Sci. (Phys./Eng.)	or Physical Sci. (Chem.)	or Life Science	and Choice of Subsidiary Subject
Year One	The Nature of Scientific Discovery	Properties of Matter	Organic Chemistry	Zoology	One choice from: Life Science: chemistry[a], geology, psychology, physiology, contemporary social problems of science and technology.
	Economic History	General Engineering Science	Physical Chemistry	Botany	Physical Science: Psychology, physiology, philosophy[b], sociology[b], mathematics[a,c], contemporary social problems of science and technology.
Two	The Rise of the Scientific Perspective Science, Technology and Industrialisation Economics	Electricity and Magnetism	Inorganic and Radiation Chemistry	Cell Biology and Genetics, with Data Analysis Or Ecology, with Data Analysis	Life Science: one choice: Physical Science: two choices: Geology[d], psychology, sociology, philosophy, computer science[d,e], decision theory[d,e], science of engin. materials[d,e], mathematics[d,e].
Three	Three from: Sociology of Science Technology and Production Science, Technology and Government Technology Assessment and Forecasting	Energy Resources and Power	Environmental Chemistry	As second year, but more advanced courses	None*

* Final year students also present a dissertation on a subject of their choice.
a For those without A-level in this subject.
b Physics and Engineering option only.
c Chemistry option only.
d Physical Science students must take at least one of these courses.
e Physical science students only.

the LSS departmental brochure which illustrates well how departments have co-operated in teaching the course and how the 'traditional' and 'social' approaches have been integrated:

CHEMISTRY

This programme, taught mainly by the Department of Chemistry, but with contributions in the final year from the Departments of Geology and Botany, is designed in the first two years to prepare students for a final year course entitled *Environmental Chemistry*. Topics covered in the first two years include kinetics, thermodynamics, chemistry of biologically important molecules, inorganic chemistry and radiation chemistry. The object of the final year course is to study some of the chemical processes which shape the natural environment, and in particular those interactions between Man and his environment which are relevant to his continuing evolution and survival. Topics covered include Geochemistry, ecological chemistry, recycling of minerals, and the chemistry of energy sources and their utilisation.

Sample Examination Questions

1. One of the most important contributions to speculation on the origins of life has been the synthesis under simple aqueous conditions of bio-

logically significant organic compounds from simpler molecules, which have been shown to be present in volcanic gases, on some of the other planets, or in interstellar space. Discuss fully such a synthesis of *two* of the following: *(a)* a mixture of simple amino acids; *(b)* cytosine; *(c)* adenine.

2. Give a chemical account of the reasons why the degradation by photochemical and other paths of polychlorinated biphenyls, or any other chlorinated hydrocarbons, raises environmental problems.

Sample Reading

1. W.J. Moore, *Physical Chemistry* (Longmans, 5th edn., 1972).
2. I. G. Gass, *et al., Understanding the Earth* (M.I.T. Press, 1973).
3. E. D. Goldberg, *et al., Man's Impact on Terrestial and Oceanic Ecosystems* (M.I.T. Press, 1971).

Finally this example also allows us to say something about the employability of graduates from broad science courses. The question most often asked when these courses are under discussion is: "Yes, all very well, but what sort of jobs will graduates from a course of this type go into?" The underlying assumption is that the employment of graduates from traditional science courses is straightforward, unproblematical, (a strange assumption when, for many years, opportunities for the employment of science graduates in jobs where they will use directly the theoretical and experimental skills they have been taught—jobs as 'bench scientists'—have been getting less and less) and that appropriate employment for broad based science graduates is hard to imagine. Manchester has now seen eight intakes through to graduation and is therefore in a position to give an answer to that question. Again we quote from the departmental prospectus where the employment of the first six cohorts is analysed:

Thirteen per cent of our graduates took up posts in the public sector, some in administrative and managerial positions (e.g., UKAEA contracts division; hospital administration; NORWEB administrative trainee), others in various kinds of inspection work (e.g., water authority; pollution control; Weights and Measures Inspector), and yet others in technical writing, information work and social work.

Thirty-seven per cent entered private industry. Most took up administrative and managerial positions (e.g. Kodak: administrative services; Barclays Bank Trust Company: graduate trainee; J. & S. Pumps: personal assistant to the Managing Director; 3M Company: personnel management; Mars Ltd.: production management). Others entered technical sales and marketing with such companies as ICL, British Oxygen, Royal Dutch Shell, and Courtaulds. Some took up information work, and others began careers based on operations research, systems analysis or computing with, for example, ICL,

British Iron and Steel Research Association, ICI and Chapman-Thompson. Some became accountants with, for instance, Touche Ross and Co.

Fifteen per cent went into teaching posts, via the Postgraduate Certificate of Education.

Twenty-two per cent entered unusual and challenging careers in, for instance, the BBC (programme operations assistant), publishing (with Penguin Books), and science journalism (with *Nature,* and the journals of the Science Policy Foundation and the Institute of Electrical Engineers). One joined the Army, another the RAF, and a third became a missionary in India.

Finally, *thirteen per cent* took up postgraduate research, either for higher degrees or as research assistants in universities.

In short, our graduates have moved into a very wide variety of occupations. There is no "typical" career route for them, this not being a wholly vocational course. What we do provide is a foundation of intellectual competence which enables a graduate to enter with confidence into a life-style of his or her own choice.

And, we might add, provide graduates better suited for the range of employment for which science graduates *are* required (as so thoroughly documented in the Swann Report) than the highly specialised output of the more traditional course.

(iv) Integrated Science Studies: Aston University

This course, as the name implies, aims at an integrated approach to a broad science course. It is an honours degree course based on pure and applied natural and social sciences. Care has been taken in the selection of topics to bring out those fundamental ideas that are common to all science. The student has to absorb much information from different areas and to concentrate *both* on sophisticated ideas that unite these *and* the necessary differences in approach when dealing with topics as diverse as economics, physics, biology or production engineering.

The course is managed by an Academic Steering Board which draws its teaching from a wide range of disciplines. In such a course as this it is essential that all concerned with its teaching and conduct have a clear idea what it is they are doing and of how each contribution fits into the whole. In this case the group concerned are explicit that they are not producing graduates who will be 'bench scientists' (although they see some bench science as an essential part of their education) but graduates who will make their careers in administration, the civil service, local government, journalism, teaching and other occupations where *both* a knowledge of the working methods of scientists and technologists *and* an appreciation of some of the urgent problems of to-day are required. While general direction remains the responsibility of the Steering Board, admissions, everyday co-ordination, student counselling and the like are in the hands of a Course Tutor.

The first year of the course provides a grounding in the fundamentals of the sciences—pure and applied—and in mathematics. Physical, biological and social sciences form three separate courses with some cross references between them. The content of the mathematical course is carefully tailored to the other courses and those students without GCE Advanced Level Mathematics are given additional tuition; a big problem in bringing together a group of students in an unorthodox course of this type is that, as the students inevitably have mixed backgrounds, some selective teaching to reduce the inhomogeneity is therefore necessary in the first year.

The main part of the second and final years concentrates on the study of three topics: 'Materials', 'Systems' and 'Science, Technology and Society'. In addition, in the second year, there are courses on the scientific method (in which the methods used in the first year are abstracted and critically discussed) and more mathematics; there is a strong component of statistics and computing in the mathematical studies of the first two years. The three principal topics are intended to provide both integrating factors across the scientific disciplines and an awareness of contemporary issues important for graduates of this type.

Materials: information from several disciplines: mechanical properties, design possibilities, economics, availability, corrosion resistance etc. is needed to decide on the choice of materials for the manufacture of an article. 'Materials' therefore deals with natural resources, metallurgy, physical properties, chemical properties, economics, design and production engineering, international trade, psychology and marketing.

Systems: provides integration in a different way. Whereas 'Materials' uses information from a wide range of disciplines and processes it into a decision, 'Systems' seeks for methods of thinking common to problems in different areas: electronics, manufacturing, biology, ecology, social organisation, economics, etc. The systems approach proves a valuable method of analysis which gives an understanding of the roles played by various parts of a system and of how a given organisation can be improved to achieve certain ends.

Science, Technology and Society: examines some of the modern dilemmas arising out of the increased use of technology with its consequent increase in consumption, waste production, pollution, depletion of natural resources, ecological problems, etc. In the final year there is an individual project, an interdisciplinary problem, which provides a further opportunity for integrating the very broad range of knowledge and skills which characterises this course.

The student may attend the course *either* for three years, full-time, *or* over a period of four years, one years industrial training being inserted between the second and final years.

(v) Undergraduate Science Course, Griffith University, Brisbane, Australia

All the course patterns used to illustrate this section are exceptional in that, clearly, they are different each from the other, and each is unique to greater or lesser extent; there are no other courses *quite* like them though there may be some (or many) which are of the same pattern as each one. But this one is exceptional exceptional in that a) it is the only illustration taken from outside the UK and b) this is not an option available to science students at this university but is *the* science. All science students entering Griffith University, Brisbane's second University which enrolled its first students in January 1975, follow a common first year course. They spend half of each working week studying a composite physics-chemistry-biology course, a quarter studying mathematics and a quarter studying Science, Technology and Society. In the second and third years the student may choose to which areas he wishes to proceed. The School of Science is committed to inter-disciplinary teaching programmes and, in a world in which tradition weights the scales heavily towards specialisation, sees this approach as necessary in order to achieve its purpose.

The first (or Foundation) year course in Science, Technology and Society (known locally as FYSTS) comprises 41 lectures and 14 tutorials covering the following topics:

The Origins of Modern Science
The Nature of Scientific Knowledge
The Scientific Community
Science and Public Policy
Contemporary Problems in Science and Society

given approximately equal weight. This course, and succeeding courses in the second and third years, are taught by a small specialist staff, the senior member of which is also Director of the Science Policy Research Centre.

To further ensure that these broadening studies are *seen* to be important, it is written into the course regulations that each student must reach a certain level (33%) in the end-of-year assessment in the STS and Maths courses to be allowed to proceed to the second year. In the composite sciences course this hurdle is set at the pass mark (45%). However if the student wishes to proceed to Honours he must gain a pass mark in *all* three first year courses. The assessment of FYSTS uses a mixture of essays set during the year and examinations held at the end of each semester.

As was to be expected this insistence on the inclusion of a broad view of science was at first met by some suspicion by the students, brought up to expect—demand—a narrow, technique oriented, approach. However, the anti-honeymoon period was soon over (probably because the lecturers concerned recognised the problem, understood the reason for it, and met it sensibly) and the level of interest and commitment grew perceptibly. Of the 87(60) students in this first (second) cohort, 8(3) achieved distinctions in STS and 8(5) failed the foundation year because of inadequate performance in this part of the course. Of the 72(55) students who proceeded to the second year, 32(17) opted for the one semester course: "Science, Technology and the Modern Industrial State"; these included many of those ranked highest overall at the end of the first year. 38 of the students in the first cohort when entering the third and final year elected to proceed to STS courses in the third year; these are two, each half a semester in length: "Science, Technology and Underdevelopment" and "Science and Government". In both the second and third years the weight given to STS courses is similar to that given in the first year; that is to say, about a quarter of the student's time during the semester. The figures in brackets show the position for the second cohort entering Griffith in January 1976 one year later, i.e. when completing their first year of study and about to enter their second. At the same time the first cohort had completed its second year and was about to enter its third.

It is worth noting that the School of Science at Griffith has extended this broad view of science teaching to the postgraduate level. In March 1976 it opened an M.Sc. course in Science, Technology and Society, of three years duration by part-time study; the first two years are formal study, the third is devoted to the production of a thesis. The course is 'managed' by the STS group, and supported by teaching contributions from Griffith's School of Australian Environmental Studies, from the School of Economics at the University of Queensland and the Federal Department of Science, Canberra. Fully subscribed, all the students have passed the end of first year assessment and, at the time of writing, are proceeding to the second year.

At the beginning of this note we graded this entry 'exceptional exceptional' for the reasons given. But the reader will now appreciate that it is noteworthy in another, more important, sense. Efforts to broaden science courses are normally conducted in a hostile climate and prejudiced thereby. Griffith has shown what can be done when the science community sets out, as an act of policy, to create a supportive environment.

(vi) SISCON (Science in a Social Context)

Although we are including SISCON as an example of what is being done to broaden science education in the particular area of the social aspects of science it is not a 'course' as such. The Project began in October 1973 as a Nuffield supported co-operative project involving eight universities and one polytechnic. It lives on in 1976, now financed by the Leverhulme Trust and involving directly nine universities (Aston, Bradford, Edinburgh, Leeds, Leicester, Manchester, Stirling, Surrey and Sussex) and three polytechnics* (Middlesex, North East London and Newcastle). It originally sprang from a realisation that the spread of science courses offering a significant component dealing with social aspects was being

---

*   to which have now been added Huddersfield, Lanchester, Manchester and Napier Polytechnics.

hindered by the lack of both appropriate teaching materials and suitably qualified and experienced teachers. The original aim of SISCON was to produce teaching-learning materials, to publicize these developments in science teaching, to encourage and assist the development of new courses of this type both within member institutions and in other universities and polytechnics, to hold conferences and to assist in the movement of lecturers between institutions in order to make the maximum use of the teaching resources available.

Since October 1973 the project's principal activity has been the production of teaching-learning materials. These have been produced on a variety of topics: Science, Technology and the Modern Industrial State (three); Sociology of Science (three); Galileo and Copernican Astronomy—A Scientific World View Defined; Society and Food; Darwin to Double Helix—The Biological Theme in Science Fiction (two); Research and Technology as Economic Activities; Science and the Environment (three); Limits to Growth (two); Aspects of Scientism; Science and Survival; The Scientist's Social Responsibility; Decisions on Technology; Health Hazards in Industry. About an equal number on equally varied topics are yet to come. They have been produced in a manner which allows them to be used flexibly; the 'unit' is conceived of as providing sufficient material to occupy a student for about one third of his total working time over a period of three weeks. Each unit is presented in a form which allows the teacher considerable freedom of choice and the units themselves can be selected and assembled to meet the needs of a wide variety of students and courses. The response to these materials has been very pleasing and they are shortly to start appearing as commercial publications. They have all been circulated to a large number of institutions (well over 100) of which about one third are overseas.

It is not envisaged that during, say, the next decade a fairly uniform pattern of socially oriented science courses will emerge in higher education. Rather will the separate institutions use the materials available and supplement them with their own resources to form first degree courses which will differ widely in the emphasis placed on the social aspects of science and in the subject matter. Already this is evident in the courses which have been developed by SISCON members. Some, for example, marry a fairly conventional study of science during part of the student's working week with a complementary study of the social and historical aspects of science. Others have produced a course pattern in which the social consideration of the subject is inextricably linked with the study of science itself. In this way a range of choice will be open to the intending student in keeping with the best traditions of British higher education. In all the courses there is considerable emphasis on seminar teaching, on producing materials in a form which will encourage students to develop their independent learning abilities and on increasing the communication between teacher and taught.

(vii) Lincoln Polytechnic: Diploma in Higher Education, B.Sc., and B.Sc. with Honours in Combined Studies

Our last example is a course which does not exist and never will. It is the brainchild of Dr. David Billings, Registrar for Science of the Council for National Academic Awards who invented this imaginary future submission to the CNAA, as one of the documents on which to base discussions at the Combined Science Conference in Bournemouth in November 1976. Both the Lincoln proposal and the report of the conference, copies of which may be obtained from Dr. Billings, make interesting and instructive reading.

The proposal is dated 1984; you must decide whether the choice of date is significant. It is not intended as a model submission but, rather, to contain (in a course of this type) as many problems as possible and to draw attention to the educational issues. The Council intends to use it as a training exercise for its Officers; we recommend it as a 'training exercise' to anyone interested or involved in broad based courses.

The scheme has a modular construction and contains within it six possible programmes:

Dip H.E. : 2 years full-time or 3 years part-time
B.Sc. : 4 years full-time or 6 years part-time
B.Sc. Honours : 4 years full-time or 6 years part-time.

—but, as will be revealed, that is not the whole story!

It contains modules contributed by ten departments:

Agriculture and Food Science
Biological Science

Business Studies
Education
Engineering
Environmental Studies
Maritime Studies
Mathematics and Computing
Physical Science
Social Studies

and assumes that four years full-time study to graduation will be the emerging norm by 1984. The author explains the underlying rationale of the submission as follows:

The aim of the course is to provide opportunities for students to follow both broad and more specialised programmes with a basic science orientation. The flexibility of the structure enables a range of science subjects to be combined, and permits students to delay their choice of any specialisation. The importance of scientists having a clear understanding of the nature of their discipline—its methods, criteria and philosophy—has been recognised within the course, as has been the need to develop scientists' social responsibility through insights into the social, political, economic and environmental context and impact of Science. It is through these studies, rather than attempts at directly relating the main science Fields that integration is attained so that students' programmes of study are coherent. However, that is not to say that interrelationships between the Fields are not developed where possible, for example through the project, interdisciplinary seminars and the academic tutorials.

The inclusion of Business Administration and Education Fields is felt to be justified in view of the need for "scientifically literate" graduates within the management of industry, and the need for science teachers in secondary schools who have an understanding of the real nature of science rather than the image emanating from most of our scientific community and currently pervasive in popular mythology. (i.e. the image of the scientist as always convergent, cold, rational, objective and myopic—c.f. C.P. Snow and Liam Hudson). It will not be possible to combine these non-science Fields so that students' programmes will all contain an emphasis on science.

The course has been designed to provide opportunities for recurrent education. So that, although it is available for full-time study, it is possible to take a part-time version of the course or to combine these two study patterns or to interrupt education by periods of work. In order to make this possible, the credit principle is incorporated in the course. Further, those students who choose may undertake periods of supervised industrial training for successful completion of which credits will be granted. Those students taking the Education Field who supplement the part-time teaching practice and the concurrent professional studies with a block period of successful teaching practice, are eligible for being recommended for qualified teachers status. In order to implement fully the recurrent concept, it is intended that no maximum duration for the course should be set down although the Polytechnic will retain the discretion to terminate studies which have taken longer than three years beyond the normal duration where it is apparent that little more is likely to be achieved. A consequence is that students cannot be guaranteed access to all of the modules or Fields which will be available when they first enter the course (although every effort will be made to maintain viability) and that modules and Fields may be modified over the period of the student's registration; such modifications may lead to students being strongly counselled to undertake additional studies. A further consequence of the recurrent principle is that the award cannot be based solely on the aggregation of credits, since the demand on students may differ according to the period over which they spread the modules. The aggregation is therefore used to establish eligibility for taking the final synoptic assessment which determines the award. Finally, it is necessary to adopt a system whereby credit exemptions can be granted or additional introductory modules prescribed so that a flexible approach to entry to the course is maintained; this should benefit particularly the mature student.

The learner's responsibility for his own education is a valued concept in this course, and one consequence mentioned above is the emphasis on counselling and guidance rather than on prescription and constraint. Thus there are no progress requirements between years of the course and the decision as to whether to repeat a failed module is the student's. Similarly the choice of Fields is made, under guidance, by the student although within Fields there are some constraints so as to achieve a coherent core; the only other constraints on content are in regard to breadth of overall study so as to provide a balanced education. Teaching methods will be student-centred, so that students have a choice of learning strategies for much of the material of the course. To this end, most of the first (full-time) semester's work is already available in the Learning Resources Centre as self-instructional learning materials of various kinds. The students can then choose whether or not to come to lectures or to use the learning resources or a mixture of these. The only aspects in which students are expected to participate are the small group sessions (tutorials and seminars) and the individual or group project work which takes place in each year; course-work marks contributing to the criteria for the granting of credits will be given for essays, problems, seminar contributions and project work. Work is progressing on learning materials for later sections of the course and will be completed in time for students who enrol in 1984.

and, later:

Induction

There will be an induction week preceding the first semester of the course, during which all students will take a pre-knowledge test, on the basis of which they will be counselled with regard to choices of Fields and modules and also any supplementary individual studies which they may need to undertake. Besides introductions to the tutorial staff and the polytechnic amenities, students will also receive guidance in regard to learning methods, information retrieval, use of the computer centre and the objectives of the course and their chosen Fields.

Modules are offered at four levels (effectively the four years of the full-time B.Sc. programme). At each level the student is required to complete 12 modules and take part in interdisciplinary seminar and

project work for a time equivalent to an additional 2 modules. Satisfactory completion of levels 1 and 2 entitles the student to the award of a Diploma; the completion of levels 3 and 4 results in the award of a Degree. The Diploma course is essentially the Foundation Course of the Degree programme. All the interdisciplinary work and 18 of the necessary 24 modules to this level are *prescribed* and form the core course of both Diploma and Degree.

The core contains:

    (i)   *double* modules in
          Life Science,
          Physical Science,
          Social Science;

    (ii) *full* modules in
          Earth Science,
          History and Developments of Science,
          Mathematics,
          Cell Biology,
          Energy,
          Molecular Science,
          Systems of Modelling,
          European Studies,
          Genetics,
          Development and Evolution,
          Languages;

    (iii) *half* modules in
          Communication,
          Statistics,
          Computing,
          Philosophy of Science.

The remaining 6 modules required to complete the Diploma/Foundation course may be selected from 18 modules covering a very wide range of subject matter.

For those students continuing to the Degree or Honours Degree a further 24 modules plus the equivalent of 4 modules of interdisciplinary studies are required. These are offered in 10 fields:

    A.   Business Administration
          Computer Science
          Education

Engineering
Mathematics and Systems

B.   Earth and Astronomical Sciences
       Environmental Studies
       Life Sciences
C.   Food Studies
       Physical Sciences

The fields in each of the groups A, B and C are timetabled simultaneously so that only one field within a group may be studied at any time. Six modules are studied by the student in each half of levels 3 and 4 and these may be selected from the 3 fields (or from 2 only if the student wishes) according to one of the following patterns:

3 : 3
4 : 2
2 : 2 : 2
3 : 2 : 1
3½ : 2½
2½ : 2 : 1½
3½ : 1½ : 1

The pattern may be varied from one half-level to the next. In practice the choice (from a large number of modules) is limited by prerequisities and is less than appears at first sight. As soon as student numbers and resources permit the college plans to duplicate some modules and thereby reduce the restrictions on choice.

It is also intended to make imaginative use of teaching methods, encouraging both student participation and independence. Back to the author:

While lectures and tutorials/seminars are available in all modules, as detailed in the syllabuses, it is possible for students to decide to learn other than through the medium of lectures. For students who make such a decision (which may vary from module to module) there will be a range of learning materials in the Learning Resources Centre—each having a set of objectives and a test. All students will be informed of the objectives of each Field and module, whether they are learning through lectures or other methods, students who choose to attend lectures may also use the learning materials to supplement their knowledge. All students will have access to academic (and personal) tutorials, and will be expected to attend seminars for those modules where these are held.

Practical work is not included in the individual modules, since it is considered to be related instead to the needs of the Field. In this way, practical work is used selectively to develop the higher levels of ability (problem solving, experimental design, analysis of results, critical awareness, creativity, evaluation etc), rather than as had been usual until about 1980 to illustrate and reinforce material covered in lectures.

Although in the early parts of the course, the experiments are fairly definitive, as the student progresses, he increasingly meets open-ended experiments culminating in the individual project. The time available for practical work (other than the project) is less than has been common, and is provided in the Fields either through special Practical Work modules or (as in Earth Science and Environmental Studies) through intensive field work courses; in some Fields provision for both is made. Through this approach, the practical work acts as an integrating agent within each Field. Additionally, throughout the course, the Interdisciplinary periods enable project work to be carried out as suits the student's development; in the Foundation Course this and the field work activities are the only timetabled provision for practical work. However, it has been stressed earlier that the course has been arranged on the assumption that private study will be undertaken to bring the total load per week to about 36 hours on average; some of this time is therefore available if students so wish to use the laboratories on open access. Additionally it is not believed that understanding of the methods and empirical base of science comes only through carrying out practical work. Thus there will be case studies and seminars, some of which will look at original research papers and seek the student's views on the validating of the experimental design and of the conclusions. In other cases, students will be given raw experimental data to interpret as assignments, or computer simulations of experiments will be available, or they will be asked to design experiments or to formulate problems so as to be amenable to empirical solution.

The submission goes on to consider the assessment and administration of this little lot.

We here have only given the reader a taste of the proposal, an appetiser. To savour its full horror/beauty (according to the reader's preferences in such matters) requires reading the submission in full and digesting it appreciatively/painfully. It is a gem, put together with great ingenuity and a sly humour which makes the reading of it as near to a delight as such a document can ever be.

Integration and Separation as a result of Unit Courses

A.R. Stokes

Introduction

The course-unit system has been in operation for ten years in London University for B.Sc. degrees, and for a somewhat shorter period for B.Sc. (Eng.) and some Arts subjects. The first courses for the new system started in 1966, and the first students completed their degrees under the new system in 1969.

In this article the system will be described, and an attempt will be made to assess its working and its effect on teaching. For this purpose the opinions of some 50 teachers of the University, from all Science departments (and some Engineering departments) and from all the ten Colleges in which Science degrees are taught under the system, were sought by means of a questionnaire. These 50 teachers were chosen randomly from among the many hundreds engaged in teaching Science subjects, and were of all grades from lecturer to Head of department.

Nevertheless, this article must be taken mainly as a personal view of the subject written by a teacher of Physics, and it has not taken into account the views of teachers in other Universities that have modular or unit systems. It was felt that it would be more useful for the author to concentrate on his personal experience of one system and to consider this from the inside, rather than to try to take an overall view of all such developments. The answers to the questionnaire have therefore been used as a check on the author's views rather than as a basis for the article. In this respect the article is different from, and in a way complementary to, a booklet entitled "The Container Revolution", which is recommended to the reader.

A further point to be made here is that some space is devoted in this article to matters concerned with examinations and other methods of assessment of students' performance, as well as with actual teaching. In any educational system teaching and examination are bound to be interlinked and to have repercussions on each other. It seemed therefore that one could not write about the course-unit system of teaching without giving a good deal of information about the examination system that goes with it.

In order to avoid confusion in nomenclature, the following terms are defined. A *course* is a series of lectures, with practical work, field work, examples classes and tutorials as appropriate, on a defined syllabus within the subject being taught. A *course-unit* is the unit of value of a course, used in calculating the minimum work-load that must be undertaken for a degree, and in setting the maximum permitted work-load for any year. A *degree-course* is a student's total selection of courses that go to make up his three (or exceptionally four) years' study.

1. The Course-Unit System in London University

The basic idea of the course-unit system is that it allows the student to choose (subject to limitations) the content of his degree-course. Each Science department provides a number of courses, suitable combinations of which will form complete degree courses in a single subject or in more than one subject. In order to provide a measure of the amount of work that will constitute a degree-course, each course is assigned a value, measured in course-units (c.u.). The course-unit is defined as being one-third of the work-load which an average student, having the necessary pre-requisite knowledge, can be expected to undertake during one academic year. Fractional course-unit values are allowed, and in fact a large

Footnote. *"The Container Revolution", a report by Tony Mansell and others, 35 pp., published by the Nuffield Foundation, April 1976, price 50p.

proportion of courses at present in operation are valued at ½ c.u. Values greater than 1 c.u. are also allowed, but are unusual. Courses valued at ¼ c.u. or less are not generally approved.

Each College department decides the contents of its own courses. In order to keep some semblance of uniformity of standards, all proposals for new courses or modification of existing ones have to be submitted to the appropriate Board of Studies (or in some cases, e.g. a course in Astrophysics, to more than one Board). It is not claimed that this procedure can ensure equal academic standards of all courses of given course-unit value, but at least it is possible to see that there are no gross inequalities in syllabus, amount of lecturing time, laboratory hours and tutorial time.

Each College is also responsible for deciding whether its students' proposed degree-courses are satisfactory. In the case of a single-subject degree, such as Physics, the decision is not normally difficult; the principal question is whether the degree-course will give a sufficient training in the basic methods and data of Physics to bring the student's knowledge up to date in at least some fields of Physics. It is also necessary to decide what ancillary knowledge is needed. Clearly, mathematics is one such ancillary requirement for physics; but is Chemistry or Computing? Can the student spend some of his time on peripheral subjects like history and philosophy of Science, or general-interest subjects like Geology, Music, or a language, without detracting too much from his study of Physics?

With two-subject degrees it can be more difficult. Taking Biology/Physics as an example, there is undoubtedly a core of physics that will be necessary for every student, but it is impossible to make this core as large as the practising physicist would like it to be. One has to recognise that the most that can be taught is a selection which will give the basis of physical laws and methods of procedure in physics. The rest of the contents of the degree-course have to be geared to the type of biophysicist the student hopes to be eventually; for instance, a fairly heavy specialization in atomic and nuclear physics and electronics might be appropriate for a future medical physicist, but the basic parts of optics, thermal physics and the general properties of matter must not be ignored. For this reason it is usual to insist that the student takes a comprehensive "core" course in Physics in his first year.

Each College holds its own examinations internally, with the usual moderation by Visiting examiners, some from other Universities and some from other Colleges of London University. In order to qualify for a degree, a student must have attended courses to the value of at least nine course-units and sat the appropriate examinations, and must have passed at least eight. It is then for the College examiners to decide what class of honours he merits. Since some students take single-subject degrees and some two-subject degrees, it is very difficult to arrive at any agreement as to how the class of honours should be determined so as to treat all students equally, and in fact a number of different systems are used by different departments for their single-honours degrees and by Joint Boards of examiners for combined-subject degrees. In single-subject degrees the questions are how to give due weight to quality and quantity as between students who have taken different numbers of course-units, and whether to weight the three years' work differently. In considering combined-subject degrees there is the further question as to whether a very good performance in subject A should be allowed to compensate for a relatively poor performance in subject B. Here one must remember that it would be wrong to give a certificate to the effect that a person has merited upper-second-class honours in Maths/Physics, and is therefore to be assumed to be a good physicist, if in fact he had obtained excellent marks in Mathematics and only third-class average in Physics. Questions such as these can only be settled by relying on the wisdom of joint boards of examiners. However, the University regulations also stipulate that in order to qualify for a degree called "A *and* B" the number of course-units passed in A must be not less than one-third of the total number passed, and similarly for the number passed in B. If the imbalance is slightly greater than this, then the label "A *with* B" may be used, provided the number of units passed in B is at least a quarter of the total number, otherwise the degree becomes a single-subject one.

Finally, if a student fails one or more courses he may re-sit them on a subsequent occasion. Whether or not he is allowed to continue a degree-course after having failed any substantial fraction of his first or second year is for his department or Faculty to decide. A limit is placed on the number of times a candidate may re-sit any particular course. This means that no candidate may ever be said to have finally failed to obtain a degree until he has re-sat all his failed courses four times and still not passed the minimum of eight course-units!

2. Changes brought about by the Introduction of the Course-Unit System

Here we list the main effects of the introduction on the course-unit system on the way in which a student is taught and examined. The merits and demerits of these changes will be considered later.

Choice of courses. The most obvious difference between the two systems is that the course-unit system gives the student a very much wider choice of subjects of study. The extent to which this is true will, of course, depend largely on the type of degree-course the student elects to take; in a single-subject degree-course there may be relatively little choice open to him, whereas in a combined course there may be a bewilderingly large number of courses available in the two main subjects and in other cognate ones. In any case, the choice of courses is limited only by what the teachers in the student's subject or subjects regard as viable combinations and what the time-table can allow. In any combined-subject degree system it is inevitable that some combinations of subjects are impossible, and are deliberately made so by the time-table: London is fortunate in that there are very few combinations of Science subjects that cannot be provided by at least one College, and arrangements for inter-Collegiate lectures can be made where necessary.

Departmental control over courses. Under the old system the syllabuses of courses were fixed by Boards of Studies whose members were drawn from all Colleges teaching the subject: teachers therefore had to bow to majority opinion in designing lecture courses. Under the course-unit system each Department decides what to teach, with the minimum of control by Boards of Studies.

Examination system. Under the old system there was an examination common to all students, consisting of Part I taken at the end of the student's second year (in the case of Special degrees), and Part II taken at the end of the third year. (Some variations in syllabus were allowed for Part II). A student who failed Part I could not proceed to Part II, but would re-sit Part I. In some cases there were examinations in Ancillary subjects to be taken at the end of the first year or the second year, and the degree could not be granted until these ancillary-subject examinations had been passed.

Under the course-unit system there is generally an examination for each course, usually held soon after the end of teaching for that course. Most examinations are held at the end of the academic year, in June, but it is permissible to hold them at any time after the teaching course has ended. Some courses are completed in a semester instead of a whole academic year, and in this case examinations may be held at the end of the semester or in the following June.

The main effect is that a student can put some of his courses behind him at an earlier stage than was possible under the old system. If, for instance, he takes and passes two course-units of Physics in his first year in a combined Biology/Physics degree, and if he elects to study no Physics other than atomic and nuclear physics during his second and third years, he can forget all other branches of physics. If, however, he has failed the Thermal physics course in the first year, this does not prevent his continuing with second-year studies, but he may re-sit the Thermal physics paper at the end of the second year if he wishes. If the system of assessment for Honours does not give appreciable weight to re-sit examination results, then a student generally will not re-sit a failed examination unless there is a serious risk that he is not going to obtain the minimum of eight course-units by the end of his third year.

The effect of this examination system is therefore that the student never has to face one very large examination on which everything depends, and for which more than one year's work is being examined. Whether this is a good or a bad feature will be considered later.

Assessment of Course-work. The old system allowed for a small proportion of marks to be awarded by the College on the basis of laboratory work or other course-work. Under the course-unit system any fraction, or even the whole, of a course may be assessed without examination, by inspection of note-books or marks given for essays, etc. Where a fixed proportion of marks is given for the written examination and the rest for some form of course work, it is for the Department to decide the proportions. In submitting a course to the Board of Studies for approval, the Department must state what combination of written papers, oral examinations, course-work assessment and practical examinations are to be used; the relative weightings, however, do not have to be stated.

Thus there is a degree of flexibility in the use of different methods of assessment, singly or in combination, that was not allowable under the old system, with its more rigid regulations.

3. Opinions

As stated above, the opinions of about 50 teachers in Science and Engineering departments were sought on the operation of the course-unit system. This sample was considered large enough to show up any overwhelming feeling in one direction or another on any aspect of the system. Those questioned were also invited to make any comments; the questionnaire was not intended to be answered like a multiple-choice examination paper, with no opportunity for qualification of the yes/no answers.

The questionnaire and its results are given in an Appendix, where it is pointed out that numerical results from this size of sample may be misleading. The main results are considered here in more general terms.

Teachers were, on the whole, very much in favour of the course-unit system, though some had reservations. They commented that it tended to fragment a subject into compartments with very little communication between them, more than did the old system with its Paper I, Paper II,.... on different branches of the subject. They point out also that it has meant much more work for teachers in examining and other forms of assessment. No doubt any system that gives the student more choice and more personal consideration will mean more work for the teacher. Students generally approve of the system, but most of them know no other system. They do however complain that the choice of courses can be bewildering. As for the opinions of employers, it was generally reported that little was known about this aspect.

There seems to be a fair measure of agreement that the first-year courses should form a "core" or foundation, being the same, apart from minor variations, for all students of the same specialization, and that a wider choice should come only in the second and third years. To a varying degree students are allowed to take courses that are not closely related to their speciality, but only a few such courses are allowed. Opinion is fairly evenly divided on whether the rules allow a student to choose a degree-course that leaves him with serious gaps in his knowledge of his subject; the interpretation of "serious gaps in knowledge" evidently varies from one teacher to another.

The flexibility of the system means that it is possible to introduce new courses or to change existing courses in the light of experience. A question as to how often courses had in fact been changed brought the reply from about half of those questioned that changes had not been very numerous since the system began; while those who said that many changes had been made, pointed out that these changes had in many cases been brought about by changes in teaching staff. A few commented that their department made changes far too frequently for their liking. It was often pointed out that small changes in syllabus were continually being made, without the need for the course to be re-registered as a whole. In Physics the overall picture is that, at the ten Colleges at which course-unit courses were taken, nearly 1000 courses have been registered since 1966, and of these nearly 500 are at present in use, the rest having been withdrawn on being superseded by other courses. However, some of these supersessions represent only minor changes; a change of title, for instance, must be registered, in order to avoid ambiguity in the student's statement of courses passed.

Some departments provide for students taking Joint Honours courses by allowing them to take courses designed for specialist students; others run courses specifically designed for those for whom the subject is not their only speciality. It was fairly generally agreed that to separate the courses so as to allow for different degrees of specialization is good educationally, but that it makes greater demands on teaching staff—demands which can be very difficult to meet in the case of smaller Colleges with small numbers of teaching staff.

Systems of assessment for awarding honours vary very much from one college to another and from one Department to another. Details of such systems are usually confidential, and therefore cannot be considered here. Some Colleges lay down a common system of assessment for all departments; others leave this to the departments, but approval by the College Board of Examiners is required. It would appear that the majority of departments use a weighted mean of marks for all courses (weighted according to the year in which the course was taken) as a starting-point. Some also bring in a requirement that, say, at least five course-units must have a mark over 60% if an upper-second-class honours degree is to be awarded, and corresponding conditions must be satisfied for other classes of honours.

Generally stûdents are given in outline the scheme by which they are assessed. Such information is necessary to help the student with his choice of courses; in particular, to enable him to decide whether to attempt the maximum allowed number of courses in a year or to concentrate his efforts on a smaller number. Too detailed information can encourage the student to try to "play the system", so as to gain the best possible class of degree with the minimum of work; most teachers were of the opinion that inevitably some students will do this, but that the practice was not prevalent. In any case it is very difficult to draw a clear line between legitimate and illegitimate manipulation of the system to give results of the greatest advantage to the student.

The course-unit system offers great flexibility in the use of assessment without written examination, where credit is given for field-work, practical projects, essays, etc. In fact answers to the questionnaire showed that such assessment was used in many departments but only to a limited extent, only one or occasionally two course-units being assessed without examination.

4. Discussion

There appears to be quite general agreement among teachers of the University that the introduction of the course-unit system in London was a step forward, and that only a few would wish to move in the reverse direction. It is a system with a very wide range of possibilities, many of which have not yet been tried, and much experience has yet to be gained before all these possibilities can be realised. If it is true, as some teachers complain, that it is being used in some departments merely as a way of carrying on the old system with its rather stereotyped syllabuses and systems of examination, then this is probably due largely to natural conservatism, a fear of losing the good features of the old system, and a feeling that innovations should be brought in gradually, a few at a time, giving opportunity for the effects of one lot of changes to be observed before bringing in the next lot.

Another thing which can be said about the course-unit system without fear of contradiction is that it makes teachers think more about the purpose of a university course. It is nowadays impossible to put everything into a science course, and it is also impossible to attain agreement as to what should constitute a complete course. One would like to give the student all the basic principles of the subject, the main experimental methods and the mathematical techniques that are in use, the most recent results of research and the newest concepts that have been introduced, and the history of ideas and experimental techniques. Such an aim may have been realistic 70 years ago, but it is certainly not possible today. Under the old system it was almost entirely up to teachers to decide what was good for students, and the natural tendency was for them to regard the tradition in which they had been brought up as being the right one. It is naturally very difficult for a physicist, brought up to regard physics as a unified whole, to accept the idea of allowing students to take a degree-course in which only the most elementary parts of a branch such as optics are introduced. Yet this is what is implied by the course-unit system, especially as applied to joint degree-courses such as Biology/Physics where any attempt to include every branch of physics would mean that it would be quite impossible to cover any one of these branches to a depth that would be at all useful.

Instead, it has to be recognised that Physics is not principally a collection of experimental data, laws and principles, but a way of analysing certain aspects of the behaviour of the physical universe. One teaches this way of analysis by means of examples drawn from various branches of physics, but it is not necessary to cover all branches in order to convey the spirit of physics. Indeed, it may be much better from the point of view of some students to cover a few branches of physics in depth. Once the student has thoroughly absorbed methods and attitudes of mind needed in one branch of physics, it is more likely that he can apply the same methods and attitudes to other branches when he needs them. As an example, quantum physics teaches the fallibility of models; it shows that although the electron may be considered for some purposes as a negatively-charged cricket ball, one must beware of giving it all the attributes of a cricket ball; it is impossible, for instance, to know both its velocity and its position precisely at the same time; it is also impossible to know simultaneously all three components of its spin angular momentum (maybe a batsman would be the first to appreciate these ideas!).

Many parts of a physics course, especially those concerned with atomic structure and nuclear structure, depend quite heavily on the understanding of ideas such as these. Thus it is quite possible that a good understanding of quantum physics along with a brief survey of solid-state electronics would equip a student better than a more superficial study of both subjects, since it will put him in a better position to gain an understanding of solid-state electronics if and when he needs it.

Although much has been written on general aspects of scientific method, I doubt very much whether this is a subject to be taught in the abstract in undergraduate courses; for just as the proper study of Mankind is Man, so the proper study of scientific method is the work of the scientist.

However, another reason can be given for teaching parts of a subject in considerable depth, and that is to give the teacher more opportunity to convey to the student his enthusiasm for the subject. Of course, in the case of a specialist student this ought not to be necessary, but it may be so if the student's choice of speciality has been arrived at for the wrong reasons, such as his teachers' influence rather than his own keeness. In the case of a Joint Honours student it may be a different matter. The student whose main wish is to become a biologist or a geologist, seeing that many important advances have been due to the application of physics, may decide to take a joint course in two subjects. He may then find that the physics is not what he expected and that it is, to him, either uninteresting or unintelligible, or both. For such a student it is very necessary that some relevant parts of physics should be explored to such depth as will show him that physics is a worthwhile pursuit.

This leads us to consider the advantages of running courses which are specifically designed for Joint Honours courses or as "ancillary" subjects for other specializations. These students generally proceed at a different rate from specialist students, and require a somewhat different selection of material. It has been suggested that these students may consider that they are being given only second-best if they are not allowed to sample the same fruits as are served to the specialist students; against this, however, a struggling Joint Honours student could argue that he ought not to be expected to keep up with those whose sole interest is in one discipline. To proceed to the logical conclusion, of course, one cannot regard as ideal a system in which the same set of courses in Physics is provided for all Joint Honours students irrespective of their other subject, be it Mathematics, Chemistry, Biology, Geology, etc, but one must draw the line somewhere in multiplying courses to suit the needs of various students. This line is inevitably drawn in accordance with the limitations of the time-table and the availability of teaching staff.

The danger of compartmentalisation of courses has been noted already, and this can be a real risk if a teacher fails to keep his own branch of the subject in the right perspective. An expert in one branch can too easily overestimate both the depth to which students need to learn his particular speciality and the amount of detail they are capable of absorbing, especially if he is not an experienced teacher. If this happens, it is probably a sign that there is insufficient co-ordination of courses within the department.

Some students find the choice of permissable courses very confusing, and to advise on this choice is not easy. One advantage of a basic "core" course in the first year is that the student is not faced with this confusing choice at the outset of his degree-course. When choices have to be made, I believe that students should be helped by being given sufficient information and by being warned of the risks involved in certain choices rather than being directed in any way. Some courses can appear much more attractive in prospect than in reality: there is a tendency among some physics students to regard theoretical physics as an easier option than those branches of physics that require laboratory work as an adjunct; in the case of students whose mathematical ability and powers of abstract thought are not strong it is necessary that this misconception should be corrected at an early stage. It is highly desirable that students should be given the opportunity to attend introductory lectures to all the courses in which they are likely to be interested, so that they can make a well-informed choice from among them. A student who is directed too forcibly into some set of courses may develop a resentment against "the system" if things do not work out well for him.

The course-unit system tends to bring examinations and other forms of assessment into a different light. Just as individual courses tend to become the domain of one teacher (or of two or three working together), so the examination of a course tends to be largely the product of one or two teachers. The paper may in fact be set by a committee of any number from two upwards, but its basic shape is likely to be influenced most by the person who has lectured on the course. In fact, only the lecturer can know whether a given question will be seen by students as book-work or as an unseen problem. This again means that care must be taken to ensure that courses are not allowed to run in isolation from each other.

Provided there is sufficient co-ordination between courses, there are advantages in having the examination so closely coupled to the teaching process. It removes one of the most serious criticisms of the examination system, namely that it causes teaching to be geared to an examination syllabus; instead, the teaching syllabus is settled first and the examination suited to it. It should also make success in the examination less dependent on memory, since the examiner, knowing his students and the course which they have studied, can more readily distinguish the candidate who reproduces uncritically what he has been told from the one who shows a real understanding of the subject. It is said that students may not like the idea that the teacher who readily gives them help with their problems in friendly tutorials and encourages them to bring out their difficulties may at the same time be making notes of their shortcomings for the purpose of assessment. However, against this it may be said that students get to know their teachers (and therefore their examiners) better, and, seeing them as persons of integrity (at least, this is what one hopes) can rely on fair treatment when it comes to the assessment of their capabilities.

The question of frequency of examinations is one on which there may be some argument. Under the old system, candidates were examined on two years' work at one time. Under the course-unit system examinations may be held at any time, and while it is usual to examine each year's work at the end of that academic year, there are departments in which courses each last for one semester and examinations are held at the end of the semester. This means that a course lasting from October to the end of January may be examined in February. Some students find that this arrangement gives them no time to think about their courses. Arguments about the interval between examinations can be pushed in both directions: the longer the interval, the more difficult is it made for the candidate who cannot take in and retain many ideas at the same time, while on the other hand the more likely it is that the good candidate will see his degree course as a whole rather than as isolated pieces. My own view is that for an average present-day student taking a Science degree, the one-year interval between examinations is about right, but there may well be cases in which one could argue for a longer or a shorter period.

A student's grasp of his subject as a whole may be tested by means of a "comprehensive" examination paper, in which the questions are of a general nature, covering all aspects of the subject. Answers to the questionnaire suggest that this has been tried but that the idea has not found favour with many departments.

As mentioned in the Introduction, this article is written by a Physicist and from the point of view of experience in the London University course-unit system. A fair amount of factual information has been included, some of which might appear superfluous, but it was felt that it was relevant in that it helps to give a background to the arguments for and against the system. Opinions on how to teach seem to be almost as numerous as teachers themselves, and it is certainly not to be expected that any statement of views such as this one will command agreement from other teachers. However, I hope it will at least serve as a useful contribution to discussion on the subject.

5. Summary of Conclusions

The course-unit system has flexibility and possibilities which have not yet been by any means fully explored.

This flexibility makes it important to consider further the purpose of a degree-course. In Science courses the study and illustration of methods and ideas are more important than the collection of facts and data.

The system makes it easier for a teacher to convey his enthusiasm for his subject provided he is allowed freedom in the choice of syllabus.

There is a danger of compartmentalization of subjects, this is especially so if teachers are expert in their own particular lines and fail to fit their courses into an overall scheme. The number of combinations of courses open to students can be very confusing, and adequate non-directive advice must be available. The examination system can be very closely coupled to the teaching system and moulded to the teaching syllabus rather than vice versa. Some drawbacks of the written examination can be removed. There is more scope for examiners to use their personal knowledge of their students in arriving at an assessment of their attainments.

Examinations are generally held at more frequent intervals under a course-unit system. Failure means that only the failed courses need be re-examined. The interval between examinations is a matter for adjustment to circumstances. There may be a risk of making examinations follow too quickly on a short lecture-course.

Appendix — The Questionnaire

The questionnaire referred to in the Introduction is reproduced below, and the answers given are indicated in brackets. Where the numbers of answers do not add up to the total of 55, some blank answers had been given. In drawing any conclusions from these numbers, it must be remembered that if 25 individuals answered "Yes" to a question, then this number might well differ by at least 5 from the number of "Yes" answers that would have been obtained from another sample of 55 individuals, simply by the fluctuations introduced by random sampling. This means that no significance is to be attached to the difference between the number of "Yes" and "No" answers to question 4, for example. Note also that some answers had comments attached. In some cases I had to use my interpretation of these comments to decide whether "Yes" or "No" was more appropriate, and in others (e.g. question 10) it is difficult to know just what significance to attach to the results.

No numbers are given for the answers to questions 8, 9 and 16. It was felt that information of this sort has to be treated confidentially, and that many of those concerned with the examination process would prefer that even statistical information were not made public. Most departments said that they give students information in outline only on the system of assessment.

Question 22 gave an opportunity for respondents to fill in any gaps in the questionnaire. Some of the suggested questions are reproduced below, but not one of them was suggested by more than one or two individuals, and it was not considered worthwhile to issue a supplementary questionnaire.

A. SPECIALIZED COURSES

1. Do your first-year students all take more or less the same course? (Yes 41, No 14)

2. Do you impose restrictions on the choice of course-units taken by a student:
   (a) in the first year:
       slight (5) moderate (17) severe (32)
   (b) in the second and third years:
       slight (31) moderate (20) severe (3)

3. Do you allow students to take course-units outside their speciality
   (a) far outside (18)   slightly outside (15)
   (b) only 1 or 2 such   several such courses (17)
       courses (29)

4. Do you consider the course-unit system, as operated in your College and in your subject, allows students to take a course in which there are serious gaps in their knowledge at the end of three years?   (Yes 27, No 25)

5. Do you treat laboratory work (or example-classes, etc.) as separate course-units (4) or as an integral part (41) of each course-unit to which it is relevant?

   Do you have strong views as to which method is better? (Separate 2, Integral 23)

6. Do you set "comprehensive" papers? (Yes 8, No 42)

   Do you find them useful in the final assessment? Or for other purposes? (Yes 6, No 6)

7. Would you like to see certain basic parts of your subject being examined by means of a paper or papers common to all Colleges of London University? (Yes 18, No 34).

8. In assessing for Honours, do you use
   (a) an average mark (either weighted or unweighted)
   (b) a system requiring a minimum number of course-units to have been passed at a given standard
   (c) some combination of (a) and (b)
   (d) some other method?

9. Are students made aware of the system of assessment
   (a) in outline
   (b) in detail

10. Do you find that some students try to "play the system", i.e. work out how to gain the best degree with the least effort? (Yes 33, No 19)

11. Do you frequently supersede old courses by new ones? (Yes 26, No 28) What has been the average life of registered courses since the system started? (3 or 4 years)

12. Are any of your courses assessed by written and/or oral reports alone, and not by examination? (Yes 38, No 15). How many? (Average 2)

13. Are any of your courses (not included above) assessed as to more than about 60% of the total marks by written and/or oral reports alone? (Yes 7, No 11) How many? (1)

B. TWO-SUBJECT DEGREES AND ANCILLARY COURSES

14. Do you run courses specially designed for Joint-Honours (two-subject) degree students and/or "ancillary" to other main subjects, and separate from your specialist courses? (Joint Honours — Yes 22, No 29: "Ancillary" — Yes 27, No 24)

15. Do you consider such separated courses educationally desirable? (Yes 34, No 11)

16. In assessing for Honours, do you use (a) (b) (c) (d) (as in question 8).

17. As question 10.
    (Yes 22, No 16)

C. GENERAL

18. Do your students like the course-unit system?
    (Yes 42, No 1)

19. What opinions have you had (if any) from employers on course-unit degrees?
    (Approval 9, No feed-back 40)

20. Do you, personally, like the system?
    (Yes 34, No 15)

21. Has the advent of the course-unit system resulted in any significant changes in the way your subject is taught in your department (apart from the fact that you are now free to choose your own syllabuses)?
    (Yes 27, No 21)

22. Are there any other questions that you think I ought to have asked?

Some of the additional questions suggested were —

Have standards fallen since the introduction of the new system?

Are there obvious discrepancies between the standards of course-units in different departments of one College, and if so, does this influence the way in which students may "play the system"?

Has there been any change of emphasis on the abilities that a given class of degree represents?

Has there been a change in the proportions of the various degree-classes awarded, since the introduction of the course-unit system?

Ought the scheme of assessment for Honours to be made uniform throughout London University?

Would you prefer to return to the old B.Sc. system (with a little more latitude in its operation)?

Conclusion or What do we do Now?

A personal reaction by a U.K. astronomer

D. McNally

By now you will have read some or all of the Authors preceding me in this series. You will have accumulated some very good advice but you will have discovered that not all of it points in the same direction or even in neighbouring directions. Do we broaden our courses or do we not? Do we have small group teaching or more project work or do we go for personalised instruction? Are you, like me, just a bit confused by it all? After all, we are the people who will bear the heat of the day, actually standing up in the lecture rooms and doing our best to "facilitate learning" i.e. the thing that up to now we have called teaching. But we cannot devote all our time to teaching. We have our research, we have our committees, whether they be University, learned society, research council or whatever. Not only do research papers multiply like Hydra's heads and the paperwork for committees accumulate like the debris of a flood, but now we have been introduced to a multitude of carefully winnowed papers on educational theory and practice. Does it not make you feel remiss that you have read so few of them? It's enough to make us all creep back to those crystal clear and delight-fully few instructions of our youth when we first started out on the tortured path of a university lecturer, e.g.

Stand up, speak up, shut up;
He, who is not one up, is one down; (with apologies to Lucky Jim).
If a difficulty is encountered, mumble to the blackboard;
Keep the difficult bits to the end of a lecture,

write rapidly on the board for the last 10 minutes and exit
with alacrity 2 minutes after the class was due to end;
Face the class for at least 50% of the duration of the class;

and for seminars and learned societies;

The more distinguished the audience, the simpler the lecture should be.

Such simple, straightforward rules must have guided many of us in our early days and indeed served us well. Generations of students have survived our unsophisticated attempts to make them learn. After all, we survived our own university days to perpetrate what we had endured on the next generation.

The issue is not "what was good enough for us is good enough for the next generation", but rather " can we do things more efficiently, more effectively, (noting that both things are not necessarily compatible simultaneously)?" While I incline to the view that great teachers are rare, (I should hate to be required to define a great teacher) there is ample scope for increasing the number of effective teachers. The story is told that students of Natural Philosophy at Glasgow did not care for the lecturing style of Lord Kelvin. His assistant Day gave splendid student orientated lectures. When Kelvin went to London to receive his knighthood, the day before his return some perspicacious student wrote on the board "work while the Day is yet with us for the Knight cometh for whom no man may work". Yet I am sure many of these same students would admit in later life that they gained greatly from the lectures of Lord Kelvin as well as referring to the excellent notes they took from Day. Here I think we reach a dilemma which has not been faced in this series — do we always try to teach students from the standpoint of the student or do we stretch them as required by the subject. While many of us do neither, I think we should tend to err on the side of stretching the student. This, I consider, should be the hallmark of university education.

In this final article, I would like to look at several issues which I consider are important in learning within the university context. Some of these considerations are incompatible with each other and produce a tension which must always be present in university teaching. My personal biases will appear and should be allowed for.

1. The subject

A university teacher is never a university teacher, full stop; he is a teacher of physics, biology or whatever. Without his subject he would not be a university teacher in the first place. His discipline is, or should be, his prime concern. In this sense, his teaching must be secondary. It is the discipline from which he derives his inspiration and drive to teach. By discipline I do not mean the 19th century divisions of scientific enquiry now ossifying into the last quarter of the 20th century. By a discipline, I mean the area of scientific enquiry which interests the teacher and towards which his research interests are directed. (I do not suppose that all university teachers are active research workers but all will have an area of science in which they have some interest.)

The research activity of a university is of great importance. It is through research that science is extended. It is also through research that the results of past research are preserved and maintained for future generations. Science subjects which are museum pieces, do not attract scientists eager to question, they attract historians. (I am not saying that historical enquiry is valueless — on the contrary, the stimulation of historical enquiry activates the historian.) We are attempting to teach in our universities sciences which are currently active and exciting. It is the activity of our disciplines which keeps us lively and up (more or less) with the chase. The feature that distinguishes universities from research institutes is that universities have the additional responsibility of passing on their accumulated expertise and knowledge, if not wisdom, to each rising generation.

Without its research to enliven and illuminate its teaching, a university could simply become a correspondence college directing reading assignments from well-established texts. A text once written, printed and published, may serve as the bible of many generations of students but no matter how authorative, well constructed, pedagogically erudite, it is but a snapshot of the field at the moment its author finally put down his pen.

A university teacher has the unique opportunity of being able to say to a class — "Hey, did you see that paper in this week's Nature which claimed . . . ." (fill in the blank to suit yourself). He can then link the new paper with work in the course. It is the possibility of students working with more experienced research workers that makes a university education worthwhile. Many students expect deep research discussion with their teachers every time they meet. This is an unrealistic expectation but contact with ongoing research should occur at least several times in a course — even a first year course. A teacher ought to have an opportunity somewhere in the course to say "Look here, while your text says 'such a thing', some recent research shows that 'such a thing' is not as reliably established as it might be". While shaking a students preconceptions can have dangerous consequences, a student who has graduated without once having had his preconceptions challenged during a degree course must either be the original immovable object or exceedingly unfortunate in his choice of discipline/university. A university exists to extend knowledge and extension demands that preconceptions be challenged. But the ways that different disciplines carry out their challenges differ and differ markedly. A teaching method of universal benefit in psychology may only have limited validity for physics and vice versa. Even in sciences thought by outsiders to be closely related, the basic attitudes may differ markedly. The same is true within different branches of the same subject. The methods employed to teach thermodynamics may be wholly unsuited to a class in computer programming. A teacher must consider carefully the nature of the topic he is to teach. The subject matter will often limit the manner in which it can be presented. However, the teacher should not accept that the traditional method of teaching the subject must be the only way. He should ask himself whether or not other non-traditional approaches are likely to be more effective, as effective, or less effective than the traditional approach. He might be surprised to find that another method does exist. A superlative text book just ideal for that course might have been recently published. In such circumstances chalk-and-talk may be out, and directed reading and tutorials may be in. During the passage of time, the text may become outdated and the proportion of talk-and-chalk may then rise again to take account of new developments.

Care should always be taken to meet the exigencies of the subject and, indeed, it is of paramount importance that the subject should always come first. In this way a healthy scientific atmosphere will be generated and provide a framework within which the student can both learn his discipline and obtain some feeling of what that discipline is about and where it is going now. A balance has to be struck between the detailed content and its overall direction. Without direction, the content quickly loses flavour; without content, direction is pointless.

2. The Student

Universities accept the obligation to provide a situation of advanced learning for their students. In this respect, they differ from a research institute. If the support of research and repair of the store of human knowledge is the primary responsibility of the universities, then their next responsibility is for their students. The aim of university teaching should be to ensure that each student realises as much of his potential as is reasonably possible. In an age which has supplanted its icons with statistics, is not the purpose of universities to see students, not as statistics, but as individuals? The intellectual cream (amongst others) of society attend university. This rare resource should not be eroded unnecessarily by rigidity in the university system. However, universities should not relax a high standard of intellectual attainment — to do so would be to the detriment of themselves as institutions, their students and so of society in general. Maintenance of high standards is not the same thing as rigidity though often the two are equated.

Students come to university with a wide range of expectations, hopes and doubts. Some hope to bend the university to further their careers, others to partake in a pleasant and free social atmosphere but, by far the vast majority, come to university to study a subject or discipline which, at the time, seems of great interest to them. Candidates for university entrance are often ill advised about university subjects and ill prepared for university life. Some universities try to counter this lack of preparedness but cannot devote adequate time to it.

It is a criticism of British educational system that it enforces a rigid specialism. (Just admit at school that you like chemistry and brother, a chemist thou shalt be. Just try to get off the conveyor belt!) Yet our Universities are making great strides towards a broader education through the sciences. The opportunities are there and more could be made available. But candidates who make a commitment to come to University are facing a formidable step into the unknown. They — wisely perhaps — show a conservatism which tends to ensure that he who does well in French in School will take French at University. He may not really want to do French at all, but cannot see any other road open. It takes courage to explore new paths in defiance of headmaster, parents, old uncle Tom Cobley and all. To embark on a new type of course is the academic equivalent of a blind date. At present, training in the sciences has reached the point where the tradition that has served so well in the past is being questioned. Does a person with ability in physics need to be educated from the point of view of the research physicist with the pious hope that education which is good for a potential specialist research worker is good education for all? Clearly, such training is not wholly disastrous as many graduates who are by no means incompetent in fields outside their university specialism clearly demonstrate. Perhaps university teachers and medical practitioners share the same dispensation — the great powers of recovery, both mental and physical, of the human animal. Certainly, universities must continue to provide what they do best — the education of the specialist research worker. They would be in grave dereliction of their primary responsibility if they did not. Yet they are criticised widely for so doing. Many subjects, having little relevance to current society are worthy subjects of university study. A subject such as Astonomy has little relevance to the real world, beyond a minor contribution to calendrical regulation, but it has survived since prehistory in any society with pretensions to civilization. Without such subjects to add new dimensions to experience, our civilization would be dull indeed. Universities must defend to the utmost the disciplines studied by their members. These members should have the right to pass on their accumulated experience to interested students.

But it also is clear that universities should not be self-perpetuating closed societies. Young people will come to university to widen their educational base. Most of these young people have no intention of remaining at University beyond their first graduation. This brings into focus another important difference between the universities and research institutes. The young people at university are looking outwards beyond their period of degree studies. This is a valuable contribution since it helps prevent introspection.

These young people bring a continuous stream of youth and vitality into their university. If it is the job of university teachers to challenge their students, the students in their turn challenge the university teachers about the realism (note: not relevance) of the education they are providing.

The dilemma of today is how the universities can maintain and advance a first-class successful scientific tradition. This requires the highly trained and motivated specialist. But with that prime responsibility there is an uneasy awareness that the education of specialists is not the same thing as a wide scientific education suitable for the administrators and managers of an increasingly technological society. Perhaps, in twenty years, we will look back and wonder why we ever had growing pains.

It is not for this article or for this series of articles to suggest ways out of the dilemma — this is something which needs to be agreed both inside and outside the universities. However, it is clear that we cannot return to the 19th century. We have to reconsider how the universities can respond to the need for provision of scientific education which will be of value in the years to come.

However, in planning for the future, despite our wealth of statistical information, it is the interaction between individual students and teachers that matters. Candidates for university need to be counselled not recruited. It is as important to advise a candidate *not* to come to university as it is to advise to come to university. The real intentions of candidates — not that of their parents, headmaster, peers — should be sought and the candidate advised which universities are most likely to suit those intentions. Each candidate should have complete freedom, subject to qualifications, to select the university which he considers will suit him best. Undoubtedly, some students, however well counselled, will make mistaken choices of subjects or of university. Such students should be recognised early and be transferred to other courses either at the university of their choice or another appropriate university. An attitude should prevail that such students are not failures — often transfer to another course brings a transformation. (Note: I am speaking here of those who are well motivated toward university study and not of the intrinsically idle.) Every effort should be made to match students to a course of study for which they are suited. Fortunately, most students can happily study a variety of subjects. Those who make the wrong initial choice should be helped to rectify that error as soon as possible. It is not a criticism of a student that he makes a wrong initial choice of course — the change of environment from home/school to university often challenges the student to wonder why he came to university at all. Fortunately, most remember that they came to study the subject they are studying.

The university student (a much criticised animal by an unfeeling parliament and people) is a valuable, natural resource, unfortunately not unlimited in either quantity or quality. Students require every help in ensuring that each individual can reach the fullest extent of his intellectual capability in order that this priceless resource is not thoughtlessly squandered.

3. Who wants a university education in science?

In his perceptive introductory article, A. Becher drew a distinction between validity and relevance. To the pure scientist, validity is of paramount importance, to the engineer it is relevance that occupies the key position. A scientist must know that what he has achieved is valid within the context of the principles accepted by his peers. If his work is invalid, say influenced overwhelmingly by some quirk in the technique he is using (e.g. the growth of error in a numerical solution), his work counts for nothing and he must start again. On the other hand, the engineer does not need to know if the scientific principle he is using conforms precisely with the latest theory in the structure of the nucleus — he wants to know if he may safely use that principle within the context and confines of a practical problem. The scientist, therefore, needs to be taught to produce work that is valid and the engineer to draw on knowledge that is relevant. However, it is impossible to isolate the purely scientific part of a course from the purely engineering. Both aspects must enter into any subject. The degree of the mix will vary from time to time and from university to university.

The current demand is for more relevance. Unfortunately, relevance to what or to whom is poorly indicated so that its positive identification, clearly above the noise, cannot be made. Long speeches about relevance are made *ad nauseam* until the word has little meaning left and all that remains is the oratorical resonance. Relevance, like beauty, is in the eye of the beholder. Yet it would be too facile to dismiss, because of lack of precision of formulation, what is a clearly felt emotion.

Many young people feel that it is entirely unrealistic to devote their lives to a single narrow specialism. They see very clearly that if one wants to earn a living in the world today, the market for intense specialism is a contracting one. They may also feel that science has not lived up to its promise of a brave, new world. Indeed, we always feel we can do a better job than our fathers did and so it was since the world began. Whether it be altruism or practicality, it is a fact that young people are cautious of specialisation in certain sciences. However, universities are discipline based and the only way to make progress with any investigation is to concentrate on it. Consequently, a tension must exist between the need to concentrate effort on certain areas of great immediate interest and the need to give a student a sufficiently wide overview so that a proper appreciation of that discipline can be arrived at. The problem resolves itself into identification of who are the consumers of university science education and what are their objectives.

It is clear that no university science department can survive on a population of those students who will ultimately enter the same department — the prosecution of science has simply become too expensive. Therefore, the majority of students will not be those who will propagate the faith. In the past, it has been assumed that the training and education offered to prospective academics will be good (if not ideal) for the rest. On the whole, this has not been proved to be an unmitigated disaster. Students did learn about the nature of their subject and, being people of considerable intelligence, adapted quickly in response to new situations by learning on the job. The argument now runs that the time is just not available to learn on the job — managerial errors while learning to manage mean lost business opportunities. Before such arguments are accepted it might be asked if the errors result from lack of knowledge or immaturity in managing people. One can argue that it is better to study something in depth than never to have studied in depth at all. Only by trying to study an unsolved problem can one really grasp how much hard work is necessary even to stand still let alone to break the problem. Too facile an appreciation of the effort needed to advance knowledge may be just as dangerous as ignorance of the latest in management techniques. In my view, it is just not proved that attendance at a specialist degree course is an inappropriate educational background for intending non-academics.

This is not to say that I consider efforts to broaden degree courses as misguided. Indeed, I would like to see them encouraged because it seems that there is an identifiable type of student who prefers this form of study. Such a student is put off by the detail of academic research but is not academically slothful as is sometimes imagined. He will not be interested in a research career. Nevertheless, he likes the disciplined approach to problems that science offers. Such people may become managers of science, governmental administrators, school teachers, financial experts, even politicians. To them, a scientific training is an appreciation of scientific method and some idea of how particular fields are developing. It does not seem to me to be a useful thing to make the sweeping judgement that science education should be broad or specialised; one should look carefully at the student population and judge accordingly.

The above problems are compounded (as problems usually are) by a further factor. The percentage of the population entering university has increased. Using an analogy with a Maxwellian gas, an increase in the university population means an increase in the numbers of lower energy students. I am not arguing the merits of taking more poorly qualified students — the fact remains that there are more, less-well qualified students in university departments of science. The question may be asked again — is a degree course designed for intending academics suitable education for these students? The answer here is probably a resounding no. But at once a dilemma is reached — how do we avoid lower level degree courses for such students getting a low-level reputation?

In our universities — at least in the U.K. — we are trying to maintain a fiction that all degrees represent the same level of intellectual achievement. That they do not is patently obvious and it is dishonest to pretend that they do. It is all the more dishonest because it is unnecessary. We have to recognise that we must cater differently for different levels of ability. The university population represents the best of a country's brain-power and we are assessing the upper ability levels. It is not right to force a student into a straight-jacket where he will always be at the bottom of a highly academic degree course. That way, we condition him to think of himself as a third class citizen. He is not. As a member of a different kind of degree course, he may even show first class ability and be a much more contented person. The sheer rush of students into university has precluded proper counselling of students which pays due regard to what the student wants to do. The status of the research oriented degree is, rightly, high — but it is not the measure of all men. A student might wish to undertake a research oriented degree even though he knows his chances of doing well may be remote — he may be content with having faced the challenge of that degree even though he gets third class honours. Such students will be exceptional. Most faced with that choice would opt for a degree where they had a chance of doing well and, in a secular world, rightly so.

It is also clear that the direction of education at school level has an important bearing on the reception of students at university. The adequacy of preparation at school for high pressure university courses is declining and the indications are that future changes in the philosophy of school education will hasten that decline. If the changes in educational practice at school decrease the incidence of mass adult illiteracy and innumeracy, the changes will be well worth while. But the universities must face the fact that their expectation of student performance will have to undergo radical revision. Students, while no less intelligent, will be less adequately prepared for three years of intensive study.

The time has come to reconsider the pattern of university education — not just in terms of specialisation or broadening or interdisciplinarity or what-have-you, but to fundamentally rethink what tertiary education has to provide. At a time when the public seems to want to cut the time spent in university education as a two year Diploma in Higher Education suggests, it seems to me that what is required is an extension of time at university from 3 years to at least 4. Since the school leaving examinations are not accurately predictive of individual performance at university and bid fair to become less so in the future, a year at university learning the ropes might well be beneficial. Students would be encouraged to study several sciences, learn how to study, be exposed to different teaching methods and to use self-paced study techniques. Students, after finding their feet at university would be asked to make a choice of direction at the end of their first year and the system should be sufficiently flexible to allow modest change of direction at the end of the second year. If one wished, stopping places at the end of second, third and fourth years could be considered. However, the status of such stopping places would need to be such that he who stopped after his second year would not be considered the intellectual inferior of he who stopped after his third year and so on. A person of great intellectual ability might decide that after two years of university education what he really wanted was specific vocational training outside a university environment.

Unless great efforts are made to see that each student receives the education he needs and is capable of taking, we may waste a considerable amount of a limited resource of talent. We must also recognise that in the transition from school to university, we also have a transition from legal childhood to legal adulthood. Taking responsibility for ones life may force a reconsideration of the dreams of ones childhood. Whilst it is heartbreaking for any academic to see a student, endowed with all the attributes of a first class research worker in ones own field, move off into some disparate field or away from university education, it is also encouraging that a spell at university has given that student the necessary back-bone to stand up against his teachers and his previous inclination. University education for that person may be deemed successful whatever the outcome.

Universities must address themselves to students as they are and not as they would like them to be. The greatest innovation would be to stop hiding behind the skirts of tradition and seek a satisfying scientific study which will encourage students back into science departments and encourage teachers to teach such classes with enthusiasm. A major change of professional ethos is required which no amount of tinkering with presentation or administration will change. Radical rethinking to meet a new situation is required. Surely, it is well worth giving our best minds our best attention.

4. But what do we do tomorrow?

Well, you will say, fine words butter no parsnips, none of us in the U.K. are going to see four-year degrees in any form for a few years yet. What are we to do to enhance learning in the existing situation? It strikes me very forcibly when reading the preceding articles in this series that what all the authors have in common, despite their predilections for differing learning strategies, is their concern for the student. So perhaps the first thing we might resolve to do is to care a good deal more for the student viewpoint. This does not mean that one should adopt every and any suggestion that students put up, but to consider these suggestions to see if they mark a deeper discontent. Students' views change like womens' fashions. What is in this year may be out next, so that our courses should always have a little in hand for tailoring purposes. Where possible, we should provide flexibility in learning so that many student attitudes to learning can be comfortably accommodated. For example, a student may experience extreme claustrophobia in a lecture theatre — is it really essential that this student attend all lectures?

Another point which strikes me forcibly about all the articles is the way the point is made that each lecturer should know what he wants to achieve by his course and what assessment of the students in that course really means. In many universities, lecturer X is told to give course y. He is given little or no guidance on how course y fits into the degree and no indication of what the students should know at the end of the course except in vague terms. So what does poor old X do? — he thinks back to what he was taught under roughly similar circumstances and then does the same, spiced to his own taste. Some lecturers give courses which are little more than recruiting exercises for research students, some give courses which are the quintessence of dullness but give good lecture notes, others give exciting courses from which the students find extreme difficulty in extracting a coherent thread. There is a very great need to organise and discuss the framework of degree courses within departments. The concept of a course team may be a useful one to explore. A team could take responsibility for a given degree course, discuss the underlying philosophy and the aims for each constituent course of lectures or practicals and decide what the assessment procedures were setting out to measure. A course team would have the advantage of being a smaller group than a department and have a chance of working together in a mutually supportive way. As members left the team, so new members could join an existing group and be given support and help within the context of a clear course philosophy.

Assessment is frequently accepted as meaning a 3-hour essay-question examination. While such examinations are excellent for measuring the amount of prior organisation and understanding the student has done and acquired (though this measurement can be negated by rote learning), excellence of memory, speed of recall, flexibility of wrist, and ability to work under pressure, examinations could be used more selectively to measure specific things. This is not to decry the 3-hour essay-question examination as useless — the phenomena listed above are all worthy of measurement and invaluable in every day life. Many subjects do not lend themselves to a wide ranging set of questions and are predictable in some degree. Why many (not all) students are so inept as not to recognise that predictability has always remained a mystery to me. The standard examination is fair to the extent that a well defined situation exists and the student knows what to expect. That person-alities exist for whom the standard examination is entirely up-setting is no argument against such examinations — there will always be people seriously disadvantaged by any form of assess-ment, e.g. there are many who would cheerfully sit through any number of standard papers than give a 20 minute project talk; there are students who are undervalued by one word answer tests. Other forms of assessment ought to be brought into general use. The project can be used to assess response to a research environment, open-book papers can be used to assess capability in marshalling documentary evidence and so on. Examiners need to be explicitly aware of what they are trying to measure by degree classification. They should perhaps design examinations which are specific to a single criterion of performance. The overall performance in the degree could be assessed by weighting the separate measurements together. Those departments setting store by research ability would weight the project highly, departments which admired library retrival skills would weight open-book papers highly, in order to produce the final assessment. Alternatively, one might stick to 3-

hour essay-question examinations which are a reasonable measurement of overall ability. All too often final assessment depends on the tradition that we have always done it this way, and to question the method is unthinkable.

However, questioning the reason behind degree assessment is a valid exercise. Even if the outcome is to do the same as before, at least some logic will be seen to be behind the *status quo*. New means of assessment require careful introduction if no discontinuity with past standards is to occur. It would be invidious to make a change of standard for award of a degree which produced a marked step either up or down from the standard achieved by previous holders of the same degree. Any change of assessment procedure should not be made until it is ascertained that the majority of previous holders of the degree, if assessed in the proposed manner, would still have been awarded the same class of honours. Such maintenance of continuity does not affect tuning of the new system as the scheme evolves with time.

Having thought about what each constituent course in a degree course is designed to achieve and how the students are assessed to measure that achievement we are brought face to face with the problem of how to present the course material to the students. The authors of the articles have given some very pertinent advice about the advantages of small tutorials, large classes, project work, laboratory work, broad courses, interdisciplinary courses, modular courses, but nowhere have they spelt out to us how we should go about presenting the next academic year's thermodynamics, or positional astronomy, or quantitative analysis, or whatever. They did not tell us in consistent units how much information will transfer from teacher to taught per unit time, per unit cost for any of their favourite methods.

We were asking a lot if we expected that sort of guidance. It is impossible guidance to give. In the first place, learning is affected by many variables which are not in the control of the university. The university today is a place where young adults may learn if they choose. These young adults are subject to many outside non-academic pressures — finance, housing, social and family problems. University students are no longer fenced off from the rest of the world only emerging at the end of term or on rag day. They are no longer *in statu pupilari*. Most students would believe that the advantages of being recognised as adults outweigh the disadvantages. However, being subject to outside pressure, the learning environment can depart from the ideal. Again, all students will not respond equally to any given teaching situation. Some students will like the anonymity of the large lecture, others will revel in small group teaching. Some students will develop an antipathy to certain teaching styles or to a particular lecturer, some small group teachers may find themselves disliking a particular student. Personalities will grate and jar somewhere. Students will change their view of the ideal learning situation as they progress through a degree course and increase in maturity and experience. A variety of learning situations should be the norm and not the exception. A student should come to university expecting to meet not just formal lectures, but a range of learning situations. At present few courses exist in alternative forms — for very good fiscal reasons. In the future, a wider structure should be aimed for. It would be an interesting experiment to find out over a ten-year period just what form of teaching most students preferred — anybody willing to make a prediction? I would suspect that the formal lecture might just be in front.

To obtain even a small amount of flexibility in teaching is uphill work. The trouble with flexibility is that it tends to ossify on the spot. New methods are tried and a successful formula is adopted and then adhered to. Yesterdays innovation tends to become todays unquestioned practice. To some extent ossification comes from a basic academic conservatism and in part from unwillingness to make an ongoing financial commitment to innovation in teaching methods. It comes down in the last analysis to graduate production at the lowest cost per student. Innovation is expensive. Other demands are made on university resources. However, is expenditure on facilities for training top minds a luxury? On the contrary, should we not accord the very best facilities for that job?

To revitalise next year's courses we must first think of the nature of the subject matter of the courses. Some subjects will not lend themselves to gross departures from formal lectures while others are ideally suited for experiment. Suppose our course has just benefited from the writing of an ideal text book that covers our course in all its detail and reflects our philosophy towards the course. Clearly, we should give up formal lectures and institute reading assignments. Lecture time should then be released for discussion of reading, examples and the detailed exposition of difficult arguments. The student is being asked to take responsibility for his own learning but with firm direction. Illustrations can be introduced in lecture time for which there would be no time in conventional patterns and the lecturer can give attention to some well directed class demonstrations. The difficulty with such a technique is, "will the students read as directed?" The answer seems to be, "no", unhappily. Sitting in a formal lecture taking notes of material which could be gleaned without pain from the text book is so ingrained that students, who loudly complain that they waste time writing notes on a lecture which is a poor imitation of the text, will procrastinate over reading assignments. If students are to accept the change they must be assiduously schooled first. Changes of technique are more likely to be successful in the second and third years when the students have more confidence in their abilities than in the first year.

The above technique could be introduced for more advanced classes if several good, but non-ideal texts exist. Texts covering the course are selected and reading assignments set as before. Discussion can then also range over the approaches, similarities and differences of the respective authors. However, the collective immaturity of the first year class probably precludes such a method being satisfactory since a first year class, above all, like stability and the confidence that the book is right — a confidence which should be gently shaken right from the first week of their first term.

Classes which are designed to impart a technique are probably best conducted informally — a lecture on soldering never teaches anyone to solder. For example, a class on computing can become completely informal. The lecturer can specify a problem to be solved and the class can break up into groups of any size to discuss how to tackle the problem. Access to the lecturer and some demonstrators is freely available and each person or group decides on a program to submit to the computer. Feedback is instantaneous — the program either worked or it did not. Consultation on diagnostics gets the program sorted out and a new program is tried. Once most of the class have got the program working, a comparison of successful programs can be carried out. Length of program, duration of computer time, etc., can be discussed and the groups asked to defend the merits of their programs. The class should try to find some criteria of effectiveness of programming since it may not be the shortest, quickest running program that is the most convenient to use. After the stage of program comparison, a new problem can be introduced and the process repeated.

Formal lectures need not become rigid. Opportunities for class discussion should be built in. It is often the case that a particular problem under discussion presents several means of attack. The class might list some of these. The class suggestions can then be developed and the reasons for a favoured approach demonstrated. For example, in a discussion of the structure of a star, the class might be asked, before discussing the equilibrium of stars, to list all the forces which they consider contribute to the equilibrium. They can be asked to segregate major from minor forces. Again, the class could be asked to suggest all the things that could happen to a photon in transit from the centre to the surface of a star or what might happen to a photon in transit through interstellar space. Such breaks allow a short rest from the business of a lecture and give the class a sense of participation. It is usually rewarding to follow up a few of the "crazy" suggestions as well as those bearing directly on the subsequent course of the lecture. The buzz-group technique can be used as effectively in lectures as in small groups. It takes a little time before a first year class may grasp what it is supposed to be doing in buzz-groups but usually there are enough outspoken members to get the ball rolling. The class soon learns, and both the scientists and the humourists rise to the challenge. Light relief, change of activity and the feeling of participation, in that order, result, with benefit to the lecture situation. Encouragement of student participation requires a confident lecturer. He will be placed on the spot and there will be questions he cannot answer. However, if the lecturer knows his subject, he can suggest reference sources for the class to look at to find the answer. He would also do well to find the answer himself.

Tutorial work is probably the most difficult area to tackle. Tutorials are ill defined, covering one-to-one teaching up to groups of 10 to 12. Commonly, a tutorial group is 3 or 4 people per tutor. The one-to-one situation is often the most efficient in exchange of information. The student has a clearly defined pathway of communication and there is no third party behind whom he can shelter.

Teaching can take place at the pace of the student and a range of techniques employed. The tutor can explain the basis of a problem, set a few examples, indicate appropriate sources and then leave the student to find some solutions which can be discussed later and so on. A single student can be effectively taught by this method in about half the time of an equivalent course of lectures. There is no reason why up to four students could not be taught in this way though as the number of participants rises, it becomes increasingly difficult to be aware of the response of each student to new information.

However, few tutorials are directed towards teaching a specific topic. Most tutorials are held with students to elucidate areas of difficulty perhaps over a range of courses. Students are not willing to expose their weakness readily even in a small group and, particularly in the first year, they worry that the difficulty may appear to be criticism of the lecturer concerned. Second and third year students have little inhibition in criticising their lecturers. Careful probing may turn the response that they are "getting on alright" into an exposure of a very considerable difficulty also experienced by other members of the group. Once difficulties are brought into the open the remedy is clearer. The root of the problem lies in making first contact. The average student is shy and finds a lecturer quite a remote person. He is not sure of how to interest his lecturer in him. It is up to the tutor to build a few bridges but it is up to the student to cross at least one of them. I have found that by introducing a few ideas which seem to have nothing to do with the subject matter, one can get the students discussing freely. For example, in an astronomy course one can ask students where they come from, what hall they are in, do they like it?, is the food good?, what is the orientation of the hall with respect to the College?, do they like travel in the rush hour?, how would they set up a way of determining the direction of the hall with respect to the College?, and so on, exploring their concepts about direction and thus, to their concepts of celestial co-ordinate systems. During such discussions, misconceptions can come out and be corrected. Alternatively, one can end a tutorial class with a problem for consideration for the next tutorial. It need not be difficult but it should be a bit out on a limb, e.g. why should Shetland Islanders be more aware of the 18.6 yr. precessional lunar cycle than Alexandrian Greeks? The answers one gets are varied but start up discussion on the next occasion. By and large, tutorials can be used to relate disparate parts of a course or several courses together. Not only is this intrinsically useful but brings out misconceptions and weakness of understanding.

Tutorials with large groups are almost useless. Most students are very shy about speaking out in a large group. A class tutorial can be a very slow business, no one wants to throw the first stone. If the lecturer indicates that it is a collossal boost to his ego for the class to be completely satisfied with his course, there is usually one individual who considers that such ego inflation should not go unchecked. Once the ice is broken, others follow on. However, although such tutorials do no more than scratch the surface, evidence for underlying discontents can be detected. X may say that he did not follow the connection between lines 5 and 6 on the second blackboard on the left. Several others may murmur assent. However, what may be the problem is not the immediate one of connecting line 6 to line 5, but a global misunderstanding of the mathematical basis of the connection. A reappraisal of that mathematical basis is then essential and this may involve work treated in another course, belonging, perhaps, to another department. Often students feel that their problem may be so trivial to the remainder of the class that it should not be brought up. The contrary is often the case and the class is delighted to have the matter aired. Large tutorials of this type are extremely difficult to run since the tutor must guard his tongue rigidly since, once put off by a nuance however slight, it may be difficult to re-establish easy two-way communications within the large group.

Tutorials are demonstrably expensive. The ratio of students to staff is small and a relaxed atmosphere does not lead to a rapid exchange of information except where the tutorial is set up for that purpose. However, the tutorial allows a flow of information which would not occur in any other teaching method. The staff and students get to know each other. It may be that the knowledge that one of ones students is an amateur weight lifter is of little academic use, but one might just want a temporary vacation technician to assist with some heavy work. The students from a tutorial can get a view of their subject which they might never get in an entire degree course. The tutorial is an area which needs further exploration both from the point of view as an aid to learning and from the point of view of student need. Not all students need the same tutorial medicine and some may even be allergic to it.

Finally, the subject of programmed learning has been scarcely touched upon in this series of articles. In many instances, a great deal has been claimed for the virtues of the teaching machine. These claims have not been realised. Possibly, the technology was not able to match the ideas, possibly too much was expected, possibly teachers did not like the threat that they could be dispensed with. Whatever the reasons, teaching machines are now held in low regard.

The biggest objection to teaching machines is their inflexibility. They represent a considerable capital cost, time and energy to programme. There is a strong compulsion not to alter things once they work. However, technology is again overtaking events and the microprocessor-chip again holds out the possibility of less inflexibility.

The replacement of teachers by machines is so absurd that it need hardly be taken seriously. The idea that a given topic could be enshrined in a programme and then be studied universally is not really a practical possibility. Like text books, programme choice would be personal. However, learning situations still require teachers for in the last analysis it is the interaction of minds that produces learning.

Students are also supposed to be unhappy with impersonal machine contact. They quickly reach the limits of machine flexibility and once that happens boredom sets in. The excitement of using a new technique wears off and so the technique gets another black mark. Nevertheless, programmed learning does have its place though one must not be over ambitious in its use. Programmed instruction can have a very useful purpose and fill a need but the need must match the technique. Instruction regarding a given technique can be programmed so that the learner can learn at his own pace and repeat the message as often as required. For example, instructions on how to use a telescope may be set out as a tape-slide presentation. The instructions are recorded and illustrated by slides of the details of the telescope the student is actually going to use. Similarly, a demonstration which requires a long time to set up, or may be potentially hazardous, can be televised and the recording played back within the context of a lecture, practical class, tutorial or by the student in his own time. Specific mathematics can be programmed with the requirement that students make the correct responses to carefully posed questions before the next bit of the programme can be accessed. In medicine, a student can use programming to improve diagnostic technique and also to learn the effects of specific drugs.

Many of these uses are not particularly inspirational and make little diagnostic use of the feed-back on student performance. Modern computers have the capability to attempt to measure student performance and so allow a more sophisticated level of programmed teaching. Even so, even the peripheral use of programmed learning techniques has hardly yet begun to make an impact on university teaching. Remedial teaching, teaching of specific concepts and techniques, use of specific items of equipment could all be taught on some form of programmed basis. The will to try again is lacking — a will which must be reduced in todays more impoverished climate.

5. Conclusion

So here we are at the end of it all and no recipe for instant lecture room success in sight. However, some clear guidelines do emerge.

1. Decide the philosophy of ones degree course — is one training future scientists or is one educating through science?

2. Consider the nature of individual courses — what is the best way of presenting the material? Read these articles before you decide.

3. Consider alternative ways of presenting the material not mentioned in these articles including combinations of methods.

4. Consider what a student should have learnt at the end of your course and tailor the method of assessment to measuring how well the student has acquired and understood that knowledge.

5. Give the student opportunities to become involved with the work of the course.

6. Change the broad presentation of your course to better adapt to the needs of different groups of students taking the course.

7. Remember that students are a valuable natural resource.

It is so obvious when you think about it.

In short, what the authors of these articles are saying is that irrespective of current fashions, pressures and fancied needs, there is nothing to beat good teaching. Good teachers care for their students and use any technique to whet the interest and sustain motivation. It does not matter if you do not know the answer to students' questions. Together you can find out. What is important is that the students feel sufficiently free and secure to ask questions. It is of great importance to get students to participate in their courses, to ask questions, to challenge axioms and to think about the nature of their science. Any technique which stimulates a student in this direction is worthy of use. In any university institution with undergraduates there should be sufficient flexibility so that many forms of teaching and learning can coexist. The gifted teacher will use many methods even within an apparently inflexible framework. Those of us who are not so gifted can see that our students are exposed to as wide a variety of teaching/learning strategies as is compatible with the nature of the subject being learnt.

But we can do one more thing — we should rethink our teaching in the light of what has been written for these articles and apply some of the ideas outlined there. It is possible that if we were more self conscious of our teaching then the students might just notice the difference. So where is that drawing board. . . . . . ?

At the end of the day, it is up to each student to take responsibility for his own learning. Whilst Universities may do their utmost to provide absolutely superlative water in the most attractive packaging that can be devised, the student still has to drink. That choice is the student's and the student's alone. All that has been written in this series of articles is designed to make the process of learning a pleasant, stimulating and rewarding experience. But, the student does have the choice and it is a choice he must be allowed. Nevertheless, it is a privilege to educate the finest minds of our time and we should see that those minds are educated in the best way possible. That is our responsibility as university teachers.

ACKNOWLEDGEMENT

I am most grateful to the Committee for Teaching of Science of ICSU for giving me the job of editing this series of articles. The previous authors have challenged me to look anew at my teaching. As someone not versed in the language of research into teaching methods, they have opened new doors for me and given me new insights.